Beyond Marx and Other Entries

Studies in Critical Social Sciences Book Series

Haymarket Books is proud to be working with Brill Academic Publishers (www.brill.nl) to republish the *Studies in Critical Social Sciences* book series in paperback editions. This peer-reviewed book series offers insights into our current reality by exploring the content and consequences of power relationships under capitalism, and by considering the spaces of opposition and resistance to these changes that have been defining our new age. Our full catalog of *SCSS* volumes can be viewed at https://www.haymarketbooks.org/series_collections/4-studies-in-critical-social-sciences.

Beyond Marx and Other Entries

David Gleicher

Haymarket Books
Chicago, IL

First published in 2017 by Brill Academic Publishers, The Netherlands.

Published in paperback in 2018 by
Haymarket Books
P.O. Box 180165
Chicago, IL 60618
773-583-7884
www.haymarketbooks.org

ISBN: 978-1-60846-102-8

Trade distribution:
In the U.S. through Consortium Book Sales, www.cbsd.com
In the UK, Turnaround Publisher Services, www.turnaround-uk.com
In Canada, Publishers Group Canada, www.pgcbooks.ca
All other countries, Ingram Publisher Services International, ips_intlsales@ingramcontent.com

Cover design by Jamie Kerry and Ragina Johnson.

This book was published with the generous support of Lannan Foundation and the Wallace Action Fund.

Printed in United States.

10 9 8 7 6 5 4 3 2 1

Library of Congress Cataloging-in-Publication Data is available.

Contents

Acknowledgements

I'd like to dedicate this book to Annie Stauber, who for forty-five years always got me to really think from outside the box. I miss her.

Preface

Beyond Marx and Other Entries is a truly original book. It explores deep areas of semiotics and philosophy joined with economics, joined with anthropology, sociology, history, political science, and Kafka's *Castle*. These are communicated by entries, based primarily on my actual blog, *Looking through the Crack* (http://economics-finance-adelphi.blogspot.nl/), from 2013 to 2017.

Entering into various entries are three writers of *social Totality*—Walter Benjamin, Felix Guattari, and John McMurtry—who do not fit into any single area in its own right. This book itself does not fit into any specific area of social-science, either, although at the same time each individual entry with some exceptions only, is indeed within discernable social-sciences.

No other structure of a book quite compares to *Beyond Marx*, the closest being perhaps simply a collection of essays, but that leaves much left out. More accurate would be equating it to impressionist art, or the bridging of *the one and the many*.

Each entry is independent; nothing in one makes an allusion to any of the others. There are 44 of them in total. All but a few are in the range of 1,000 to 3,500 words. Readers however cannot help but to look with depth into connections in the entries, and by themselves come into the grips of dystopian possibilities, and the manner in which the social Totality is moving into them.

This is communicated in the book by grouping the individual entries into 8 chapters. However, the entries are never melted together; rather the book serves up a dialogistic study, an aspect of which is a critique of economics, one based on Benjamin's basic assertion; that mathematics is a language among other languages. There is no mathematics of language per se, it is only *a* language.

The book at hand is a critique then of the dominant classical and neoclassical schools of economic thought as well as that of Karl Marx. It calls for us to finally go beyond an economics in isolation. Contemporary economists since the fifties have been immersed in econometric modelling with more and more complexity due to increasing digitalization. As seen in PhDs in economics for instance—topics, for the most part, are about studying quarterly prediction of corporate sales or prices and interest rates in the financial markets—very few in life-needs.

Amazingly, the core understanding of the economy by these economists date back some 300 years ago, in the eighteenth-century imagination of a market-economy exclusively functioning sealed off from all other areas of social life, not to say of nature. Stepping back slightly the economy has taken out of economics anything from other social-sciences.

In *Beyond Marx* it is the reverse. Dialogism is expressed through various dialogues that super-cedes mathematical problems with ongoing dialogues. There is no static solution in the sense of a mathematical reduction of language that is offered. Dialogue is ongoing as is the movement of the social Totality.

Felix Guattari succinctly captures in his important 1989 piece, *The Three Ecologies*, the basis of my work:

> The logic of intensities is concerned only with the movement and intensity of evolutionary processes. Process strives to capture existence in the very act of its constitution, definition and de-territorializing.
>
> Praxes strive to scout out the potential vectors of subjectification and singularization at each partial existential locus. They generally seek something that runs counter to the 'normal' order of things, a counter-repetition, and an insensitive given which invokes other intensities to form new existential configurations. (p. 30)

The Summer Before the War

All on a Saturday, bright as a bell
Early and just for the ride
We took a trip cycling down to the sea,
You and your lady and I

And oh, what a summer, and oh, what a sun
Bright to the blue sky it clung
One day at Whitsun, the sea and the shore,
The summer before the war

Warm summer places where you could taste the country air
Chasing our shadows we'd fly
Down through the narrow lanes, racing the slow trains,
And the last of an age going by

And we had a good time, and we had some fun,
There was time then when we were all young,
One day at Whitsun, the sea and the shore,
The summer before the war

Young hearts and young souls, young minds to unfold,
Knowing the untold somehow
One day at Whitsun, the sea and the shore,
The summer before the war

We found a small cove by the sand and the water
The salt air was brushing your skin
With your hand in her hand there was nothing to say,
Just watch the sea rushing in

And oh, what a moment, and oh, what a day
We held it and it never slipped away
One day at Whitsun, the sea and the shore,
The summer before the war

Words & music: Hue Williams (PRS).
CD, The Wishing Well, sung by Connie Dover

CHAPTER 1

Industrializing Capital: Classic Works of the Twentieth Century

Harry Braverman's *Labor and Monopoly Capital*

Harry Braverman's *Labor and Monopoly Capital* (1974) is a seminal study of changing forms of capital over the course of a capitalist social system. He points out that in the period of the late-17th through much of the 19th century, emergent *production-capital* commonly took the form of sub-contracting, notably putting-out arrangements and the like, between capitalist and craftsmen, or not-yet displaced peasants. And it was common to be paid in piece-rates for product, rather than wages.

Thus, the craftsmen still were playing a central role in the organization and regulation of the production process. Along with that, capital continued to generate in large part a return to both merchant and banking capital; exchange but not production. These other forms came to the fore around the 14th century. Profit generated by production and sale was not conceived of as a fundamental form of capital until roughly the mid to late-19th century (Braverman, p. 62–63).

In turn, it was not until mechanization had spread across industries that the basic principles articulated by two major figures, Frederick Taylor (1911) and Charles Babbage (1832), could be put into practice on an ever-larger scale. At that point *industrializing capitalism* became established, perhaps the chief tenet of Taylor being: "There is an almost equal division of the work for which they (management) are better fitted than the workmen, while in the past almost all of the work and the greater part of the responsibility were thrown upon the men" (Taylor, p. 37).

The employed then are simply to carry out management orders, according to a division of various tasks dictated and assigned by management. According to Taylor, "All possible brain work should be removed from the shop and centered in the planning or lay-out department" (p. 113). Management-determined production is in closed time. It is an idea. This creates not only a clear separation of what management activities are, as opposed to those of employees, but a splitting of the very time dimensions along which these separate agents are experiencing the process.

It bears mentioning that there is a curious juxtaposition in Marxist thought, here, at least as far as it is reflected in Braverman's exposition. Braverman begins his book with Marx's famous assertion that what distinguishes humans from all other creatures is, we humans alone imagine and design, after which we actually create. Industrializing capitalism can be seen then as an historic leap (akin to the domestication of animals), the tailoring of production imagined and designed so as to create what amounts to mechanized activity; that is, activity requiring of the subject as little thought as possible. Ideally, it is purely physical, robotic.

Babbage's Principle, as it is known, complements that of Taylor. It is predicated on the dividing up of the employees' activity in such a way that each subject's identity derives from a set of tasks they are assigned to do. Those tasks are literally the occupation of the employed. And in unrestricted markets the nature of the occupation—not the product per se—is what the payment of the employed is for.

In short, the individuals employed within the process of production capital are not to be producers as such. Babbage's principle, then, is to design production always with a mind to further simplifying the sets of tasks—what Braverman calls de-skilling—thereby reducing costs. It is easily seen that mechanization along these lines fulfills Taylor's call for strictly defined tasks imagined and designed by management. They are designed for and by the machine. Babbage's principle of simplifying tasks of the employed furthers the mechanizing of the employed as championed by Taylor.

Braverman makes a striking assertion concerning the period prior to industrial capitalism, the late stages of the enclosures, the ending of the 17th century, in Britain, and within another fifty years industrializing capital was happening throughout Western Europe and the US.

> The early domestic and subcontracting systems represented a transitional form: a phase during which the capitalist had not yet assumed the essential function of management in industrial capitalism; for this reason it was incompatible with the overall development of capitalist production, and survives only in specialized instances. (1974: 63)

The current crisis of 2006/2009 has brought home to many another reality from what it was before. Industrializing capitalism, as a particular social system, has been rapidly transforming into something else.

Braverman rightly concludes that there is an essential function of management in industrial capitalism. The questionable Hegelian notion of an overall development of capitalist production, however, obscures the possibility that the social system in the period preceding industrialization was not, at the partial existential locus of open time, necessarily a transitional form at all. Certainly, it can be understood to have been a social system in its own right, one that indeed lasted some 200 to 300 years.

Along the same lines, industrializing capitalism seems to have greatly weakened around 1980. Thus, it had been a dominant form of capitalism for some 150 years. And the transition is clearly seen in the radical change of the function of management. Much of capital now takes the form of a financial asset and is taken away from all but ever-growing oligopolies in production for profit.

The transition is exemplified by two contemporary aspects of virtually all the major industries: extreme concentration seemingly leading in a few cases already into duopoly and even monopoly; and secondly, expansion of scale to a global level. Conjointly, the new reality is seen directly in production industries evolving into quasi-banking institutions, the revenues from production and sale effectively treated as deposits.

Karl Polanyi's *The Great Transformation*

In his classic work, *The Great Transformation: The Political and Economic Origins of our Time* (1944) Karl Polanyi locates the sharp turn between 1795 to 1834 in England as a decisive moment when an industrializing capitalism took shape.

1795 is marked by the passage of the Speenhamland laws. The latter constituted a major reform of existing Elizabethan laws. It changed the basic allowance arrangement by which the State provided economic support of the needy, notably assisting for the first time the lowly paid employed in addition to the needy unemployed. Like the preceding Elizabethan laws, however, Speenhamland was administered by the localities in which individuals were registered. As such, the State continued to be a kind of federation going back to the peasant villages possessed by Lords, prior to the enclosure movements.

1834 is marked by the complete repeal of Speenhamland and beyond that the elimination, on principle, of State allowance-giving. No longer were governing institutions to have the social responsibility of insuring necessities to the needy.

A theoretical basis of this change was initially articulated by Bernard Mandeville in his *Fable of the Bee* (1714), summarized in his saying: *Private vices are social benefits*. It is of course at the core of Adam Smith's celebrated *Wealth of Nations* (1776). By that time and thereafter more moderate ways were found of expressing the principle instead of vice: laissez-faire, individualism, liberalism, free market, free enterprise, and of course capitalism.

It is believed in by most people in the world, including well-respected economists, up to this day. It is taught to be the first and only *efficient* economic system and, as well, the most just. Indeed, this is as robust and widespread a view these days as any other in the 300 years after the time of Mandeville and Smith.

The radical removal in 1834 of all State obligations to the lives of its citizens is generally treated as a great triumph of the classical school of economics. David Ricardo—the leading thinker of the school—spearheaded the drive against Speenhamland, calling for the adoption in its stead of a laissez-faire policy.

Polanyi quotes a populist writer of the time, Joseph Townsend, who voices (much like Ayn Rand) a faith in the principle so strong that sacrificing for others to be harmful socially.

> Hunger will tame the fiercest animals, it will teach decency and civility, obedience and subjection, to the most perverse. In general it is only hunger which can spur and goad the [poor] on to labor. (p. 118)
>
> The Poor Laws proceed from principles which border on absurdity, as professing to accomplish that which in the very nature and constitution of the world, is impractical. But once the indigent were left to the mercy of the well-to-do, who can doubt that the only difficulty is to restrain the impetuosity of the latter's benevolence? (p. 123)

Control of production processes by private banking financiers, able to fund massive production capital, was not significant until the mid to late 19th-century, in tandem of course with accelerating mechanization. The repeal of Speenhamland could be taken as a tactic of severing the rural poor from their localities by taking away the allowances. Beyond that it was just one part of the larger erasure of the peasant village, the cultural attachment of peasants to the land.

Without income support, many were thus forced eventually into the newly industrializing cities. In doing so the employed were established as what Polanyi calls a fictitious commodity: An actual human activity whose purpose is to be bought and sold as an object of capital.

The sharp movement toward the employed as object clearly was driven by control, through ownership of production processes within corporations, and the thrust of mechanization driving down unit costs. Taylorism was still being diffused across industries at the turn of the century. For what it is worth, the repeal of Speenhamland back in 1834 certainly was a factor, but two other forces in their own right were far more powerful in freeing the supply side of burgeoning industrial employment markets.

To Polanyi the effect of the repeal in freeing up early-19th century markets was secondary in any case. Rather he sees in it an historic cultural shift. This is the darker meaning of the early classical school followed in the late 19th century by the neo classical school. The sadness though not his regret, Polanyi juxtaposed an infinite loss to humanity, the degradation of life, but on the other side, the great harm to be done by trying to recoup the loss.

> Under Speenhamland society was rent by two opposing influences, the one emanating from paternalism and protecting individuals from the dangers of the market system; the other organizing the elements of production, including land, under a market system, and thus divesting the common people of their former status, compelling them to gain a living by offering their labor for sale... By 1834, there was a general conviction—with many thinking people a passionately felt conviction—that anything was preferable to the continuance of Speenhamland. Either machines had to be demolished or a regular labor market had to be created. Thus, was mankind forced into a utopian experiment. (pp. 80–81)

This leads to the conclusion that the repeal of Speenhamland in a certain sense does mark a transition. The larger historic removal of the State's responsibilities was the enclosure movement, first in England, which peaked well before 1834. The separation of peasants on-mass from the land was led by merchant and banking capital, spawned around the 12th and 13th century. Mercantile capitalism was established by the 15th century in much of Western Europe and continued through the enclosure movements into the 18th century.

The repeal of Speenhamland, then, can be understood as a major sign of the first transformation of an existing capitalist system. 1834 is at the edge of the industrializing capitalism. It depends crucially on employed subjects whose activities are controlled by corporate owners, and where accumulation and circulation of merchant and banking capital are now directed toward industrial production.

From a contemporary vantage point there is, perhaps, something that Polanyi could not have seen. One major transformation of an existing capitalist system into another, after around some 200 to 300 years, suggests that a second transformation of an existing capitalist economic system is not out of thinking. Industrializing capitalism may well have turned into yet another capitalist system.

Addendum

Polanyi's economic analysis of Speenhamland is his basis for asserting the impossibility of any direction taken except laissez-faire that did not make things worse. Unlike the Elizabethan laws allowances were now designed to provide all the employed with putatively livable incomes. At a set-income level or below the employed allowances became the amount needed, beyond the payment by the owner, to reach that income level. It was required that the able-employed had to qualify for the allowance.

According to Polanyi, the crucial years of Speenhamland were an economic disaster. It caused such great harm to both would-be owners of production and the impoverished that there was no choice but to embrace laissez-faire. As he sees it, the owners during the period could do nothing to stop a great fall in unit production under Speenhamland. And in the range below the set-income level the owner lacked the leverage to do much about it. There was no way of raising payment as a carrot, or reducing it as a stick.

This last statement however begs a question not posed by Polanyi. Would not a raise of the set-income, increase payment for subjects functioning as object? It would seem to suggest an alternative road from that of laissez-faire. And indeed, starting with the Depression of the 1930' such a road was to be travelled for over forty years in the US, and then it was over.

Adolph Berle's & Gardener Means' *The Modern Corporation & Private Property*

In the final section of *The Modern Corporation & Private Property* (1932), Berle & Means write that the pre-industrial system of capitalism is a union of financial and productive elements of capital. The first is risk-taking in the form of investment in the capital stock of the *business—production-capital*—and the second one is entrepreneurship in pursuit of profit.

However, by the late-19th century the dominant structure of the corporation, as Berle & Means would have it, had become a clean separation of the financial as ownership, on the one hand, and on the other, control of the production process is paid to executives who independently take on the responsibilities of the corporation.

Berle & Means do not give significant consideration to the crucial union of finance and industry early on. It wrested control out of the hands of the employed by the turn of the 20th century. This neglect exposes a lacuna in their account. The separation they now refer to has turned the financial into investment in debt ownership, notably shares in the corporation, while the other includes management of the employed as objects. The latter is a new element, uniquely basic to industrializing capitalism. The subject/objects run on increasing mechanization simplifying the employed.

Karen Ho in her otherwise extremely insightful book, *Liquidated: An Ethnography of Wall Street* (2009) criticizes Berle & Means for unwittingly giving support to the claim that a clean separation of ownership from control of the corporation betrays a transcendent principle of capitalism: to honor the sanctity of private ownership. She claims that corporations never were controlled by owners of debt prior to the 1980's.

This apparently would include the direct ownership of the firm's capital stock, more common in the 17th and 18th century. During the 19th century ownership of debt instruments, stocks, bonds, futures, and derivatives were becoming prominent, and have remained so.

Unfortunately, much of Ho's argument is restricted to the stock market. As a consequence she does not sufficiently take account of the incipient years of industrial capitalism, roughly from the 1880's to the stock market crash of 1929.

She describes three characteristics of what she calls the modern corporation: "Complex organizational structure, multiple constituencies, and burgeoning sense of paternalistic responsibility" (p. 169–170). As such, she envisages what came to be known in the post-World War II golden age as *welfare capitalism.* But as she herself eventually discusses, the welfare state comes into existence in the US only with the crash of the economy. The response to it was both the New Deal restructuring of the US financial system and the strengthening of the rights of the non-management employed.

But in the forty years prior to the crash of 1929 the corporation as an institution accelerated up to and then during and after World War I, in the 1920's. The so-called robber barons in concert created a new industrial structure, corporate oligopolies with major market shares, coupled with competitive businesses that have marginal market share, and are forced to take the price of the oligopoly.

The barons of course were Morgan, Carnegie, Rockefeller, Vanderbilt et al, and in general the privileged few and their courtiers. These were owners of vast amounts of debt-instruments including shares of stock. They accumulated money generated in and through private and largely unregulated banking operations.

Adumbrating the current period, i.e., the years since roughly the 1980's, this handful of banker industrialists arranged mergers and acquisitions, expanded and often cornered a speculative market, were able and willing to significantly corrupt the State in their own private interests and so on. Further, oligopolies in those years too exploited child employment. There were extremely unhealthy and otherwise dangerous environments, payments to the employed were barely enough to live on, and their power over the State prevented any significant unionization, hence the leverage the employed attained under the New Deal.

Ho's error in this regard is matched by Berle & Means' fierce conviction that the industrial form of the corporation in the context of a capitalist economy, would not go back in the end to the principle, the sanctity even, of private ownership. And yet the owners of corporate debt—including but not restricted to stock—continued to retain the legal right to control the corporation through the New Deal and the post-WWII Golden Age period.

Berle & Means indicate that a wide spread of debt ownership among the public is what renders necessarily-passive shareholders, whose ownership is that of a consumer.

> "We cannot project into the future the trend here... The likelihood of a reversal of trend, however, seems so slight as not to inquire our serious attention. To think that the individual will place his savings in private business on a large scale in defiance of the ever-spreading corporate system is again to expect the most improbable.
>
> We must conclude, then, that parallel to the growth in the size of the industrial unit has come dispersion in its ownership such that an important part of the wealth of individuals consists of interests in great enterprises of which no one individual owns a major part". (p. 63–64)

It does seem that Berle & Means, like many thinkers of the time, unconsciously believed that there is only one true system of capitalism, at least in the sense of long-run stability. Mercantile capitalism is seen as an underdeveloped form of industrializing capital, as is the gilded age. But as early as the mid-1970's the corporation was reverting back to robber barons, although the context of it has radically changed, notably the onset of digitalization.

By the 1990's there has again been amassed huge holdings of debt-instruments in the hands of a tiny number of families trapped inside their own cultural bubble, who are anchored in powerful private and loosely-regulated financial, industrial, and military institutions. As in the early 20th century, these families have established themselves once again as sole creators, rulers, and constituents of the large-scale oligopolies and their ancillary industries.

This non-development, if you will, exposes Hegelian-type premises upon which rests conventional views of a capitalist system. There may be said to have been now a third capitalist system that has emerged, for a second time. Each reflects its own financial and industrial institutions in the light of the nature of the capital.

An important aspect of this is mathematical modelling of the capitalist system as the basis of economic theory. It has a deadly blind spot. It cannot see changes in the system itself. Economic theorists are still trapped in a general theory of an economy that hasn't existed, even ideally, for at least two hundred years.

Concerning this, Berle & Means wrote an interesting footnote literally a few pages before the end of their famous work, and somewhat out of the blue.

> It is frequently suggested that economic activity has become vastly more complex under modern conditions. Yet it is strange that the concentration of the bulk of industry into a few large units has not simplified rather than complicated the economic process. It is worth suggesting that the apparent complexity may arise in part from the effort to analyze the process in terms of concepts which no longer apply. (p. 308)

The Conclusion of Marcel Mauss's *The Gift*

Marcel Mauss, author of the seminal book, *The Gift* (1950) is one of a number of anthropologists in the 20th century, reaching a peak in the inter-war period, seriously studying archaic economies, that is, in cultures that do not have specific words for money. Notables along with Mauss are Bronislaw Malinowski, Raymond Firth, and Mary Douglas. Much of their studies are based on extensive observations of various existing tribal societies.

Raymond Firth, in his article, *Themes in Economic Anthropology* (1967) locates the heart of Mauss's book: "Mauss notes in essence that giving is an extension of the self, and hence the obligation to give is bound up with the notion of the self, its social bounds and social roles" (p. 10–11).

Mauss himself cites a 1906 report of observations of rules of generosity:

> In spite of the considerable volume of these exchanges, since the local group and the family know how to be self-sufficient in tools, etc., these presents do not serve the same purpose as commerce and exchange in

> more developed societies. The goal is above all a moral one, the object being to foster friendly feelings between the two persons in question, and if the exercise failed to do so, everything had failed. (p. 19)

However, when Mauss presumes the gift is really an exchange for social acceptance then the gift is a purchase by the gift-giver. This is to say the giver is not a debt-owner. In any contemporary market economy, why would one need to give things they possess, a gift, in return for a previous gift—especially outside the family—for one reason or another? And in the family, as an example the exchange of gifts at Christmas-time is an unpleasant obligation for many at best.

Mauss, in the last chapter of the book, the second section entitled *Conclusions for Economic Sociology and Political Economy*, introduces observations and interpretations that do not seem to fit the obligate-reciprocate explanation of gift-giving found in the three previous chapters. The obligation if anything is now expressed in terms of ritual and myths, or in our language, religious belief, i.e., that which is not a commodity.

> Several times we have seen how far this whole economy of the exchange-through-gift lay outside the bounds of the so-called natural economy, that of utilitarianism. All these very considerable phenomena of the economic life of all peoples and all these important vestiges of those traditions in societies close to our own, or of our own customs, fall outside the schemes normally put forward by those rare economists who have wished to compare the various types of known economies.
>
> The notion of value functions in these societies [is such that] very large surpluses, speaking in absolute terms, are amassed. These are signs of wealth and kinds of money are exchanged. Yet the whole of this very rich economy is still filled with religious elements. Money still possesses its magical power and is still linked to the clan or to the individual. The various economic activities, for example the market, are suffused with rituals and myths. They retain a ceremonial character that is obligatory and effective. It is indeed something other than utility that circulates in societies of all kinds, most of which are already fairly enlightened. The clans, the generations, and the sexes generally are in a perpetual state of economic ferment and this state of excitement is very far from being materialistic. (p. 72)

Mauss removes here the premise of the gift as *transgredient*—i.e., experienced as—commodity exchange. Thus, the giver can be seen instead as experiencing liberation in the form of separation of the self from the social other. From the other individual, clan, or even perhaps the tribe: "A perpetual state of economic ferment, far from being materialistic."

Along these lines, a sacrificial ceremony, giving back to the natural world, is not experienced as an obligatory reciprocation, but rather as fulfillment of individual debt to the social Totality, a liberation not a form of commodity purchase. In giving, the gift fulfills the individual's debt to the community, and in that way the individual can free the self from the social other.

In the first section of the last chapter, entitled *Moral conclusions*, Mauss applies the question raised and discussed in his monograph, concerning archaic money to the industrializing capitalist economies of the early 1920's, primarily of course in Western Europe and the US.

> It is possible to extend these observations to our own societies. A considerable part of our morality and our lives themselves are still generated with this same atmosphere of the gift, where obligation and liberty mingle. Fortunately, everything is still not wholly categorized in terms of buying and selling. (p. 65)

Hedge funds and trusts and, particularly after WWI, holdings of corporate stock, multiple forms of debt ownership, were in a few hands during the gilded age, from the late-19th century up to the last few years of the 1920's. Liberty in this context, is an adumbration of contemporary neo liberalism, exemplified in the part played by the enormously rich giving some of their *wealth earnings* to the poor, university, arts, and the global citizenry. That is, to the social collective in which private financing opens up a major non-governable space, filled by privately-owned financial institutions.

Mauss sees the rich as sources of non-reciprocated gifts, *charity*. The relation is neither commodity exchange nor debt accrued. He expresses, in this ending of the book, disapproval of such a means of supplying needs to the needy. He clearly is resisting such a movement, arising in the economy. His reasoning initially is genteel, however, enough perhaps to reveal his own condescension to those in need. "Charity is still wounding for him who has accepted it, and the whole tendency of our morality is to strive to do away with the unconscious and injurious patronage of the rich alms giver" (p. 65).

At the same time, Mauss is advancing a moral position that becomes a major basis of Roosevelt's *New Deal* of the 1930's.

> All our social insurance legislation, a piece of State socialism that has already been realized, is inspired by the following principle: The workers have given their life and labor, on the one hand to the collectivity, and on the other hand, to their employers. The State itself, representing the community, owes them as do the employers together with some assistance from themselves a certain security in life, against unemployment, sickness, old age, and death. (p. 67)

Welfare capitalism, and a mixed economy, ran through the US golden age of capitalism, from the post-WW II period in the fifties, peaking in the early 1960's, and lasting up to the mid-1970s. Mauss indicates that welfare capitalism in the Western European States had been established in as early as the mid-19th century.

But one sees through Mauss in his book—published in 1950—where he attempts to resist the realization that social guarantees of all, is threatened by ever-more powerful interests in massive *product capital* financed by deep-pocketed bankers and more generally owners of debt.

> All such morality and legislation corresponds in our opinion, not to any upheaval in the law, a return to it. On the one hand, one is seeing the dawning, and even the realization, of professional morality and corporate law. The compensatory funds and mutual benefit societies that industrial groupings are setting up in order to finance corporate charitable works, from a purely moral viewpoint are entirely admirable, save on one score: they are run entirely by the employers. (p. 68)

Addendum

The famous poet Ralph Waldo Emerson wrote an essay, *Gifts,* 1844 (mentioned by Mauss briefly.) A poem is attached that precedes it, signaling the lightness of the subject in the waning years before industrialization was in full force.

> *Gifts of one who loved me,—*
> *T'was a high time they came;*
> *When he ceased to love me,*
> *Time they stopped for shame.* (p. 180)

The Great Failure of 20th Century Economists

Economics as an academic discipline suffers from models that—for the most part unknowingly—are used for contemporary application, but are based on an atavistic system of the late-17th to the early 19th centuries. There is an implicitly *ergodic* premise that an essential capitalism exists indefinitely. Deep economic research is taken to be a project of uncovering ever-more sophisticated mathematical models of a purely market-driven economy.

It has long been clear to Marxists that since industrializing capitalism became established, markets have been dominated by corporate oligopolies. The latter strategically set prices in conjunction with production levels aided of course by mass marketing, collusion, political corruption and so forth. Hence *perfect competition,* which gives life to the *invisible hand* has long been invalidated.

A deeper critique, however, aimed at Marxist thought no less than the classical and neoclassical schools of thought, is about an assumption so basic to each school that it is seldom made explicit. Ricardo in his major work, *Principles of Political Economy and Taxation* obliquely, but succinctly, articulates it:

"The rate of interest, though ultimately and permanently governed by the rate of profit, is however subject to temporary variations from other causes" (1821: 349–50).

A very influential introductory undergraduate textbook in economics was written by Paul Samuelson in the late-forties. Over many editions it was a fixture throughout the golden age (circa 1952–1976). It qualified the notion of a pure market-economy solely driven by competition, by emphasizing that *in reality* there are only *mixed economies.*

However, what was meant by this amounted to no more than mere variations and exceptions to be expected within any system. It is true that in the golden age there were some nationalized industries, particular outside the US, as well as wide governmental services, regulated monopolies, genuine non-profit private institutions and so forth. Nonetheless the economic system itself was deeply understood by economists to be a singular entity both across nations and over time.

Unexpectedly, the post-golden age has been marked by a grand homogenization—an unmixed economy so to speak—approaching a universal privatization of production, dominated by large-scale global corporations that form oligopolies. And economists of almost all persuasions cannot perceive that this homogenization of production, spanning the last forty years, is an aspect of a different system of capitalism than the industrialization of the previous century.

By conceptualizing multiple systems of capitalism, an 18th century enlightenment belief in progress is found to explain the unified but terribly mistaken confidence of an essential capitalism. In the midst of the golden-age, economists expressed little doubt that the clear separation of speculative capital and production would be strengthened in the years to come.

But the post-golden age is in fact marked by the power of global corporations to generate infinite finance capital, an ever-growing and concentrated debt ownership. And indeed the military industrial complex—along with the State-insured private banking oligopoly—serve as key locations of State power wholly contracted out to corporations. This has in many respects created a hollowed out and seemingly helpless government body in its own right.

And yet, the uncontested premise of a singular capitalism remains, to wit a necessary vehicle by which owners of debt expand money is thought to be always for profit-motivated production of commodities; *i.e.*, a dominance of *product capital.* But money now is accumulating by a financial system that can generate money internally, independent of product capitalists. It forms a vast web of money circuits that do not include industry capital in the traditional sense of thinkers like Ricardo, Marx and Wicksell.

As clearly expressed by McMurtry in his book *The Cancer Stage of Capitalism* (2013); second edition

> On the surface, quasi-religious belief in a providential invisible hand assumed to convert selfish pursuit of money profit to promotion of the social good as a natural law. Yet what distinguishes the pure $-$’-$″ circuit today is that: (1) There is no *use-value* production between the transformation of money into more money; (2) This pure $-$’-$″ circuit has become for the first time in history the dominant form of capital investment. (p. 175)

A sign of historic change in the industrial capitalist is the self-identification of securitized corporations as insttutions owned by share-holders. The object has become to leverage flows of money coming into the corporation whether through sales or by taking it out of the corporation itself via junk bonds, equity firms and so forth. The cost of generating these flows of money is of course minimized.

But it is in order to maximize net revenues, not profits per se. In particular cases the self-multiplication of leveraged revenues is maximized with little or no profit from production at all, but nonetheless maintain enormous share value. Google, Apple, and Amazon, are leading instances of this.

It is not often commented on in the academic literature that the classical school of the late-17th through early 19th century—associated with the writings of Smith and Ricardo—conceived of capitalism in a context prior to mechanization let alone digitalization. At the same time, basic concepts framed in this very early period of capitalism have come to constitute an increasingly atavistic foundation upon which current economic theory heavily, and at the same time uneasily rests.

The three major schools of economic thought have been variously taught in university economics departments over the past sixty years or so. By date of arrival: Marxist political economy, neoclassical economics (Austrian and Walrasian) and Keynesian macroeconomics (neo-, new—and post-). Each was spawned in the context of mechanization, spanning the mid-19th century to the second decade of the 20th.

While the three are usually considered distinct approaches to economics, a fundamental concept at the start of each of them is: *All markets are competitive.* In other words all economic agents are price-takers. That leads (by hook or by crook), to the normative principle of Pareto efficiency and in turn the normative notion of an ideal set of prices, over any given (finite) time-horizon, that uniquely clears all markets.

Inferred then are stability forces drawing the system to this set of prices. And from this is inferred a systematic movement to *full employment* and a *uniform rate of return on capital* across industries. Also, but tacitly, the return on capital is commonly understood to be generated by the production and sale of *goods*.

The core models, whichever of these schools one singles out, mostly neglect, analytically, the striking difference between the pre-industrial and industrializing capitalist systems, and more to the point for that matter between contemporary digitalization and industrialization. Envisaged as early as the late 17th century, capitalist businesses were seen in a pre-industrial context, taking in the main the form of individual entrepreneur, family businesses, partnership etc., and including financial relations involving silent partners, local bankers, issuance of bonds, stock companies of various sorts and so on. The capitalist is understood to be engaged in employing primarily manual activities, and selling the goods produced primarily in local markets.

McMurtry:

> The real free market was a great advance of the communities' control of its own life when it was no longer subjugated to kings, lords or municipal monopolies for the privilege of its existence. It was an opening of

> liberty when ordinary individuals could freely exchange with each other in a public space to acquire the foods or crafts they chose to produce or buy. Money here was not a weapon to reduce others to instruments of bosses. Real money in the real free market is a universal medium that enables individuals to transact across differences of jobs and goods without incommensurables of worth standing in the way of their free exchange. What remains of a publicly established legal tender and credit for individual exchange among citizens in the global corporate system? (p. 112)

Addendum

Alan Blinder reviewed, in the New York Review of Books, a book by Jeff Madrick, author of: *Seven Bad Ideas: How Mainstream Economists Have Damaged America and the World.* Blinder asks the question *What's the Matter with Economics, and Exchange,* Dec.18, 2014.

Blinder is an accomplished, highly-respected mainstream economist, a professor at Princeton. In the end, he replied to the replies of his review which were rather critical. The details are not of interest here, but there is a point of contention that touches on how irrelevant elite orthodox economists like Blinder have become. In very clear language Blinder makes mainstream assertions in response to an attack on his review:

> I don't think any mainstream economist doubts that free, competitive markets perform their core functions far better than any alternative mechanism.
>
> Mainstream economists do normally view the invisible hand as the best mechanism for delivering the right goods and services to the right people at the lowest possible costs.

There is no doubt that there has not been a capitalist system composed of free and competitive markets for at least since the industrialization, including corporate control of the production processes. In the contemporary scheme of things virtually all industries are dominated by oligopolies. This fact means markets are not competitive and in that sense are not free, as that term is understood by economists in general. In short, corporations in an oligopoly, given demand limitations, can collectively set its price.

Recently, for instance, US is calling upon Saudi Arabia to purposely raise the prices of oil, so as to prevent higher cost producers, fracking operations, from losing their share of the market. No one reporting this question the fact that the oil industry is a global oligopoly. It is understood that if Saudi Arabia chooses to cut back production it can unilaterally drive up the market price.

Of course, there is a whole legal structure delineating market relations. To a large extent this is constructed by corporations and States that are largely governed by corporations. It is in the power of both therefore to affect, at times determine, market activity. There is simply no meaning then to either of Blinder's assertions.

Suppose it were true that a system of free and competitive markets would generate an ideal price system, it still remains that the present system is definitively not one of free and competitive markets. That is to say, Blinder is applying a deep model relevant at best to another ideal system, but not the system at all that exists.

Blinder put up something of a defense, writing:

> The invisible hand is an approximation, usually not applicable in the real world without significant modification. And those modifications point toward, inter alia, antitrust laws, consumer protection, fair labor standards, health and safety regulation, financial regulation and much more.

As it happens one of my very favorite professors at the Columbia graduate school when I was a graduate student there was the late Kelvin Lancaster, well-known mathematical economist within the profession. For a while he thought about an invisible hand, in his words that had a bit of arthritis. The hand has to be given some help, but not necessarily much, just the minimum. That's certainly better than socialism, isn't it?

Lancaster called what Blinder is appealing to *the theory of second-best.* He showed mathematically, using a standard general equilibrium model that if there is any deviation at all from even one market that was not free along with competitive markets, there is no coherent way of ranking the remaining price outcomes. In other words, based on the model there is no second best.

And so, Blinder exemplifies the dependence to this day of an 18th century concept that has come to constitute an impossibly weak foundation upon which current economic theory, some three hundred years later, still heavily, and at the same time uneasily, rests.

CHAPTER 2

Corresponding Thoughts of Benjamin: Kafka, Bakhtin and the Prague School

The Role of Language in Trauerspiel and Tragedy

Walter Benjamin, age 22, over the next seven years (1914–1921) wrote intensely short pieces, transcending academic disciplines. He later organized them somewhat in a book, *The Origin of German Tragic Drama*, finished around 1925. In these early writings Benjamin goes deeply into *sui generis* lines of thought. And as it happened, two others, unknown by at least one of them, possibly both were travelling along side of him: Franz Kafka and Mikhail Bakhtin.

Kafka was in fact a close friend of Benjamin's in these years of his youth. Kafka's own literary career took off (so to speak) in 1913 with the publishing of the story *The Judgment*, and he finished a true master-piece of literature, the novel *The Castle*, in 1922, two years before he died. There is nothing, at least that I know of, that is left of any of the myriad discussions the two must have had. One can only imagine.

Mikhail Bakhtin, leader of the *Bakhtin circle* in Russia, three years younger than Benjamin, published a book in 1919, his important early work, *Toward a Philosophy of the Act*. It and many other writings of Bakhtin amazingly run parallel to the early Benjamin writings. Bakhtin also as Benjamin did, continued to work on this set of unusually critical ideas, particularly in the realm of *social semiotics*, throughout the 1920s.

According to Tim Beasley-Murray, in his book *Mikhail Bakhtin and Walter Benjamin: Experience and Form* (2007), there is no evidence of Bakhtin having knowledge of Benjamin's writings, nor the other way around (p. 4–8). Both, in those early years, were rather obscure figures and Benjamin travelled only once to Russia for a few months in 1926, while Bakhtin in those years did not leave Russia at all.

And yet Bakhtin begins *Philosophy of the Act* with the observation of shapes of what Benjamin terms *open and closed times* which are not commensurate. He further notes that for both of them, interestingly enough, social semiotics is approached through aesthetic intuitions.

Bakhtin:

> The moment which discursive theoretical thinking (in the natural sciences and in philosophy), historical description-exposition, and aesthetic intuition have in common, and which is of particular importance for our inquiry is this: all these activities establish a fundamental split between the content or sense of a given act/activity and the actuality of its being, the actual and once occurring experience of it. (p. 1–2)

Benjamin, in his piece Theological-political Fragment (1920–1921):

> Only the Messiah consummates all history, in the sense that it alone redeems, completes, and creates its relation to the *Messianic*. For this reason nothing historical can relate itself on its own account to anything Messianic. Therefore the Kingdom of God is not the telos of the historical dynamic; it cannot be set as a goal. From the standpoint of history it is not the goal but the end. (p. 312)

The messianic, in other words, is in closed time, exemplified by the scriptures and learned from the prophets. Hence, as told in the story of Job, there is no room to judge a subject's guilt, i.e. *answerability*, on the basis of how they have acted in open time.

Benjamin, in his piece Fate and Character (1919):

> In the Greek classical development of the idea of fate, the happiness granted to a man is by no means understood as confirmation of an innocent conduct of life, but as a temptation to the most grievous offense *hubris*. There is therefore no relation of fate to innocence. (p. 306)
>
> It is not therefore really man who has a fate; rather, the subject of fate is indeterminable. The judge can perceive fate wherever he pleases; with every judgment he must blindly dictate. (p. 307–308)

In that context, Benjamin points to a "demonic stage of human existence, when legal statutes determined not only men's relationships but also their relationship to the Gods," in particular sacrifices to the Gods. He infers, then, that the demonic law was free of any ideas of guilt and innocence. Sacrifices to the contrary were gifts to the Gods.

Kafka imagines the human others whom we cannot experience or they us, others as we might have been and who in some ways we still are, but by definition we cannot communicate it.

Benjamin, in his piece Trauerspiel and Tragedy (1916):

> The idea of closed-time appears in the Bible, as its dominant historical idea: As *messianic time*. The idea of closed time, that is, is not understood as the idea of an individual time. What differentiates *tragic* from *messianic—time* is that the former relates to the latter as individual relates to divinely closed-time. (p. 242)

The mythic tragic heroes of antiquity, e.g., Agamemnon or Oedipus, are reduced to the Shakespearian Hamlets and Macbeths, no longer touched by the Gods but rather signs of witches and ghosts who are left unknowable. It is all-knowing and all-encompassing fate, which Benjamin describes as "the idea of closed-time," and that eventually becomes the Laws of Nature.

> Shakespeare tragedy resides in the mastery with which it sets off the different stages of tragedy from one another and makes them stand out, like repetitions of a theme. In contrast, classical tragedy is characterized by the ever more powerful upsurge of tragic forces. The ancients know of tragic fate, where Shakespeare knows of the tragic hero, the tragic action. Goethe rightly calls him Romantic. (p. 243)

Hence, Shakespeare connects the idea of the individual in the moment when the tragic hero is revealed, captured in the image of the tragic mask suddenly torn off. Open time, in this moment, is usurped by the individual's fate, but it is bereft of a divine truth. It is not messianic, that is, in the sense of the Gods' taming of human *hubris* writ large.

Benjamin sees this as "almost a paradox" inured in the structure of Shakespearian tragedy. Decisive stages in open time, culminating in—"when tragic-time bursts open"—the revelation that in essence the individual's experience of open time is no longer and never was. Benjamin, then, suggests that *messianic reduction* fosters science, insofar as now it assigns the answerability of *hubris* to be within nature.

Benjamin, in Trauerspiel and Tragedy, emphasizes that the messianic reduction is at one with tragedy in one crucial sense. Each implies the death as the end of the subject. In *both* cases open time is swallowed by revelation.

The tragic hero's fate is seen by Benjamin as an ironic immortality. The tragic hero dies twice, first as active subject in open time, the moment of the tragic revelation, and second, no longer existing in open time, a being that must cease to be alive "because no one can live exclusively in closed-time" Benjamin concludes, somewhat ironically, one presumes, "It is the real expression of the hero's guilt" (p. 243).

Benjamin, then, focuses on the Trauerspiel, as an historic break from tragedy.

> Historical life, as it was conceived at the time is the Trauerspiel's content, is its true object. In this it is different from tragedy. For the object of the latter is not history, but myth, and the tragic stature of the *dramatis personae* does not derive from rank—the absolute monarchy—but from the pre-historic epoch of their existence—the past age of heroes.

Benjamin perceives the dialogical articulation of social relativity embodied by the Trauerspiel, one that recalls the conclusion reached in an earlier piece: Two poems by Friedrich Holderlin (1914–1915):

> It cannot be a matter of investigating ultimate elements, for the ultimate law of this world is precisely connected—as the unity of the function of that which connects and that which is connected. But an especially central site of this connectedness must still be noted, one in which the energy of the inner form shows itself all the mightier, the more surging and formless is the life that has been denoted. (p. 32)

This is to say, in open time there is no closure. And as such there is no existence of open time, only closed time. Benjamin sees the shape of time in the Trauerspiel as "one branch of a hyperbola, whose other branch lies in the infinite." The inner-life of the social Totality, the infinite, is revealed by its active subjects in open time, each residing in "the restricted space of earthly existence," each engaged in dialogue with and within the infinite, until death.

Benjamin calls attention to the *dialogical* aspect of the Trauerspiel by noting its characteristic even number of acts. And he observes that the characters in the Trauerspiel being royalty, is another expression of the form's dialogical foundation. Even in this limiting case of the royal subject—Kafka's emperor of China—there is no escaping "the peculiar mirror-nature of game and play." The Trauerspiel, itself, which is either historical drama or re-enactment, is the art of re-creating experience in open time.

> The *Trauerspiel* artistically exhausts the historical idea of repetition; it thus fastens on a problem that is completely different from that of tragedy. (p. 244)

The mirror-nature of the two branches of a hyperbola, by which Benjamin imagines a work in the form of Trauerspiel, functions as an example. It marks "temporal repetitions" of the social Totality in closed time. The artistic exhaustion takes the reflection in the mirror to the infinite, the historical-philosophical equivalent, perhaps, of the poetized whole in two poems, the *social Totality*. Repetition is known only in the limit. As written by Jean-Francois Lyotard, "Repetition escapes from repetition in order to repeat" (p. 153).

Thus, while a particular work in the form of the Trauerspiel contains a dramatic resolution it is never an absolute one. The content of the work comprises self/other dialogues of active subjects that exist dramatically in open time, implying that the state of the Totality in closed time is fundamentally uncertain.

> The nature of temporal repetition is such that no closed form can be based on it. And even if the relation of tragedy to art remains problematic, even if it may be both more and less than an art form, it nevertheless remains in every case a closed form. But the Trauerspiel is in itself unclosed and the idea of its resolution no longer lies within the realm of drama. And here is the point where—proceeding from the analysis of form—the distinction between tragedy and Trauerspiel decisively emerges. The remains of the Trauerspiel are called music. Perhaps it is the case that, just as tragedy marks the transition from historical time to dramatic time the Trauerspiel marks the passage from dramatic time into the time of music. (p. 244)

Shapes of Time

Peter Fenves in his book *The Messianic Reduction: Walter Benjamin and the Shape of Time* (2010) has observed that the mathematician Hausdorff, at the beginning of the twentieth century, found formulations of continuous functions that are nonetheless non-differentiable at any point (pp. 106–118). This suggests that as a mathematical expression of *historical time*, the social Totality at any point is determined. It is the dependent variable. The continuous acts of subjects can be in turn undetermined, the independent variable.

Gershom Scholem, Benjamin's chief mentor in his youth, turned this around, rendering it messianic by positing that closed time is determined by the Gods, and open time is undetermined: A great differential equation that expresses the world, and is found in Kafka's works, especially the three novels.

Benjamin's premises, however, are such that spoken language subsumes mathematics, the latter itself being the language of a particular logic. In the language of Bakhtin, Language is the *transgredient of experience*. It is what thoughts and feelings are communicated in, as distinguished from what thought and feeling are.

Tim Beasley-Murray:

> Bakhtin's point is that language cannot be reduced to abstract, logical or mathematical expression alone. The utterance always bears some of the traces of its genesis in a particular, historically, and socially located context. Benjamin similarly argues that Kant's inability to account for the fullness of possible experience is the result of his tendency to seek the model of knowledge not in language but in mathematic formulae. For both Bakhtin and Benjamin thinkers, language contains a fuller form of experience than the minimal experience that is grasped by abstract thinking. (p. 88–89)

Benjamin's understanding of semiotics is that language goes beyond mathematics by way of two basic truths from which social applications prove fruitful. Benjamin draws an ontological distinction. In open time the activities experienced by subjects are infinite in every direction and unfulfilled at any moment. On the other hand, in closed time the subject communicates in language. It is the being of experience, in the sense that experiences can be sustained in the mind.

This signifies the fundamental incommensurability of these shapes of time. The act in open time, as such, is singular, and therefore the tragic revelation is purely that which the act communicates to the subjects in the course of dialogue in language.

Benjamin, in his very short but important piece, The Role of Language in Trauerspiel and Tragedy:

> The tragic rests on a lawfulness governing the spoken word between two humans. There is no tragic pantomime. A corollary is that language exists *only* in closed time. There is no tragic pantomime. No tragedy exists outside human dialogue, and there is no form of human dialogue other than the tragic.
>
> The *word in transformation* is the linguistic principle of the Trauerspiel. There is a pure emotional life of the word in which it purifies itself by developing from a sound of nature to the pure sound of feeling.
>
> How language in general can fill itself with mourning, and be the expression of mourning is the basic question of the Trauerspiel, alongside that other question. How can mourning as a feeling gain entry into the linguistic order of art?

> The essence of the *Trauerspiel* is already contained in the old adage that all of nature would begin to mourn if ever it were endowed with language. (p. 246–247)

It needs to be added that Benjamin's description of the Trauerspiel is the same as important respects of the works of some of the great playwrights from the late-19th Century well into second half of the 20th; Chekhov, Ibsen, Arthur Miller and several others come easily to mind. The latter certainly probe the linguistic confusion when the social Totality is sharply moving and therefore the lingual communication is akin to the tower of babel.

Benjamin's discussion of the Trauerspiel points directly to the striking convergence of his thought and that of Bakhtin, within the *Bakhtin circle.* Each arrives at the conception of language as transgredient of experience, thereby constituting the active subject, their existence of self-evident consciousness. Bakhtin, like Benjamin, find the roots of the transgredient in the dialogical. Language is the sole "plane of consciousness" in which self and other connect and differentiate.

In one of Bakhtin's early pieces, Author and Hero in Aesthetic Activity (1919):

> In life we do this at every moment: We evaluate ourselves from the standpoint of others, and through other we try to understand and take into account what is transgredient to our own consciousness. But all these moments or constituents of our life that we recognize and anticipate through the other are rendered into its language. (p. 15–16)

Benjamin, in The Role of Language in Trauerspiel and Tragedy illustrates language as transgredient by citing the emotional effect on the audience during the dramatic course of the Trauerspiel.

> The dialogue in its pure manifestations of tragedy is neither sad nor comic, but tragic. To that extent, tragedy is the classic and pure dramatic form. For mourning is not like the tragic; it is not a ruling force—the indissoluble and inescapable law of orders that attain closure in the tragedy. Rather, it is a feeling. That is the riddle of the Trauerspiel. What inner relation at the heart of mourning releases it from the existence of pure feeling and lets it enter the order of Art? (p. 246–247)

In the open time of the Trauerspiel emotions are generated by the transgredience, what Benjamin terms the *word in transformation*, which is intrinsically dialogical, or, as he would have it, it becomes symphonic, musical.

> The word in transformation is the linguistic principle of the Trauerspiel. There is a pure emotional life of the word in which it purifies itself by developing from a sound of nature to the pure sound of feeling. For this word, language is only a transitional phase. It describes a path from natural sound, via lament, to music. (p. 247)

The dialogical nature of the Trauerspiel is revealed, then, in the "musical principle of language" of which it is constituted. It is fundamentally "symphonic." The transgredient is "splitting the drama into characters." These are experienced by the audience members as a web of self-other dialogues in open time that enter their own dialogues, which enter others and, in that way the Trauerspiel provides a glimpse, it poetizes the social Totality.

The larger point that Benjamin makes in this context is that the emotional effect ultimately derives from the stark uncertainty of open time, in which the characters are being observed by the audience.

> Midway through this passage nature sees itself betrayed by language, and that tremendous stemming of feeling becomes mourning. These plays represent the stemming of nature, a tremendous damming up of feeling as it were to which a new world suddenly opens up in the word of meaning, of unfeeling historical time. (p. 247)

Benjamin concludes the Role of Language in Trauerspiel and Tragedy with a brief one-sentence annotation: "Whereas in tragedy the eternal immobility of the spoken word prevails, the Trauerspiel gathers the endless resonance of its sound" (p. 249).

In contrast to Peter Fenves' conclusions in *The Messianic Reduction: Walter Benjamin and the Shape of Time* it is clear that Benjamin, rather than giving up in the end his ideas as failure for lack of mathematics, to the contrary it provides a critique of existing neo-Kantian semiotics, linguistic theory, the latter associated primarily with the contemporary position of Charles Pierce, itself rooted in Edmund Husserl's phenomenology.

At the outset of On Language as Such and on the Language of Man, he makes it clear that since that which communicates itself in language is a thought or a feeling, a "mental entity," it is *not* language itself, it is a set of signs.

> All that is asserted here is that all expression, insofar as it is a communication of mental meaning is to be classed as language. To understand a linguistic entity it is always necessary to ask of which mental entity it is the direct expression of. The view that the mental essence of a thing consists precisely in its language—this view taken as a hypothesis—is the great abyss into which all linguistic theory threatens to fall, and to survive suspended precisely over this abyss is its task. (p. 315)

In this context, then, Benjamin begins by setting out the chief semiotic issue the resolution of which needs to be reached. He asserts that if the initial approach to linguistic theorizing is to *prove* the hypothesis that there is a qualitative distinction between the subject's ideas ("mental essence") and the language that communicates it, an identity of conscious being and linguistic being seems to create "a deep and incomprehensible paradox."

The logic is that such an identity, *a priori*, rules out the existence of ideas exogenous to the subject's consciousness. Therefore, it would appear to contradict the hypothesis. This is to say, the identity of conscious and linguistic leads to the abyss, threatening Kantian and the neo-Kantian thought of Husserl, and indeed going back to Descartes. It all plunges into solipsism.

As said here, Benjamin instead takes as given the distinction between a mental entity and the linguistic entity in which it communicates. This distinction indeed seems so unquestionable that it is rather the frequently asserted identity between mental and linguistic being that is problematic. Nevertheless, that seeming paradox is found by Benjamin at the center of linguistic theory, by removing the hypothesis (p. 315, On Language as Such and on the Language Man, 1916).

Language, in that sense, both is based on and refers solely to ideas that are communicated. Any particular spoken language absorbs ideas into itself, via dialogue, via the renewal, alteration, creation and disappearance of words. Thus, it is only in words that the subject has access to not only the *other*, but to the *self* as well.

Semiotics of the Social: Karcevskij's Principle and the Imaginary Community

The article by Sergej Karcevskij of the Prague school, "The Asymmetric dualism of the linguistic sign" (1929), addresses the problem of the *differential character* of the phonetic sign.

> On the one hand language must supply a means of communication for all the members of a linguistic community. But on the other hand it must serve equally as a means of self-expression for each of the individuals in this community, and however socialized the forms of our psychic life may be the individual cannot be reduced to the social. The semiotic values in a language necessarily have a potential and hence general character so as for language to remain above the whims of the individual above individuals as such. At the same time, these potential signs must apply to a concrete reality that is constantly changing. (p. 49)

Karcevskij advances a "general semiotic principle," as an explanation of how language meets the requirement that the phonetic sign be an intersection of these two dimensions, "coordinates"; that is, a conveyance of meaning to the subject, through the latter's unique transgredient of experience, and the unique inter-change of meaning between self and other implicit in self/other dialogue.

> Every linguistic sign is potentially a homonym and a synonym at the same time. It belongs simultaneously to a series of transposed values of a single sign and to a series of analogous values expressed by different signs. Homonymy and synonymy constitute the two most important relational coordinates of language because they are the most dynamic, flexible and adequate into concrete reality. (p. 51)

This is to say, for a given language sign—existentially a specific complex of sounds—there is a corresponding set of values, i.e., meanings. Different meanings in a set are homonyms if they share the same sign: peace, piece, peas, and pees. A set of synonyms have different signs but share the same meaning: peace, unity, amity, accord.

Since meaning derives from experience the set of synonyms is composed of "different variants of the same phenomenological class." The set of homonyms are, by contrast "psychological in essence" (Galan, 1984: p. 84–88). Apart from trivial exceptions—for instance puns—and like an aesthetic object, a set of homonyms as such does not impinge upon the existential.

Karcevskij puts forward the fact that the flexibility of language comes from the openness of both relational coordinates of language—homonyms and synonyms—since both sets are open, always being potentially new synonyms and homonyms respectively.

Thus, through synonymy, novel experiences of existential reality are incorporated analogically into the existing set of phonetic signs associated with a phenomenological class. Through homonymy, a new class does not require a new phonetic sign, so that semiosis is always pragmatic; it cannot be fully detached from its existential context.

> The fluidity provided by synonymy and homonymy enables the semiotic transgredient to accommodate experiences of the existential in during the subject orientating self and other. This accommodation is virtually continuous, but we do not notice this unless the gap between the adequate (usual) value of the sign and its occasional value is sufficiently large to strike us. (p. 52)

In these regards, EW Galan, a leading historian of the Prague school, asserts in the chapter "Semiotic reformulation," of his book *Historic Structures: The Prague School Project 1928–1946*:

> It is impossible for reality as such to be totally new, since it would be incomprehensible *as well as without name*: there is, in short, no perception without immediate categorization. Just as a unique fact is fated to be unintelligible, so too a unique word is inconceivable, for like a fact, it is the outcome of a particular crossing of two general coordination, this time the formal or grammatical and the semantic. It follows that a word likewise a genus, not what is individual, in the more exact terms of modern logic, a verbal sign always presents a token of an existent type. (p. 85)

Given the coordinates of synonyms and homonyms in terms of words corresponding to phenomenological classes, I suggest then social *identity signs* corresponding to self and other.

If we were to put this on an individual level, an identical sign attached to a set of subjects, is like a set of homonyms. Each has the same sign. And, like the meaning of words, the particular *subject values* in the set vary. Karcevskij: "The exact semantic value of a word can be adequately established only as functions of the concrete subject" (p. 52).

Subject value is akin to dialogical meaning, that is: *Who is the subject*, both internally and in relation to others. The identity signs on the other hand are shared names of subjects in the set, each a multi-dimensional token of an existing type, *e.g.* I am a White Jewish American man with a wife and one child; I am (named) David Gleicher.

It would seem that the dialogical coordinates lead to homonyms, like the word. Such a homonymic set of subjects is an instance, then of an *imaginary community*. The relation of the subject and the imaginary community hovers over virtually every aspect of Dialogism, even as it is rarely addressed explicitly. Bakhtin's approach implicitly requires the social-as-community to be understood inter-subjectively. The subject is oriented by its experience of another individual as that which the subject is not, *and* as that which the subject is. In order to fix a point in a self/other coordinate system the inter-subjective must be an experience of both.

Karcevskij:

> It has become a commonplace to affirm that linguistic values exist only by virtue of their opposition to one another. So stated, this idea leads to an absurdity: a tree is a tree because it is neither a house nor a horse nor a river. Opposition pure and simple necessarily leads to chaos and cannot serve as the basis of a *system*. True differentiation presupposes a simultaneous resemblance and difference. (p. 51)

Conceptually, then, the *imaginary community* is a transfiguration of the task each subject faces orienting self and other. It is a set of individuals, each individual inside the community being experienced by each other one as self, and individuals outside the set, as other. Freud, in *Civilization and Its Discontents* (1930), hits upon a major root of the imaginary community, by dialogically applying the "pleasure principle" to the detachment of self from other, early in the life of the subject.

> Normally, there is nothing of which we are more certain than the feeling of our self. This appears to us as something autonomous and unitary, marked off distinctly from everything else.
>
> Further reflection tells us that the adult's feeling of self cannot have been the same from the beginning. It must have gone through a process of development. An infant at the breast does not a yet distinguish self from the external world as the source of the sensations flowing in upon it. The infant must be very strongly impressed by the fact that some sources of excitation can provide sensations at any moment, whereas other sources evade it from time to time and only reappear.
>
> A further incentive to a disengagement of the [self] from the general mass of sensations—that is, to the recognition of an 'outside', an

> external world—is provided by the sensations of pain and unpleasance the removal and avoidance of which is enjoined by the pleasure principle. A tendency arises to separate from everything that can become a source of such unpleasance, to throw it outside and to create a pure pleasure-self which is confronted by a strange and threatening outside. (p. 12–14)

The imaginary community separates others from the community of the self, effectively providing the social subject a global self/other orientation. There are certain synonyms of the social subject and some not. The individual subject then experiences its own unique self/other dialogue inside a homonymic set of social subjects inside the community.

The individual subject, of course, has the absolute freedom to witness and judge the ongoing orientation of the community somewhat like its own self/other dialogues. However, crucially, the subject lacks the relative freedom to authorize acts of the community, as it can—and must—the self. There is no communal answerability in other words.

Michael Bakhtin in *Art and Answerability: Early Essays* (1919):

> To be sure, in life, too, we do this all the time: we evaluate ourselves from the standpoint of others, and through others we try to understand and take into account what is transgredient to our own consciousness. Thus, we take into account the value of our outward appearance from the standpoint of the possible impression it may produce upon the other.
>
> But all these moments or constituents of our life that we recognize and anticipate through the other are rendered completely immanent to our own consciousness, and they do not disrupt the unity of our own life—a life that finds no rest within itself and never coincides with its given presently exiting makeup (p. 15–16).
>
> Insofar as I participate in the world of otherness in a justified manner, I may become passively active in that world. A luminous image of such passive activity is the dance. In dancing my exterior, visible only to others and existing only for others, coalesces with my inner self-feeling organic activity. Passive self-activity is conditioned by the already given, available resources: it is predetermined by given being; it does not after the meaning-governed countenance of being. Passive self of activity does not transform anything formally. (p. 137)

The subject's experience of the imaginary community is aporetic for the reason that its unity derives from the community-as-self. It is the social as uniquely experienced by individual subjects. But it enters into each subject's experience of the existential as an identity sign. It is neither a natural or aesthetic object, nor a unitary subject. Try to locate its acts purely in the existential, and you will only find individual subjects, each engaged in its own unique self/other dialogue

This is, then, a core dialogical critique of political economy. It is succinctly summarized by the Italian philosopher Giorgio Agamben in in his *State of Exception* (2005), who refers to Benjamin's written letter to Scholem and in an essay on Kafka, respectively:

> Benjamin: "The Scripture without its key is not Scripture, but life."
>
> Kafka's most proper gesture consists not in having to maintain a law that no longer has any meaning, but in having shown that it ceases to be law and blurs at all points with life. (p. 63)

Addendum

Of note Karcevskij makes the point that what he terms, in the context of linguistics, "homonyms," are technically 'homophones', insofar as the set of meanings that share a phonetic sign, is arbitrary; it is not a unit, existentially: "The transposed value is no longer felt" (p. 54, n.3).

Keys to Kafka's *Castle*, a Guideline for the Innocent Reader

The Narrative. Each of Kafka's three novels lives simultaneously in *closed* and *open time* (as we all do more or less). These terms come from the early writings of Walter Benjamin. The latter also uses for the same dichotomy the terms *fulfilled* and *unfulfilled* time. And he refers to the two intertwined as the time of history. The latter is "infinite in every direction and unfulfilled at every moment" (p. 241).

The Russian founder of dialogism, Mikhail Bakhtin—whose early writings in many respects run parallel to Benjamin's, and in turn to Kafka's works altogether—expresses this more concretely, *Toward a Philosophy of the Act* (circa 1922–1924):

> An act of our activity, or our actual experiencing, is like a two-faced Janus. It looks in two opposite directions. It looks at the objective unity of a domain of culture and at the never-repeatable uniqueness of actual lived and experienced life. (p. 2)

In reading a Kafka novel, an innocent reader, heretofore referred to simply as 'the reader', is confronted by a third person narrative the very being of which is non-sensible. The narrative—with, perhaps, rare exception—is inhabited in K.'s experiences. These are encapsulated in a series of marginal moments, each chapter, roughly speaking, a once-occurring event. The *transgredient* of experience, language, is applied to K.'s experiences as subject, in open time. However, within Benjamin's semiotic conceptions, this contradicts the fact that experiences are uncommunicable in unfulfilled time. Language is only in, and, by definition, necessary to fulfilled time. In short, the only framework of the narration conceivable to the reader is not-an-I communicating to not-a-you.

The realm of Kafka's novels suggests itself in a saying of Jesus from the *Prologue to the Gospel of Thomas* (1992).

> Know what is in front of your face and what is hidden from you will be disclosed to you. For there is nothing hidden that will not be revealed. (p. 23)

Kafka effectively is revealing to the reader a spiritual, aka mental, realm "in front of the face," and a wall blocking out the other. But he does so by creating its absolute absence; a narration solely on the other side of the wall. It inhabits K's experiences in open time, sensed in the moment through eyes, nose, ears, skin; a world only knowable through the transgredient of language.

This is described eminently well by J. Hillis Miller, in an article "The sense of an un-ending: the resistance to narrative closure in Kafka's *Das Schloss*." This is clear only in open time, however, and it is not true that when closed time is included.

> The narrator never explicitly passes judgment on K.'s judgments, K.'s may be right or he may be wrong. The narrative voice never says anything about that. Indeed, it never says anything at all on its own hook. The narrative voice just transposes first-person present tense narration into third-person past tense narration.
>
> K. does not remain the same from one narrative segment to another. Nor do the characters. The strict rule of the narration is that neither K.

> nor the narrator ever has direct access to the minds, feelings or bodily sensations of the other characters. (p. 110–111)

Thus the reader can only follow K's experiences in a context of non-communication, in open time: always marginal. Words about things happening to K., decisions he seems to be making about them, his activities, what he observes, are encompassed in sequences of K.'s dialogue with various others. These exchanges are what the writing for the most part is literally comprised of. Each moment (chapter) of the novels, is marked by one or two or so prolonged exchanges, primarily one to one. And the spoken words of the dialogue thus seem to be means of communicating to the reader. But in open-time, paradoxically, the words spoken are only a fact of the dialogue, a running transcript so to speak. In common parlance, there is no exposition, either subtle or obvious. The dialogue is simply an experience K. is having.

This is a distinctive element of Kafka's writing, immediately sensed by the reader, although what exactly is behind the effect is not so obvious. Kafka's trick is that the words of the dialogue are being reported verbatim, but do not dually communicate to the reader as a traditional narrator would. Unlike K. the reader can hardly say with any certainty what the gist is of any particular dialogue from beginning to end and anywhere in between. But it is not that the language is foreign.

The style of Kafka's writing is rather direct, unadorned, always with a straight-face. However, with respect to the reader, what is being said is replete with obscure references, unspoken motivations, unknown expectations, inappropriate gestures; even the identity of K. himself is uncertain from the first page of the novel and on. Hence the reader has little access to actual meaning in the usual sense.

On many occasion K. seems to be experiencing his own thought during an exchange. But while the reader vaguely might discern what seem to be tactics or strategies in open time, K.'s thought remains uncommunicated, if for no other reason than the reader cannot fathom K.'s objectives, so that any tactic let alone strategy, as is, is inscrutable.

An important notion of Benjamin's runs parallel, semiotically, both to Kafka's unique narrations and the pure realm of the mind

> It is fundamental to recognize that this spiritual essence communicates itself in language not through it. Hence there is no speaker of languages. Spiritual being communicates itself in a language, it is not outwardly identical with linguistic. (p. 252–253, As Language as Such and on the Language of Man, *Early Writings*)

Kafka's invitation into the mind's pure realm is via absence. It reveals a realm that cannot be known, because there is no true transgredient. It does not exist in language. Kafka reveals it in the negative. The dialogue consists of words that exist in the moment. Thereby Kafka effectively creates pseudo-transgredience. The sequences of dialogues filling each of the novels are in a language known to (of) the reader, but communicate to the reader only language.

As Benjamin would have it, then, the Kafkaesque narration cannot be. The words of the text in open time are not being told to the reader, because that would be closed time. In other words, K. is not telling a story, and he is not speaking after the fact to the reader about his experiences. Nor by extension can there be an omnipotent author, Kafka for instance, telling a story of K. Instead, to the reader, the language of the characters and K. in dialogue is a kind of Platonic form, amidst infinite forms inhabiting an unknowable realm between being and knowing.

The reader of a Kafka novel is faced from the beginning with unexplained contradictions and general vagueness. As the pages turn, the reader can be expected to feel the oppressiveness of pseudo-transgredient communication. There is simply no exposition subtle or otherwise. Many readers of course decide in vain that there is never going to be the awaited and ever-distant accounting, the vehicle by which it all makes sense, the unscrambling of the inscrutable words (If nothing else: And then K. woke up. It was all a dream).

The discussion here thus far points to what is powerfully missing from Kafka's novels. The so-called *Kafkaesque* is generated by this unique absence of closed time. Everything is exclusively on the margin. Nonetheless, there has proved to be certain readers over decades that savor Kafka's fiction. For them there is simultaneously, and crucially a mysterious sense of determinism, of hidden purpose, forces outside of but reflected by the serial cast of characters engaged in dialogue with K. It is to locate these forces for the reader, then, that we offer up keys to the Castle.

The sets of keys: Deleuze and Guattari in their important work *Kafka: Toward a Minor Literature* (1986) analogizes Kafka's text to a spider ever-spinning itself into an ever-more elaborate web, a more and ever-more complex *rhizome*. They begin their book with a brief reading of "The Burrow", Kafka's story of a mole building into its underground tunnels ever-more hidden entrances and exits; infinite ways to get out but also ways to get in.

> How can we get into Kafka's work? We will enter by any point whatsoever; none matters more than another, and no entrance is more privileged even if it seems an impasse, a tight passage, a siphon. We will be

> trying only to discover what other points our entrance connects to, what crossroads and galleries on the passes through to link two points, what the map of the rhizome is and how the map is modified if one enters by another point. Only the principle of multiple entrances prevents the introduction of the enemy, the signifier and those attempts to interpret a work that is only open to experimentation. (p. 3)

Deleuze and Guattari effectively base their notion that Kafka's novels are literary rhizomes on the insight that that there cannot be a unified understanding of texts that exist solely in open time: "A work that is actually only open to experimentation." At the same time, they focus on characters' expressions and gestures, implicitly treating them as signs, vehicles of communication, rather than simply character-description as such. And they go further, seeing meanings expressed by inanimate objects, photos and messages for the most part, inferring that they are signs as well.

It is not too much of a stretch, then to re-direct Deleuze and Guattari's train of thought toward an amazing discovery. Uncovering a secret—as far as I know—that Kafka has more or less kept for almost a hundred years now, a way by which Kafka's novels can communicate to the reader in closed time. There is hidden in the words of the dialogues a complex pictographic translation tightly woven into the narrative. And this translation serves to foreground what one might call the pseudo-transgredients of K.'s experiences in open time.

The keys needed by the reader to unlock this other language, to consciously read the living pictograms, clownishly exaggerated activities, gestures, expressions and so forth, which once noticed can be seen in each of the characters, to some degree, not excluding K. Thus, if read very carefully the narrative is transformed before the reader's eyes into moving pictures.

As a good starting point, the reader might pay close attention to the details of various passages involving K.'s side-kicks: Karl's two fellow-travelers in *The Man Who Disappeared*, his two guards in *The Trial* and his two assistants in *The Castle*. You will find a dark slapstick cartoon miraculously coming into being in each case, living pictograms presenting in closed time what is fated.

Once having unlocked that gallery of living pictograms with one key, there are keys that unlock other rooms, each filled with a set of animated and inanimate beings each forming its own translation of what is going on. Some of the more common sets of inanimate pictograms present throughout each novel are: 1) architectural forms, e.g.: balconies, buildings, doors, gates, rooms, walls, windows; 2) forms of communication, e.g.: files, folders letters, messages, paintings, pictures, photographs, telephones; 3) forms of physical human features, e.g.: gestures, expressions, facial hair, especially beards, facial traits, noses, mouths, hair, postures of the head, ways of walking, ways of sitting, ways of looking at K.

Thus, these objects—animate, inanimate, conceptual, visual and so on—serve as other to K.'s self, communicating to the reader behind his back in closed time, often Cassandra-like in their relation to K. communicating a tragic finale. In the end Karl—*The Man Who Disappeared*—went into servitude, betrayed by his fellow-travelers. K. of *The Trial* is executed by his guards. In each case, it is indicated that K. has been reduced to a dog. Only in the case of *The Castle* is K.'s fate, or perhaps one should say non-fate, is it left unanswered.

Character and Fate: Walter Benjamin. If the social Totality were absolutely lawful in open time then, entrance to the Law—*The Trial* and *The Castle* respectively —is unexplainable. In the Castle, K. has broken free, or more precisely, due to an ergodic event K. has escaped closed time. He appears to be determined to transform his being, and if he can get inside the Castle either to liberate the time of history itself, which is to free the world of closed time altogether, or capturing the Castle and becoming its all-powerful agent.

Benjamin, Fate and Character (1919):

> Fate shows itself in the view of life, as condemned, as having, at bottom, first been condemned and then become guilty. Goethe summarizes both phases in the words "The poor man you let become guilty." It is not really man who has a fate; rather the subject of fate is undeterminable. The judge can perceive fate wherever he pleases; with every judgment he must blindly dictate fate. (p. 307–308)

In the two novels names, *Trial* and *Castle* respectively, are attached to the self-creating Totality in which all comes about. The whole however, following Benjamin's semiotics, is an idea that cannot be comprehended, having language itself within it. Thus, it has a shadowy, dream-like existence, meaning bereft of language. The messianic reduction, the subjectivity of the Gods having been reduced to scientific law, while the names that conjure up certain associations do not communicate; they do not constitute therefore language. In each novel K. refuses to be answerable, to be interrogated by this shadowy other called Trial in one and Castle another, but in so doing K. in the latter cannot bear his own refusal. It is the center of the novel.

> And now when after finishing his work in the stable the coachman walked straight across courtyard, closed the large gate, then came back, then locked the stable behind him, and all the electric lights went out—for

> whom should they have shown?—as if they had broken all contact with him (K.), but as if he were freer than ever and could wait as long as he wanted in this place where he was generally not allowed, and as if he had fought for this freedom himself in a manner nobody else could have done and as if nobody could touch him or drive him away, or even speak to him, yet—and this conviction was at least equally strong—as if there were nothing more desperate than this freedom, this waiting, this invulnerability. (p. 106)

In open time the narrative has the effect of flattening K. considerably and of shrinking the dimensionality of the other characters even more than it does. At the extreme of such shrinkage are the Assistants, who through most of the novel are akin to cartoon characters, to whom K. only gives one name. There are of course long sections of the novel taken up by K.'s spoken dialogues with others; the two chapters with the landlady of the Bridge Inn, the chapter with the Village Chairman and the crucial chapter with the connecting-secretary Burgel, are chief examples. With the significant exceptions of K.'s surprising five-chapter dialogue with Olga and his heart to heart talk with Frieda in the chapter just prior to that, these extended dialogues are lacking in any but the most basic exposition. Much of what the reader is listening to in these dialogues cannot fail to be abstract and puzzling.

Into this flat persistently enigmatic rendering of open time Kafka weaves a Talmudic tapestry; multi-textual sets of metaphorical encryptions throughout the novel that communicate in closed time. The tapestry constitutes effectively a grand rendering of archaic inscription. There are five major sets of encryptions, listed roughly in order of their extent, the first one being by far the most extensive: 1. architectural forms, e.g., balconies, bridges, buildings, castles, doors, gates, offices, rooms, sieves, walls, windows; 2. modes of communication, e.g., dictations, files, folders, letters, messages, paintings, notepads, pictures, portraits, photographs, reports, telephones, etc.; 3. gestures of the head and body postures e.g., bowing and kneeling; 4. Coverage/exposure of the face or the body, notably all manner of facial hair and features, body shapes and movements, and various modes and states of dress/undress; 5. sources, degrees, and qualities of light and dark.

This tapestry in open time blends with and often absorbs K's activities, although his motivations and apparent strategies and goals to the reader remain rather murky, at best. The encryptions are metaphorical, rather than allegorical, in the sense that, for instance, physical architectural elements given the context communicate visually the architecture of closed time; or, to take another case, facial hair can communicate visually how easy it is to see inside someone from outside. It is to be noted that each of these sets contain metaphorical elements found in the gnostic sayings (aphorisms) of Jesus, notably *The Book of Q* in addition to *The Gospel of Thomas*, and most of which in altered form are also found in the Gospels of the New Testament itself. This serves in part to point the reader to the realization that these are metaphors to be decrypted in closed time even as they serve as things that communicate themselves as such in open time.

Grounded by the set of architectural forms, these repeated metaphorical elements of The Castle—and of the other novels as well—are sending messages throughout the text in closed time, an encryption of the Law, but these messages are rarely received by the reader. By the nature of the narrative it is not clear as to whether K. in some sense reads these encryptions. The reader does experience a strange sense of the time in the novel. Gunther Anders, 1960, calls it "time-paralysis" (p. 42).

But the reader does not grasp that the narrative moving in open time is being re-casted over and over in myriad ways across varying spans of closed time, in different patterns and ratios of open time to closed time punctuated by various interconnecting revelations.

Take a very simple example, the "young man" Schwarzer. At the very outset of the novel, in open time, the innocent reader is led to believe he is acting as an "authority of the Count" (p. 2). He introduces himself to K. as the "son of the Castle steward." A handful of pages later, in closed time, the landlord reveals to K. that "his father is only a sub-steward, and one of the lowest at that" (p. 7). And, then, many pages later, over halfway through the novel, it is revealed to the reader that Schwarzer is not authorized by the Castle but rather "according to what K. has been told at the Bridge Inn" is merely an assistant teacher in the village (p. 163).

In general, the shape of time in the Kafka novels are complex symphonies of alternating and merging communications to the reader in open and closed-time; a symphony that may or may not be transcended and always threatens to be a wall of sound. It corresponds remarkably to Benjamin's story as cogently interpreted by Dimitris Vardoulakis in his book, *The Doppelganger: Literature's Philosophy*, of a automated chess player, first written in Theses on the Philosophy of History by Benjamin (p: 253–264).

Vardoulakis:

> The image of the Turk, as the automation was known, provides a complex temporality. In terms of movement, the machine can go on forever, while the man only as long as he can cope. Whereas in terms of the game, its perpetuation is dependent on the calculating man while the puppet

> is incidental. Thus, the complexity of time is created by the juxtaposition—the parataxis—of man and puppet. Thereby, the subject becomes an integral part of the act performed by the automation, but the medium of that act is time itself. (2010: 144)

Both, *The Trial* and *The Man Who Disappeared*, sneakily provide at least a few clear signals to the reader, indicating the novels are not communicating simply in open time as the narrator would have you believe. However, these signals to the reader paradoxically cannot be recognized until one has almost read the entire novel. This in turn is an indication that each of Kafka's novels is a parable, but one that itself is hidden from sight. As for the *Castle* where it seems to be a similar signal in the end, K. in the un-end seems to have possibly defied it.

In *The Trial* the clear signal is the revelation, toward the end of the novel, by Josef K's lawyer that a defense was impossible if the one charged is not interrogated within the Law. The very careful reader then might remember that Josef K. rejected such an interrogation early in the novel, at the hectic conclusion of his first and only actual hearing, and despite the fact that, as K. was holding the handle of the door to leave, the chief magistrate specifically informed him (and the reader) that by such a rejection "you have deprived yourself—although you can't yet have realized it." The lawyer reveals that the reason a defense becomes impossible is that the only way for K. to defend himself is to find out what he is charged with, and this requires that he be interrogated within the Law, since the only way for him to know the charge is to infer it from the questions that are asked of him within the Law. After the lawyer's revelation K. re-affirms (to the artist) his own judgment that he is innocent, to which the artist replies "then you wouldn't need help from me or anyone else" (p. 152). Subsequently, K. dismisses the lawyer, and at that point, except for the carrying out of the sentence, the trial that never occurred is over.

There is a similarly over-arching and therefore clear signal of closed time in *The Man Who Disappeared*, except the reader needs to have read the book first before it has meaning. As the novel is ending—just prior to his disappearance—Karl Rossman is revealed to himself in the form of a perennial student, one whose only interest is to study what is, and who thereby lives vicariously in closed time. A man suddenly appears on a balcony neighboring the one imprisoning Karl. Karl thinks "Could this man be a student?" and immediately enters closed-time.

> Could this man be a student? He gave every appearance of studying in much the same way—a long time ago now—Karl had sat at the table in his parents' home, doing his homework, while his father read his paper

> or did the bookkeeping and correspondence for a club, and his mother busied herself with some sewing pulling the thread high up in the air, even as a little boy, Karl had always liked it in the evening when his mother locked the front door with her key. What would she say if she knew that her Karl was now reduced to trying to pry open strange doors with knives? (p. 177)

The reader may well be reminded by this of the ambiguous affair, described at the outset of the novel, concerning Karl and his parents' maid, and perhaps to then further recall that Karl's parents' own judgment of his guilt (and the innocence of the maid) caused him to be banished to Amerika, and hence never to be a student, but instead to disappear.

The keys to the Castle. The key to *The Castle* is K. himself. K. personifies a violation of the *ergodic axiom*, upon which Cartesian/Kantian logic is grounded, and which thereby grounds, among other things, modern science, including neurobiology and the science of human action. If the axiom holds there ultimately is one degree of freedom. If the Totality is absolutely lawful, then the Law—the Castle—possesses, in castle jargon "control agency".

In Benjamin's terms, it is the unknowable subject of fate. This is reflected throughout the novel by the fact that an individual's exposure however indirect to the exclusively open time of the Castle invariably induces one kind of sleep or another and/or brings on a purely sensual state. The Castle in effect sifts the elements of consciousness from the individual experience, closing the inner eye.

The *ergodic* nature of the Totality is broached by the ("clean-shaven") Village Chairman who tells K. early on in the novel that an operating principle of the Castle is: "The possibility of error is simply not taken into account."

This leads K. to ask "Didn't you mention a control agency? As you described it, the organization is such that the very thought that the control agency might fail is enough to make one ill."

The chairman answers.

> Are there control agencies? There are only control agencies. Of course they aren't meant to find errors, in the vulgar sense of the term, so no errors occur, and even if an error does occur, as in your case, who can finally say that it is an error?

To which K. "cries", declaring to the reader his striving for a purely non-ergodic existence, "That would be something completely new" (p. 64–65).

In the climactic scene leading into the novel's conclusion, it is revealed, by the connecting secretary Burgel, though not without ambiguity, that K. has crossed the boundary from outside the Law:

> There is an opportunity, despite all the precautionary measures, for the parties to take advantage of the night-time weakness of the secretaries, assuming as always that it actually is say one that virtually never arises. It entails the party's arriving unannounced in the middle of the night. It may surprise you that this opportunity, which appears to be a matter of course, should arise so rarely. (p. 265)

> And now, Surveyor (K.), consider the possibility that a party does succeed somehow or other, despite the generally adequate obstacles I have already mentioned, in surprising in the middle of the night a secretary who does have some jurisdiction in that particular case. But in any case there's no need to think about it since it virtually never happens. What a strange, precisely shaped, small, clever little grain such a party would have to be in order to slip through that incomparable sieve. You think this can never happen. You're right, it can never happen. But one night—who can vouch for everything—it does happen. (p. 268)

A crucial aspect of this is that K., like Joseph K., refuses to be drawn forever inside the Law by submitting himself to interrogation within the Law. Man's being in chains, his determinateness, thus has its origins in the fact that he lets himself be put into a limited, defined position and allows himself to be bound and committed thereby.

Therefore—hearkening back to what the Village Chairman said above—it can be inferred that the Castle through its control agents is forced to cut and stitch up the boundary so as to contain K.'s actions (and perhaps those of others like him). To do so is the ergodic incumbency placed upon the Totality, so that as the Chairman says, "even if an error does occur, who can finally say that it is an error?" On the other hand, in a non-ergodic world the boundary spatially is a sieve.

In the depiction of the Castle, Benjamin's messianic reduction is married to the ergodic axiom. The Castle guards against the non-ergodic. But the unknowable purpose of the Greek gods or the single God of the scriptures has given way to a lawful Totality of individual fates. Kafka's joke is that the majesty, omnipotence, and law-giving gift of the ancient God(s) have been replaced by what presents itself to the reader as a bureaucratic organization armed with inexorably dedicated but over-worked staff, always prone to sleep, who seem to be, between them, the daunting task of keeping the fate of every single individual in accordance with the lawful Totality. As aptly put by Marthe Robert in her book *The Old and the New: From Don Quixote to Kafka* (1977):

> Built in a human way, not in some ethereal space but on earth, out of the crude and perishable materials at man's disposal, this Castle violates its very name; for it is neither, ancient, majestic or graceful—absolutely unsuited for idealization. It even lacks that imperfect ephemeral beauty of earthly things where one can sometimes read a divine message in distorted way.
>
> The Castle is structured like an enormous industrial or commercial enterprise. It represents something like the cosmic version of an anonymous society responsible for the management of the world. (p. 184–186)

K.'s triumphant moment, in the midst of his dialogue with Burgel, is one of Nietzschian joy. It takes place in Burgel's office, a room with a large bed taking up most of the space, and K. asleep experiences an absolute freedom from the Law; that is, the non-ergodic, completely new. But Kafka reveals here something that was adumbrated earlier in the novel, in the pivotal scene in which K. chooses to stay alone in that courtyard below the Castle offices, having failed to make direct contact with Klamm, the representative of the Castle in the village. In a rare observation of K.'s deep inner thoughts, K. observes himself talking to himself. The reader sees the Nietzschian messianic-reduction joke at the expense of the ancients in closed time that proves to be a cruel joke on K. in the limit, purely open time. There can be no answerable subject in isolation. The answerable subject is a social subject.

But now in the room with Burgel:

> K. slept, but it wasn't really sleep, he was still hearing what Burgel was saying, perhaps better than earlier when he was still awake though dead tired, one word after another accosted his ears, but that irritating awareness was gone, he felt free, it was no longer Burgel who kept him, but he, K., who now and then groped about for Burgel, he had not yet reached the depths of sleep, but he had dipped into it and now no one was going to steal this from him. And it seemed to him as though in this way he had achieved a great victory and a group of people was already there to celebrate it and he or even somebody else was raising a champagne glass in honor of the victory. And in order to let everybody know what it was all about, the battle and the victory were being repeated but were

> taking place for the first time and had been celebrated earlier and kept on being celebrated, because there was fortunately no doubt about the outcome.
>
> A secretary, naked, very like the statue of a Greek god, was being hard pressed by K. in battle. That was quite comical, and in his sleep K. smiled gently at the way the secretary was being constantly startled out of his proud posture by K.'s advances and quickly had to use his raised arm and clenched fist to cover up his exposed parts, but he was not yet quick enough. The battle did not last long, for step by step, and very big steps they were too, K. advanced. Was this even a battle? There was no real obstacle, only every so often a few squeaks like a girl being tickled. And then finally he was gone; K. was alone in a large room; ready to fight, he turned around and looked for his opponent, but there wasn't anybody there anymore. The group of people had scattered as well, only the champagne glass lay broken on the ground, K. stamped on it. But the splinters hurt; with a start he woke up feeling sick, like a small child on being woken up. (p. 264–265)

Stephen Dowden in the introduction to his intelligent and comprehensive survey, *Literary Criticism in Perspective: Kafka's Castle and the Critical Imagination* (1995) no doubt echo's many Kafka scholars when he asserts "At this late date in Kafka studies it has become clear that *The Castle* is not likely to give up its deepest secrets, if indeed it has any. The narrative may well be pure surface" (p. 1).

That assertion is disputed here, but in a limited way, and the interpretation just summarized in the preceding section is offered up as an initial response. To be clear, however, all the novels and short stories of Kafka's are coherent parables, but along many dimensions they go much deeper than the narrative in its own right. As opposed to allegory there is no meaning per se of the parable, in the sense of that there is no meaning in the pure sound of language. Put another way the parable is like the sounds not the translation. The latter is what this has been about.

To locate and elaborate the parable of *The Castle*, guiding the innocent reader through never-ending entrance problems planted by Kafka in the first sentences of the first chapter and which doom almost all readers immediately to unresolvable perplexity. Since these problems are always read initially without guidance, as the novel continues the reader's perplexities rather than resolving are compounded exponentially, increasingly less and less likely for the reader's confusion ever to be addressed and therefore for the parable ever to obtained coherence. Upon reading the novel for the first time the readers, then, are left early on to their own devices; either to disregard larger and larger pieces of the narrative so as to retain coherency, or to experience an increasingly excruciating babble of words and sentences threatening to devolve into meaningless sound.

The book begins:

> It was late evening when K. arrived. The village lay under deep snow. There was no sign of the Castle hill, fog and darkness surrounded it, not even the faintest gleam of light suggested the large Castle. K. stood a long time on the wooden bridge that leads from the main road to the village, gazing upward into the seeming emptiness.
>
> Then he went looking for a night's lodging at the inn they were still awake; the landlord had no room available, but he was willing to let K. sleep on a straw mattress in the taproom, K. agreed to this.
>
> A few peasants were still sitting over beer, but he did not want to talk to anyone, got himself a straw mattress from the artic and lay down by the stove. It was warm, the peasants were quiet, he examined them for a moment with tired eyes then fell asleep.
>
> Yet before long he was awakened. A young man in city clothes, with an actor's face, narrow eyes, thick eyebrows, stood beside him with the landlord. "This village is Castle property, anybody residing or spending the night here is effectively residing or spending the night at the Castle.
>
> Permission is needed." (p. 1–2)

As soon as permission from the Castle required for him to stay the night, K. states unequivocally, that is for Schwarzer, the landlord and the peasants in the taproom of the Bridge Inn to hear:

> "Be advised that I am the land surveyor sent for by the Count. My assistants and the equipment are coming by carriage." (p. 3)

Soon thereafter, hearing on the phone from the Castle telling Schwarzer that an initial mistake had been made, and that a surveyor was expected, K. thinks "So the Castle had appointed him land surveyor," which to the reader should already be a bit perplexing. It goes on:

> On one hand, this was unfavorable for it showed that the Castle had all necessary information about him, had assessed the opposing forces, and

> was taking up the struggle with a smile. On the other hand, it was favorable, for it proved to his mind that they underestimated him and that he would enjoy greater freedom than he could have hoped for in the beginning. And if they thought could keep him terrified all the time simply by acknowledging his surveyorship—though this was certainly a superior move on their part—then they were mistaken, for he felt only a little shudder that was all. (p. 5)

A quick inspection on the surface of the narrative, but in closed time, uncovers a game that K. and the Castle are playing in open time, a game that begins exactly with the novel: "It was late evening when K. arrived." In the closed time of the novel, Burgel has revealed that K. is the "strange, precisely shaped, small, clever little grain that slips through that incomparable sieve" in the dead of night. To have made it into Burgel's room means that K. crossed the boundary from outside the Law at that moment. In open time, K. is from the outset quintessentially non-ergodic, disturbing the otherwise fully-determined village.

The first move made by the Castle in the game, via Schwarzer, is to not let K. in on the grounds that he does not have permission to stay. "You must leave the Count's domain at once." But K. quickly parries this by announcing "I am the land surveyor sent for by the Count." This can be interpreted as an aggressive counter-move amounting to a declaration of war: I, the non-ergodic, am the one designed to draw the boundary. K. is thus seen as the surveyor in a larger sense. After apparently some indecision the Castle makes the unexpected counter-move of slightly altering the parameters of the fully-determined village to fit in K. The village seems to function as a kind of barrier island, providing the Castle's control agents some leeway in preserving the ergodic world, in so doing bearing both the scars and prerogatives of the villager's service. In another move in the game by the Castle, at the end of the first chapter K.'s assistants appear from within the village, and he is henceforth referred to as "the surveyor."

K. says to himself "So the Castle had appointed him land surveyor" he is pondering over this unexpected and crucial move in response to his announcement of who he is. The game continues, still in the very first pages of the novel, but which will continue in various ways until K. makes clear that he will never be interrogated within the Law. Right in the beginning:

> After waving aside Schwarzer, who was timidly approaching, K. rejected their insistent pleas that he move into the landlord's room, accepted only a nightcap from the landlord and a wash basin with soap and towel from

> the landlady, and did not even have to request that the room be cleared, for all rushed to the door, averting their faces so that he wouldn't recognize them tomorrow. (p. 5)

The landlord's room is the place in which the Castle wants to contain him, just as K. had thought, like the landlord he would be terrified all the time simply by acknowledging his surveyorship. K.'s thought that he was being underestimated by the Castle and thus would be given more freedom than he might have expected, also proves to be correct. He is able not only to have "rejected their insistent pleas that he move into the landlord's room," but also to lay private claim to the taproom, at least for the night, chasing out the animals from the manger.

This guide has relied on Burgel's revelation that K. is the "strange, precisely shaped, small, clever little grain [that slips] through that incomparable sieve." The guide can only be helpful in closed time, going back to the very beginning of the novel based on what is revealed near the end. This is analogous to the signals of closed time, cited earlier, with respect to *The Trial* and *The Man Who Disappeared*, but here it is not at all clear, since the interpretation of the revelation can only come from the realization over the course of the novel that the Castle is the Law, the ergodic mechanism if you will of the Totality.

By bringing into the guide another revelation of Burgel's, one that also goes back in closed time to the first few pages of the novel, the reader can now comprehend the continuation of the game K. is engaged in at the outset of the novel until the moment that he finally makes direct contact with the Castle, in the twenty-first chapter, and which then seems to be resumed in the final twenty-fourth and twenty-fifth chapters. Burgel describes—in the putative context of him telling K. how improbable it is to "slip through the sieve"—what it takes to make direct contact with the Castle.

> Everyone who has a request to make, or who for some reason must be interrogated about something receives immediately, without delay, usually even before he has thought the matter through, indeed even before he knows about it, a summons. This time he isn't interrogated, generally the affair usually isn't sufficiently mature for that, but he has the summons and can no longer arrive unannounced.

One sees that either knowingly or by luck K. has taken advantage of a loophole in the law. When K. announces himself as a surveyor, the Law presumes he was summoned by the Castle. It is also the case as Burgel suggests is possible, that in closed time the summons has come before K. even knew that he had "a request to make, or for some reason must be interrogated." It should be noted, in this context, that later in his dialogue with the Village Chairman this is re-casted in closed time. A surveyor was summoned to come to the village but it was an error. The aspect of Burgel's revelation central to the game is that to be fully within the law K. must now indeed request something of the Castle, or he must be interrogated, otherwise there is indeed an error. Much like Benjamin's insight into tragic revelation, "there is no tragedy in pantomime," K.'s fate is seen to be essentially a matter of the Word.

The game, directly following from what was just said, moves along a few tracks. One involves attempts of certain village authorities—the landlady of the Bridge Inn and the Village Chairman, respectively—to absorb K (and the error) into the village community. The tactic is to induce K. to marry Frieda, while offering him a proper place in the community, but not as a surveyor. Along a second track, the tactic is to get K. interrogated by Klamm's village secretary, Momus, offering K. the possibility of a path into the Castle in exchange. This would correct the error and bring K. inside the Law without intervention by the Castle outside the village. Each of these tracks ultimately leads to a dead end.

The second culminates in the eighth and ninth chapters: "Waiting for Klamm" and "The Struggle against the Interrogation;" with K. refusing once and for all to be interrogated. This finally ends with the break-up of Frieda and K. and therefore the ruling-out of their marriage. This is just prior to K.'s entrance into the Castle, and subsequent dialogue with Burgel.

Over these many chapters K counters the moves of the village authorities by moves to engage the Castle first from the Village Chairman and thereafter from outside the sphere of the village, his main effort being to contact Klamm the Director of Bureau 10 of the Castle. The following words are used in the oral message that K. conveys to Klamm, dictating it to Barnabas in the tenth chapter, but which Barnabas belatedly delivers in the twenty-first chapter:

> The surveyor K. asks the director for permission to call on him in person and accepts in advance all stipulations that that might be attached to any such permission. He is obliged to make this request because all previous intermediaries have utterly failed. (121)

As soon as Barnabas starts to leave the Castle, having delivered this request, he is given a message to deliver to K. in return, from Erlanger, Klamm's Castle secretary, scheduling K. to "speak with Erlanger" in the Gentlemen's Inn. The treatment of K. once the message is delivered is seen to follow exactly the process described by Burgel.

His request has been granted immediately (if not sooner). Here we see what Burgel means by the description of K. as "that clever little grain that slips through that incomparable sieve." He seems to have followed (in reverse-order) another Saying in The Gospel of Thomas (#94: 59): "One who seeks will find; for one who knocks it will be opened." In this case K. announces himself to be a surveyor and he is a surveyor and by making a request to be in touch with the Castle he gets in touch with the Castle.

A sign of something in the novel is the very brief physical description of K. the only word-picture in the entirety of *The Castle*. It is spoken by Schwarzer, when he describes K. on the telephone and was overheard by K. who is in the dark nearby: "A man in his thirties, rather shabby looking, sleeping quietly on a straw mattress, with a tiny rucksack for a pillow and a knobby walking stick within reach." (p. 4)

CHAPTER 3

On the Fringe

Liberal Keynesianism and *Modern Money Theory* (MMT)

A *NY Times* article, in July 2013, by Annie Lowrey appeared on the front page of the Business Section under the heading *Warren Mosier, A Deficit Lover With a Following.*

Never mind the hook that Warren Mosley, a hedge-fund manager, is a leading advocate of a contemporary economic school of thought one deemed unfavorable to members of his class (the 1%), the piece is unusual in that it provides a fairly accurate, if oblique landscape of academic economists when it comes to the current economic crisis.

> Mosley has ideas that go under the label of *modern monetary theory*, or MMT, are clearly on the fringe, drawing skeptical reactions even from many Liberal Keynesian economists who agree with some of their arguments. But they have attracted a growing following, flourishing on the Internet and in a handful of academic outposts.

This is all well and good, but how many of the relatively-educated readers of the *Times* know what liberal Keynesianism is any more than they do MMT? That is, it speaks in a sense of a fringe of what has become itself a fringe. They share an understanding of two foundational problems of achieving full-employment in the face of recessions. These were first being posed in the post-WWI period by those associated with the well-respected John Maynard Keynes.

1. *The problem of effective demand*:
   A firm does not generate products more if it projects that more will not be sold.
2. *The problem of unemployment:*
   The less products being generated by firms the less (private) employment there will be.

Neo-liberal economists, then, advocate an *austerity policy* at-odds with Keynesian theory and hence its policy implications. To some extent neo-liberal thought falls back on various long-run macroeconomic analyses that presume full-employment equilibrium growth.

Thus, any number of blind spots are found in orthodox economic textbooks with respect to models of under-employment equilibrium. This even with the longer and longer terms of under-employment, to the point that day to day discussion of policy is at best relative, absolute full-employment having not been achieved over any long term post-WWII since the 1950s to the late-1960s.

In the very early years the US policy was controlled by *post-Keynesians* (as they were called). They came out of an experience of the 1930s, and followed a demand-led increase in employment through more products being sold, aided by a complementary Federal Reserve monetary policy stabilizing bank interest rates. They would be called liberal Keynesians now.

By the mid-sixties control went to so-called neo-Keynesians. They include Robert Solow, Willian Nordhaus, Edmond Phelps, Joe Stiglitz, among many other economists. They view Keynesian policy as exclusively short-run, while in the long-run there is the familiar invisible hand, a natural force moving the efficient economy into its state of full-employment. Neo-Keynesians were part of the baroque period at the end of what were long intervals of full-employment, and under-employment were explained as illogical decision-making on the part of those employed, confusing nominal wage rates from real.

An extremely long-term of under-employment economy came with the Reagan administration, which suffered a severe recession right away and followed for rest of his presidency under-employment that at a steady but slow rate, falling for some six years, and by the end there still was not full-employment by any means. George H Bush for the first year and a half of his one term after Reagan saw the underemployment equilibrate at that left by Reagan. However, a recession came in the remaining years of the Bush 1 presidency that sharply raised the underemployment by 1992 at the peak rate of under—employment under Reagan (Coleman, 2016).

Keynesian policies during the first 30 years preceding Reagan, are unknown to many, and misunderstood by much of the rest. And flowing from that has emerged what can only be identified as a *Messianic* economic thought, with the name Austerity, a mixture of Smith's invisible hand and Calvin's God.

The long-term under-employment equilibria since the end of the golden age of economics after WWII have appeared at the end of recessions, due to the bursting of financial bubbles. While negative growth stops eventually, the products being generated do not increase sufficiently, or at all, for there not to be any significant movement of long term high percentage unemployment nationally and in major labor markets.

Neo-Liberals cannot see that firms in the aggregate employ the number of workers needed to generate products they expect buyers will purchase: the *effective demand.* The problem is no necessary connection exists between effective demand for products and the number of individuals in the labor market, whether employed or not.

If the latter is more than workers needed by firms then there is unemployment. And in under-employment equilibrium, the products generated are equal to effective demand. There is no force, then, moving firms to either increase or decrease products absent a significant exogenous change in demand. In other words, there is no movement toward *full-employment.*

This blindness of neo-liberal thinkers in the realm of macroeconomics has resulted in a quiet return to a darkness that Keynesians had lit up in the late 1920s and early 1930's: *The fallacy of composition.* Keynes critiqued the *neo-classical school of thought* on this ground in his most influential work, *The General Theory* (1936).

In recent years this has set off actual public protests by Harvard students, demanding that Keynesian thought be included. Massachusetts Institute of Technology (MIT) in its economics programs, like Harvard—each of course considered by orthodox economists the crème de la crème of economics departments—also leaves out for the most part Keynesian macroeconomics.

From microeconomics, supply and demand of any industry, President Hoover long ago made the famous statement, with its unspoken allusion to Smith's invisible hand: "Prosperity is just around the corner." It was the beginning years of the Great Depression of the 1930s triggered by a great burst of bubble. The neoclassical economists, writ large, from 1929 to 1932 were sure the private market system hit by such an exogenous force, would nonetheless have the strength to move the economy back toward full-employment in the short-run.

The analysis was straightforward, if flawed, subject as Keynes pointed out to the *fallacy of composition.* The very high unemployment-rate is due to a sharp exogenous reduction of industry products and therefore a decrease in demand for labor. The supply of labor is now more than the demand. This causes, on the supply-side of the labor market (nationally) the bidding down of the wage-rate. That in turn causes the price of labor to fall and the firm's demand for labor therefore to rise. Thus, unemployment is lessened until there is full-employment equilibrium.

Exploring the above, with respect to the neoclassical, microeconomic logic, if the price of labor goes down, the industry will move toward labor-intensive hence cost-efficient techniques of production. The very thought of this argument in relation to the problem of under-employment caused Keynes famously to respond: "In the long run we are all dead." In the heart of industrialization, the solution of unemployment here would be a transformation over decades and doing what? Scrapping its machinery to employ more workers?

In any case, being microeconomic, the price of a specific form of labor employed by certain industries is relative to the price of labor employed by other industries. It is incommensurate with an economic system nation-wide. The fallacy of composition is seen more clearly when Keynesian macroeconomic lenses are put on to wear.

By observation of the latest and greatest bursting bubble since the Depression, real wages paid to employed workers across markets plunged quickly, creating the recursive movements. Due to the layoffs of workers across labor markets demand for products have been squeezed, lessening products generated by firms who see unplanned inventories lead to more unemployed workers.

The process is recursive in time, indicated by the relation:

$$Y > D(Y).$$

Y is the total products generated nationally, per time-period.
D(Y) is the effective demand, purchasing products, as a function of Y, per time-period.

Over time both Y and D will fall, but the economy's abilities to create debt ownership demand will fall by less than Y, so that eventually the two become equal.

$$Y = D(Y).$$

At that point is under-employment equilibrium. Demand is not enough for firms to generate products requiring full-employment. And firms do not generate products that will not be demanded.

The center of Golden-age Keynesian policy is for the government then to increase its purchases, or reduce individual and/or business tax-rates, leading to new effective demand.

Products meeting those demands require increases in labor demand and therefore labor incomes among others increase and in turn effective demand, and a reduction of debt, causing firms to increase their products. Here there is a recursive relation in the reverse direction as before.

$$Y < D(Y).$$

At the start of the crisis of 2008, Keynesian policy came to the fore of discussion as to what should be done for virtually the first time since the days of the Gerald Ford administration. President Obama went forward despite many handicaps quickly attached to him by neo-liberals. There was enough, perhaps, to speed the end of the negative growth. The latter equilibrated in the US after one or two years. The under-employment equilibrium, however, has then lasted for six or seven years and shows only slightly the possibility that anything near full-employment is going to be seen in the short-run.

The Modern Money Theory MMT is not at all on the fringe of contemporary Keynesian thought. Indeed, *modern* can be taken to go back to the establishment of the Federal Reserve along with proto-Keynesian thought associated for instance with JA Hobson's *The Science of Wealth* (1911).

Aside from MMT economists themselves, liberal Keynesians are professors in many universities and various non-profit institutions. Also, there are many economists who would not describe themselves as Keynesian but nonetheless concede the short-run Keynesian policy, creating effective demand, if an ongoing under-employment equilibrium to remedy the large population of workers who are unemployed or under-employed, or under-paid.

The modern money theory economists are bringing to the fore what was a Keynesian understanding of State money that had come into the foreground in the US in 1913 with the establishment of the Federal Reserve. Bank money—checking account deposits of the sovereign-currency came into a solid existence lasting still, over more than hundred years later.

Keynes articulates this in the chapters at the beginning of *A Treatise of Money; The Pure Theory of Money* (1930):

> It is a peculiar characteristic of money contracts that it is the State or the community not only which enforces delivery, but also which decides what it is that must be delivered as a lawful or customary discharge of a contract which has been concluded in terms of the money of account. Knapp's Chartalism—the doctrine that is peculiarly a creation of the State—is fully realized.
>
> Thus, the age of money had succeeded the age of barter as soon as men had adopted a money of account. And the age of State money was reached when the State claimed the right to declare what thing should answer as money to the current money of account—when it claimed the right not only to enforce the dictionary but also to write the dictionary. Today all civilized money is, beyond the possibility of dispute, Chartalist. (p. 4)

There is a wide denial led by neo-liberals but including many others who are not, of the fact that the State via the Federal Government can and does create money at will, without cost. This is the true basis of government spending. The

Federal Reserve—the national bank—can lend money that swells the deposits in large banking institutions, or by borrowing money, tightening the amount of deposits in the banks and raising interest rates. As such it has been at the heart of monetary policy.

Depending on how much it wishes to spend, the Federal government transfers a sufficiently large number, constituting money, from the Fed to the Treasury Dept.'s account at the Fed. Just like any checking account you or I might have, the Treasury can either write checks on that number, make electronic transfers, or it can even turn it into cash, famously known as printing money. These transfers into the Treasury's account are marked by the issuing of State-guaranteed securities, new equity given to the Fed.

No less an authority than the CBO (Congressional Budget Office) measures the so-called national debt by subtracting the government securities held by the Fed from the total. Thereby the official measure is reduced, as it should be around half of the supposed debt. The State-issued securities held by the Fed require interest payments. These come out of the Federal budget. The government can pay the interest, like any other payment, by shifting a money number into its account, marking this by issuing new securities of course. That money number then is shifted back to the Fed as payment of the interest.

To Annie Lowrey, the *Times* reporter: You might report on a culture that cannot face the truth that the State does not need to borrow or even collect taxes to pay for things. In the words of a leading MMT thinker, L. Randell Wray, "*the Government does not face an affordability constraint.*" [*The government can afford anything for sale in its own currency*] (p. 184).

For this reason, MMT economists are critical of someone like the well-known Princeton economist Paul Krugman, op. ed. writer as well in the *NY Times*, on the edge of being a liberal Keynesian one might say, who is still qualifying his call for a demand-led Keynesian policy at the moment by saying that when the crisis has ended there will be a need to deal with the national debt.

The response to Krugman is not that the debt is limitless. It is that there is no such thing as State debt at all, at least in the normal sense that repaying a debt—if it is to be a debt—must have a cost to the borrower. There is a total of outstanding government securities measured in money that the State is obligated to make payments on. Rather than debt, leaving out those held by the Fed, the public has available to it uniquely risk-free assets precisely because the State can create money at will.

There is a much deeper implication of the disconnection, however, surprisingly rejected by many MMT economists. It takes us well beyond the fringe, not to say the scope of this blog. The fact that the State creates money at will implies that there is no necessary purpose in the Federal government collecting taxes out of private income at all (Federal taxation of corporations as means of internalizing negative externalities would of course continue to have a purpose however). Both money creation and connected to its sale of risk-free securities are a sufficient basis of government spending.

Eliminating taxes unties public discourse on the State from issues of spending and tax receipts, the lynch-pin of neoliberal austerity policies. It is freed to address how best the State can meet its real debt, its obligation to promote the general welfare, insuring basic entitlements like health care, education and living incomes, in general life and the pursuit of happiness.

Robert Eisner in his pamphlet *Social Security: More Not Less* (1998):

> The accountants can just as well declare the bottom line of the funds' accounts negative or positive—and the Treasury can go on making whatever outlays are prescribed by law. The Treasury can pay out all that Social Security provides while the accountants declare the funds more and more in the red. (p. 81)

In an article by Stephanie Kelton—entitled, Eisner's *Radical Approach to Social Security, Tell the Truth!* (2008) she concludes by commenting that even among liberal Keynesians there is a great difficulty coming to the truth communicated by Eisner that US government spending is not limited, or even necessarily known.

> There is still considerable disparity on the issue of government finance and macro stabilization policy. Many still treat the federal government as if it were subject to the same constraints as a household or a private business. Only a handful of liberal Keynesians have embraced the modern money approach, which emphasizes functional finance and the irrelevance of concepts like government solvency. (p. 202)

Of note, neo-liberals have succeeded to some extent in regulation of the Treasury by law that protects private banks in relation to their depositors. Since roughly the 1980s, and established with the repeal of the 1930's Glass-Steagall Bill in 1999, the separation of the oligopoly, into commercial versus investment bank, has ended. The oligopoly is composed now of *full-service global banks*.

Keynes's analysis of the banking oligopoly in *A Treatise on Money* concerns the pre-Depression period and therefore for many years seemed irrelevant, given the reforms in the 1930's. Looking back now, however, Keynes's insights into the bank oligopoly are strikingly the same as those observed over the last two or three decades.

In particular at the center of both is the ability of the bank to create a debt ownership of its own and to transform it into a checking account deposit use of it by initially depositing the loan in the bank.

> We shall become concerned in what follows with banks of the fully developed modern type existing as going concerns. A bank claims against itself for the delivery of money, from deposits in two ways. In the first place a member of the public comes along with cash in their pocket or with a check drawn on a bank, which they have hands in on the understanding that their entitled in return to a claim to cash which he can either or transfer to someone else.
>
> But there is a second way in which a bank may create a claim against itself. It may itself purchase assets, and pay for them by establishing a claim against itself. Or the bank may create a claim against itself in favor of a borrower in return for his promise of subsequent reimbursement; i.e., it may make loans or advances. (p. 20–21)

The second way leads to the ability of the bank oligopoly to create money, which Keynes asserts is not passive as is that of the first way. Instead it is new debt ownership and with it the payment in money of the debt. This is to say, the bank lends money, purchasing assets from an investor, and converts the loan into a checking account deposit of the investor, the borrower. And beyond the limitation of reserve requirements and/or capital assets, the deposit can be lent, and so on.

Keynes goes further, describing a closed macro-banking system that fits with the bursting bubble of 2008, some 78 years later, and ongoing underemployment equilibrium for six or seven years with only the slightest hint that genuine full-employment is anywhere is seen in the horizon.

> It is evident that there is no limit to the amount of deposits which the banks can safely create *provided that they move forward in step*. Every movement forward by an individual bank weakens it, but every such movement by one of its neighbor banks strengthens it; so that if all move forward together no one is weakened on balance. Thus the behavior of each bank, though it cannot afford to move more than a step in advance of the others, will be governed by the average behavior of the banks as a whole. Each chairman sitting in his parlor may regard himself as the passive instrument of outside forces over which he has no control.

> A monetary system of this kind would possess an inherent instability; for any event which tended to influence the behavior of the majority of the banks in the same direction, whether backwards or forwards, would meet with no resistance and would be capable of setting up a violent movement of the whole system. (p. 23)

From the post-war period of the 1950s to the current crisis (of 2008 and thereafter) Keynesian economics has been a lynchpin of so-called *macro-economics*, even during its decline beginning in the mid-1970s. A marker of the post-golden age, indeed, is the official abandonment of basic Keynesian fiscal and monetary policies by both major political parties in the US at that time.

The long-standing erosion of economic thought that ensued is no better exemplified than the abandonment of basic macroeconomic demand policies by the mid-70s. The latter were first instituted of course in the mid-1930s, in response to the Great Depression. Almost immediately atavistic seeds were planted in Keynes's conceptualization, and surprisingly, to some extent by Keynes himself.

In the *General Theory* (1936) Keynes advances a notion of *money illusion* related to aggregate labor supply (money illusion was coined earlier by Irving Fisher but within a financial domain). According to it, workers only act with respect to their nominal wage, literally the money they make in income, without taking account of existing prices, i.e., what the money can actually purchase.

This purely speculative hypothesis is clearly motivated by a felt-need on Keynes's part to account for an excess supply of labor over any significant time span. His argument is that lack of goods demanded, as in the Depression, causes price deflation in goods markets, raising *real wages* and hence lowering labor demand.

In the context of competitive markets this in turn should put downward pressure on nominal wages. But the illusion causes workers not to respond. The nominal wage has not changed. However, absent the illusion the unspoken implication is that unemployed workers will eventually bid the nominal and with it the real wage down. The effect would thereby be to increase labor demand and reduce labor supply until full-employment equilibrium is reached.

To parse this reasoning differently, Keynes feels compelled to justify a State-run demand policy regarding unemployment, because he is (uncharacteristically for him) seeing the macro-economy in the context of a pre-industrial economy. In the latter, unless something exogenous interferes—such as money illusion—all agents are price takers, and all markets including the labor markets therefore inexorably move toward a general equilibrium. In all markets supply and demand move toward equality; in other words, State policy is not needed then to attain full-employment.

As said, Neo-Keynesianism ruled macro-economic policy during the golden age period, following WWII. It was effective in preventing extreme recessions and expansions of production, providing some assurance to the public of available employment, along with price stability. State management of interest rates, and more broadly the regulation of the private banking oligopoly were instituted as well.

The ISLM short-run neo-Keynesian model that still inhabits many advanced undergraduate macroeconomic applications is the basis of federal government estimates of in the US of future movements of growth and employment. The model combines fiscal policy, federal budgetary decisions, and monetary policy concerning money creation by the Federal Reserve, the central bank.

The leading neo-Keynesian economists of the time—e.g., Hansen, Heller, Kuznets, Modigliani, Okun, and Tobin—paid lip-service to a long-run full-employment equilibrium absent the State. But in designing policy the long-run theory of aggregate supply and demand was ignored; as it should have been, since it obviously suffers from the *fallacy of composition*.

With the rise of neo-liberalism in the post-golden age period, there has been a new focus on long-run aggregate supply and demand model, despite its obvious faults. It was derived generally from the ISLM model—within which money supply is exogenous of the banking oligopoly—and purports to show that the macro-economy internally equilibrates in the long-run at full-employment.

Many neo-Keynesians as a consequence—for instance, Joseph Stiglitz—have spent much of their academic careers putting forward other exogenous factors to account for ongoing unemployment. In doing this, however, they validate aggregate supply and demand analysis, while at the same time hollowing out and stultifying the Keynesian notion of an endogenous variable of the Government in its own right in achieving full employment.

It is easy to overlook these days that empirically Keynesian demand policies were effective for over twenty to thirty years (post-WWII). They dealt very well with one of, if not the major economic issue that has been faced by industrializing, and digitalizing, capitalist economies: the unavailability of income with which the vast majority of people have enough money to avoid a life of accelerating debts over and beyond their life-time.

The policies have been lost in part by the historic failure of the prominent economic theorists over at least the last forty years. There has grown an unwillingness to confront capitalism as it really exists. Rather they play with extravagant models positing such fantasies as an economy of perfectly competitive markets, perfect foresight on the part of all agents, a uniquely ideal general equilibrium price outcome based on an imaginary clearing house and no money, models that mathematically cause within the profession much sound and fury, but nonetheless in the end signify nothing.

The term macroeconomics itself, not to say the basic categorization and therefore measurement of the *national economy* remains Keynesian. But what is seen through Keynesian eyes is very close-up, no further than the nose. The problem of unemployment seems solved by increasing products generated and thereby increasing the demand for labor.

A critical term is *growth*. It is conceived not only by Keynesians but both neoclassical and Marxist economic thought as well. It means generating more and more *things* (including services). But this, one cannot help but see, is causing an accelerating rate of disruption and unimaginable destruction of the living natural world for whom humans clearly have significant responsibility.

To provide sources of income heavily based on employment, Keynesians implicitly advocate unlimited and universal quest for more and more things in the foreseeable future. One can imagine that this could not be sustained without cruel lives for more and more humans, shut off from a relative few who enjoy debt ownership, a social Totality built on bank oligopoly and the military industrial complex. These institutions have gained unthinkable power in the first two decades of turmoil in the 21st century.

The destruction of a wonderful natural world is emblematic of the narrowness of all three major schools of economic thought: Marxist, neo-Classical, and Keynesian. In terms of macroeconomics it is known in a sense, but has long been put aside that the individual prices attached to the homogenized annual products—The National Product—generated and sold in the year, are arbitrary. Therefore, the numbers associated with growth, changes in the national product over time, lacks the meaning attached to it.

For example, the fact that a certain design pocketbook during a given year is sold per unit for $50,000 does not mean that more has been produced, in the aggregate, than, for instance, $500 a week that year of good-tasting nutritious meals, $26,000. In the same way, destruction of the natural environment beyond a certain point is catastrophic. No amount of money can represent the loss.

The Pope and a Respected Orthodox Economist

Dialogue

Pope Francis. Source: Laudat Si, Encyclical, June 2015
William Nordhaus, long-time Yale professor and highly-respected economist within the profession. Source: The Pope & the market, New York Review of Books, October 2015

Pope Francis

The alliance between the economy and technology ends up sidelining anything unrelated to its immediate interests. Consequently, the most one can expect is superficial rhetoric, sporadic acts of philanthropy and perfunctory expressions of concern for the environment, whereas any genuine attempt by groups within society to introduce change is viewed as a nuisance based on romantic illusions or an obstacle to be circumvented.

Dr. Nordhaus

The *efficient performance of a market economy* does not depend upon the ethics of individual behavior: "It is not from the benevolence of the butcher, the brewer, or the baker that we expect our dinner, but from their regard to their own interest" (Smith, Wealth of Nations, 1776).

Pope Francis

Some forms of pollution are part of people's daily experience. Exposure to atmospheric pollutants produces a broad spectrum of health hazards, especially for the poor, and causes millions of premature deaths. People take sick, for example, from breathing high levels of smoke from fuels used in cooking or heating. There is also pollution that affects everyone, caused by transport, industrial fumes, substances which contribute to the acidification of soil and water, fertilizers, insecticides, fungicides, herbicides and agro toxins in general.

Dr. Nordhaus

The *idealized world* of Adam Smith ignores two major shortcomings of a *realistic market economy.* The first is the presence of market failures such as monopoly or unregulated pollution that distort market decisions and outcomes, and the second is inequality of opportunities and income.

So far as the environment is concerned, the most important market failure is called an *externality*. This is the term for by-products of economic activity—such as pollution—that cause damages to innocent bystanders. These externalities occur because those who pollute do not pay for that privilege and those who are harmed are not compensated.

Putting a low price on valuable environmental resources is a phenomenon that pervades modern society.

Pope Francis

Caring for ecosystems demands far-sightedness, since no one looking for quick and easy profit is truly interested in their preservation. But the cost of the damage caused by such selfish lack of concern is much greater than the economic benefits to be obtained.

Many of those who possess more resources and economic or political power seem mostly to be concerned with masking the problems or concealing their symptoms, simply making efforts to reduce some of the negative impacts of climate change. However, many of these symptoms indicate that such effects will continue to worsen *if we continue with current models of production and consumption.*

Dr. Nordhaus

Laudat Si has an eloquent discussion of many local, national, and global environmental problems. But the discussion of solutions in *Laudat Si* provides little guidance on effective policies. ... Unfortunately, *Laudat Si* does not recognize *the fact* that environmental problems are caused by *market distortions* rather than markets per se.

How does cap and trade work and why is it effective? Cap-and-trade begins with actions by which a country, through its government, caps or limits its carbon dioxide emissions. The country then auctions a limited number of emission permits. ... Firms that own the permits can use them or sell them on carbon markets, while firms who need them can purchase permits. The advantage of establishing a market in permits is that *it ensures that emissions in the most productive manner.*

Pope Francis

The strategy of buying and selling carbon credits can lead to a new form of speculation which would not help reduce the emission of polluting gases worldwide. This [cap-and -trade] system seems to provide a quick and easy solution under the guise of a certain commitment to the environment, but in no way does it allow for the radical change which present circumstances require. Rather, it may simply become a ploy which permits maintaining the excessive consumption of some countries and sectors.

Keynes and CH Douglas

Major Clifford Hugh Douglas:

> If an attack were leveled at a treatise on the game of cricket on the grounds that the author's theory did not conform to generally accepted

> views on stool-ball, it would be necessary to stress some general differences between the games, if for any reason an answer to such criticism were deemed to be desirable. (p. 29)

Douglas is unappreciated, relatively unknown in the US, but nonetheless an important figure in economic thought during the inter-War period and once again in the post-Golden Age. The pamphlet quoted above is one of three pamphlets he published in the early 1920s, and have been reprinted in 2009 and 2012, and are of great interest in relation to Keynes, who was of course introducing a "macroeconomics" at the same time as Douglas, who was introducing his own "macroeconomics" in those same years.

Douglas's ideas are distinctively *macroeconomic* and were formed around the same time as Keynes's were. One might say they were like Keynesian thought in the way cricket is like stool-ball. For instance, both understood that with the establishment of industrializing capitalism at the beginning of the 20th century—particularly the establishment of the Federal Reserve in 1913, prior to Glass/Stegall in the 1933—the bank oligopoly that formed in the 19th century was now enabled to create money-capital.

Douglas:

> There is the idea that a bank only lends its own and its customers' money. But a bank lends new money. Bank loans create bank deposits. The rise in the figures of total deposits during the past twenty years proves the dynamic theory up to the hilt, if any proof is needed. (p. 7 *The Douglas Theory; a Reply to Mr. JA Hobson*)

Keynes:

> Practical bankers have drawn from this the conclusion that for the banking system as a whole the initiative lies with the depositors, and that the banks can lend no more than their depositors have previous entrusted to them. Even from the standpoint of one bank amongst many, it is apparent that the rate at which a bank passively creates deposits depends on the rate at which it is actively creating them. This illustrates, a little, of what is happening to the banking system as a whole. (p. 22, A Treatise of Money, Vol. V)

The ideas of Douglas and Keynes however are in important respects homonymic. They sound alike but are widely apart. For example, unlike neoclassical economists, each refers specifically to an industrialized market economy. But that which Douglas thinks the social system's *is*, is fundamentally in conflict not only with Keynesians, but with neoclassicals and for the most part Marxists as well.

Each of these others treats social credit as, if anything, an exogenous variable. At the center of the social system in the post-Golden Age is the private accumulation of debt ownership supported by the State. Douglas sees the State's responsibility instead to provide social credits in lieu of debt where it is needed. What John McMurtry in his book *The Cancer Stage of Capitalism* (2013) calls the "life-capital base."

> The most basic axiom of the life sequence of reproduction and development: Life refers specifically to sentient life. Sentient life, in turn, is life which can move, feel, and think in concepts as well as images. (p. 195)

Douglas's meaning of money is *pure credit*, meant to be realized in the acquiring of something good. Social priority is given to insuring life-capital. This is expressed clearly by Douglas in his book, *The Control and Distribution of Production* (1922), written for the larger public. In doing so he includes a critique of debt ownership, that it corrupts the social system by eliminating the role of the State, as was happening then and has returned in the late-20th century into the 21st with weak signs, at its best, of it being reversed or replaced with something new.

> The primary object of the overwhelming majority, of persons who co-operate in industry is to get goods. It is not employment, and it is only money in so far as money is a means to these things.
>
> If the distribution of the goods is dependent on the doing of work then it follows that either it takes all the available labor to provide the requisite amount of goods or an increasing number of persons cannot get the goods, or goods or labor must be misapplied or wasted, purely for the purpose of distributing purchasing power.
>
> We know that the first is not true. The means developed during the past century by which solar dynamic energy (steam, water, oil-power, etc.) has been made available to the extent of thousands of more times than are done by human muscular energy, is sufficient basis for such an assertion.
>
> If wages and salaries, forming a portion of costs, and reappearing in prices, are to form the major portion of the purchasing power of society, then modern scientific progress is the deadly enemy of society, since it aims at replacing the persons who now obtain their living in this way, by machines and processes.

> The prevalent assumption that human work is the foundation of purchasing power is the root assumption of a world-philosophy which may yet bring civilization to its death-grapple. (p. 12–16)

Along these lines elsewhere, Douglas's pamphlet, *These Present Discontents* (1922):

> At the present—time the struggle for existence is yet probably more intense than ever it was, and large classes of the working population live under conditions which are frankly abominable. This is an anomaly why they—working hard for comparatively long hours, with marvelous tools and almost unlimited mechanical energy at disposal—seem yet powerless to achieve even elementary economic security. (p. 8)

Keynes, in the *Treatise on Money* (1930), conceptualizes the bank oligopoly and the various private investment funds (money markets, derivatives, securitizations, hedges, equity and so on) as macroeconomic, a mutual dependence of interconnected financial institutions. The key is the whole must always be expanding via creation and destruction of individual debt ownership.

> If we suppose a closed banking system, which has no relations with the outside world, in a country where all payments are made by check and cash is not used, and if we assume further that the cash reserves but settle inter-bank indebtedness by the transfer of other assets, it is no limit to the amount of bank money which the banks can safely create provided that they move forward in step. Every movement forward by an individual bank weakens it, but every movement by one of its neighbor banks strengthens it; so that if all move forward together, no one is weakened on balance.
>
> A monetary system of this kind possesses an inherent instability; for any event which tended to influence the behavior of the majority of banks in the same direction, whether backwards or forwards, would meet no resistance and would be capable of setting up a violent movement of the whole system. This tendency towards sympathetic movement on the part of the individual elements within a banking system is always present to a certain extent and has to be reckoned with. (p. 23)

Of note, there is no reference in Keynes's writings to a system that includes social credits armoring individuals from debt ownership needed by all. Keynes himself wryly pointed to how perverse his own conception of effective demand is, half-jokingly that it would be fine policy to pay for workers to dig holes all day and then fill them up again the next, as long as they are paid wages to do it.

Douglas implicitly raises what should be—except for a deep-rooted Calvinist theological belief that keeps it hidden—an obvious question: Why not just pay the individual, without linking it to unpleasant activities that have no purpose and who could be doing something worthwhile instead?

In another pamphlet, The Douglas theory, *A Reply to Mr. JA Hobson* (1922), Douglas confronts a well-known proto-Keynesian of the early 20th century who had criticized his unusual questioning of the role of effective demand, a key unifying element of Keynesian policy recommendations.

Setting out the homonymic relationship:

> "It is to be noted that, as might be expected from a critic possessing Mr. Hobson's qualifications, there is no disagreement with my statement that the root factor in the whole industrial crisis and problem is lack of effective demand. But at this point the fundamental divergence begins." (p. 3)

He then addresses Hobson's Keynesian under-consumption assertion of a lack of effective demand, due to excess saving, *i.e.*, withholding money. That is, the problem according to Hobson is over-production of capital goods and net exports. And, without explicitly saying so, this is manifested as unplanned inventory, excess capacity, reduced production, and therefore in the end, under-employment.

Douglas's sees Keynesian theory as not so much wrong, but in its own limited social space. Within a broader sphere lack of consumer demand has another meaning, that is too many unrealized credits are being accumulated within the financial system, in various forms of debt ownership, and hence they are not available for purchase of goods. Lack of demand becomes "a fact arising out of a defective credit system" (p. 3).

Price as Douglas sees it serves a purpose prior to and exclusive of the replication and creation of capital in the form of credits. Conjointly, the premise that credit-allocation is centered in individual sales of labor is removed. Hence if goods that would otherwise constitute a decent standard of living for all are not being purchased, it is because the price of goods per credit being allocated is too high for significant numbers of people, people who do not make a living wage sufficient to acquire basic needs.

In the first instance, then, the question of lack of effective demand calls for new policies of distributing credit. Such policies may or may not include fostering economic growth so as reduce unemployment thereby providing more credits, i.e., via the labor markets.

By contrast, as a first principle the State might assure all individuals and families enough credits, in the form of income and insurance for each to enjoy a decent standard of living.

> Considered as a fact, it [implicitly Keynesian demand policy] is one of the many premises of which to take cognizance in suggesting methods by which to achieve the greatest enhancement of opportunity of the greatest number. In other words, both Mr. Hobson and I see a world whose financial mechanism is failing to deliver the goods. Mr. Hobson implies that a change in the nature of the steam which provides the motive force is required; I suggest that the valve gear wants re-designing. (p. 4, *The Douglas Theory; a Reply to Mr. JA Hobson*)

An illustrative case is the current debate over unemployment benefits in the US. These come in the form of a money income—not a living wage—for six months, transferred from the government to individuals laid off through no fault of their own. The issue at hand is whether to continue to extend benefits to those whose six months are up, due to the high rate of unemployment.

The latter itself is connected to the low of rate of economic growth since 2008. The homonymic relationship of Keynesian theory and that of Douglas is seen in the fact that both point to extending unemployment benefits, under the circumstances, continuing to provide new credits (government spending) to these individuals.

The Keynesian understanding of this, however, is to increase effective demand, contribute to growth and with it the decline of unemployment. Along those lines, to follow the existing practice of ending the extensions once the rate of unemployment becomes acceptably low (around an official 5%).

Like those who are against extending the benefits in the first place, the Keynesians do not even consider Douglas's notion that credits be provided by the State to individuals and families who cannot sell their labor for any of various reasons. Douglas understanding is that credits be provided by the government to individuals whose income from labor is otherwise not a living wage. And following this logic leads to a social system that ultimately finances all of an individual's or family's basic goods and services, separate from profit-making capital and labor markets as we know them.

A Keynesian premise, Douglas avers, is that a major objective of the industrial system is employment, seen to mean maximum growth, itself necessary on the grounds of employment. This objective is at the very least rhetorically championed by an amazingly vast majority of political forces acting in the US from the Green and Tea Parties, and the Chamber of Commerce and the Progressive Caucus, even Bernie Sanders and Elizabeth Warren, and of course both the Democratic and Republican parties, not to say the Working Families Party.

> The practical object of the whole economic and industrial system is to deliver not *more*, but the *right* quantity of the right goods to the whole of the people, with the minimum of discomfort to all concerned. After that object has been attained, the productive organization may legitimately be an outlet of creative activity. At no time is it a legitimate object of the general productive process to *provide employment* for the purpose of distributing wages—to make things which the public do not need and the makers do not enjoy making, in order that some canon of obsolete theological morality or the premises of an effete financial system, may thereby be satisfied. (p. 12, The Labor Party and Social Credit)

This brings the homonymic relation of Keynes and Douglas to the fore. Douglas however goes astray in referring to social credit as a macroeconomic dividend. It is based on an imaginary "universal unearned increment," due to (sic) exploitation of the machines' productivity on the part of, presumably, workers and owners of the industry.

The dividend is the vehicle for the distribution of this unearned increment, and it is in the universalization of the dividend and not in its abolition (p. 13, The Labor Party and Social Credit).

Despite this, however, Douglas is clearly pointing in a direction far off from Keynes and most others. And this is seen in the position of the owners of machine production where basic needs—life, liberty, and the pursuit of happiness—are fulfilled by social credits. It means labor relative to private capital would become more expensive and the great movement away from labor toward machinery continues.

Might This be Done?

The current creation of money, in the aftermath of the crash of 2008, by the banking oligopoly is something other than a pyramid scheme to the extent it is insured by the central bank's willingness to add to the deposits in the banks by purchasing their bad debt.

This is being done with the consent, indeed the collaboration of the US and other leading sovereign-currency States. The State is being absorbed it appears into the oligopoly. It is not clear whether or not it is actually a collection of *zombie banks*, selling debt that only the State is willing to purchase, such sales then enable banks to repay depositors and accumulate debt ownership, but not enough to do too much in term of commercial loans.

On the other hand, the Federal government's creation of money could instead be used to spending on goods, through social credit. This is especially true of entitlements, social credit that flows directly into households or as payment to providers of fundamental goods. In addition, the government finances its expenditures through sales of guaranteed securities to households and corporations (the private sector), who are thus provided with ownership of risk-free debt backed by the government.

These plain facts have been twisted into a neo-Liberal Alice in Wonderland conception of the malapropos *national debt.* In Wonderland, the debt is money owed to the borrower, since the central bank is a creature of and ultimately under the authority of the State. Moreover, the national debt is also money lent to the lender, since the securities purchased by households and corporations are deemed to be ultimately owed by households and corporations, and in the end paid by them (the private sector) through higher taxes.

The accounting practices of the Congressional Budget Office (CBO) regarding the national debt are interesting. Transfers of money from the central bank into the Treasury's accounts are subtracted out on the grounds that they are *intra-governmental* transactions. But in doing so, the CBO does not see, or perhaps does not wish to, that this confirms the fact that the government does create money at will.

The CBO is indecisive about it and therefore inconsistent in its practice. Outstanding Federal government securities held by the domestic private sector *are* treated as a component of the national debt, despite the fact that the liabilities putatively incurred by the State are offset—when one speaks of the nation's debt—by the money-valuation of the government securities held by the private sector.

What is left of the debt after both of these components are subtracted: The government securities largely held by foreign States as well as private entities. In the case of the US, this remainder is presently about 25% in a recent year of a 16 trillion-dollar national debt. Even these foreign-owned US government securities are not national debt either, because the payments to the creditors are in dollars.

The simulation of a government debt since the 1980s has been catalyzed into a great semiotic/political force, linking the national debt to income flows into households and corporations, and which then in turn flow out as Federal taxes into what are conceived of as State revenues. The crucial catalyst is the Federal income tax. It has gone hand in hand with the radical transformation of the financial system.

The devastating consequences of these false linkages are only beginning to be understood in the wake of the global economic crisis. In terms of fiscal policy in particular, the simulation of government debt underlies one of the most important tenets of *austerity*, reducing government expenditures in order to eliminate budget deficits, so as in turn to reduce the debt to a minimum.

Removing the lens of the simulation, austerity in this respect is seen to be, instead, a policy of preventing the State from creating social credits, in lieu of debt ownership. This is supported by the telling neo-liberal resistance to *entitlement expenditures* over the past three decades. They are programs by which the State effectively insures certain basic services and incomes: broadly speaking, infrastructure, health-care, living incomes, and quality education.

A primary neo-liberal policy aim has been to weaken, or even better to do away with existing entitlements, and at the least to halt any expansion of them. The social credit policy implies in most cases capital conversion, suggesting that hidden beneath the fear of State debt, is a fear of State insurance to which each citizen is entitled. Such State insurance payments constitute money that does not involve capital, and the same is true of public investment that is not contracted out by the State.

Steeped as neo-liberal thought is in classical liberalism, the idea that the State would openly and meaningfully take on this responsibility toward its citizens *for free* is anathema, despite the State's promise of fundamental goods to all. It would be the return to Speenhamland and the reversal of Polanyi's famous transformation, the poor again provided for by the State.

The reader is asked here to remove the blinders of simulated government debt and the dissimulated power of any sovereign-currency State to create money. The Federal government by monetizing the so-called debt, eliminates the neo-liberal catalyst.

There would be no need and no purpose in Federal taxation as means of financing State expenditures (On the other hand, Federal taxation of corporations as means of internalizing negative externalities would continue to have such a purpose). The State would simply acquire money through the central bank, as it does now.

Taxation can revert to what it had been prior to 1913, for the most part a practice of states and municipalities of various sorts. In the words of a leading MMT thinker, L. Randall Wray: "The US [Federal] government does not face an affordability constraint. The government can afford anything for sale in its own currency" (p. 187, 2012).

An exemplification of this crucial—for some perhaps unthinkable—disconnection of government spending and income tax collection, is *Social Security*, the most successful Roosevelt era entitlement program. It is characterized by the feature of a fund established that is ever-replenished by dedicated tax receipts. Supposedly, payments are made to beneficiaries by the government out of this fund, as if households create money and the State transfers it. Thus, in neo-liberal fashion the State's actual ability to create money at will is dissimulated by the dedicated payroll tax.

But once the State's ability to create money at will is acknowledged, then Social Security is easily seen for what it is: State financing of basic retirement and disability incomes. The entitlement is not supported by a tax dedicated to a Social Security fund. This is confirmed by the fact that the State can and does transfer money from that fund, transferring it to the Treasury account, adding, in return non-negotiable State-guaranteed securities to the fund; a process no different in principle than monetizing the debt.

The State can just as easily make Social Security payments directly to beneficiaries by transferring money into its account from the central bank. There's no purpose to the tax. A retiree, in the current system, is not guaranteed payments because there is a net surplus in the Social Security fund. What matters is that ultimately the fund itself is guaranteed by the sovereign-currency State.

Along these lines, consider the following by a leading father of post-Keynesian thought, Robert Eisner, in a pamphlet *The Great Deficit Scares* (1997), responding to the great fear voiced of there being a shortage in the Social Security fund:

> Since Social Security checks come from the Treasury in any event, there is no real reason to go through the accounting procedure of building up the computer balances and then drawing them down. The funds could be abolished and the Treasury ordered to go on paying the benefits prescribed by law, borrowing to finance these expenditures if necessary, just as it does now to finance the US military or anything else. (p. 44–45)

Randall Wray, in his book *Modern Money Theory: A Primer on Macroeconomics* (2012) writes in a heading: "Just because government can afford to spend does not mean government ought to spend." The two chief reasons he then gives for this warning are in fact diametrically opposed to two objectives of State policy as understood by CH Douglas and John McMurtry. That is, fulfilling the State's obligation to ensure life and pursuit of happiness to which all citizens are entitled, and secondly, placing strong constraints on financial capital-driven products.

Wray:
The first objective:

> A strong social safety net might send the signal that individuals do not really need to work because they can always live well enough on government handouts. (p. 189)

And with respect to the second objective:

> The more resources we remove from private use to allocate to public use, the greater the likelihood that we could have a bloated government sector and a private sector that is too small. We need to leave an adequate supply of resources for the private sector to achieve the private purpose, given as even as we allocate sufficient resources to achieve the public purpose. (p. 190)

The first proposal of ours here, then, is the disconnecting of taxes and government spending means that an albatross hanging over the State since around the 1980s—taxation as the catalyst of neoliberal austerity policies—would quickly fly off into the night. Rather than a burden on the private sector, the State's issuance and sale of securities to the public provides risk-free future liquidity to households through savings out of income.

Returning to Social Security, one sees that doing away with the dedicated payroll tax essentially does not alter anything. The State creates the money needed to furnish mandated retirement income. Without the income tax the government overtly transfers money into the Treasury Department's account to make payments either to providers, or, as in the case of most Social Security payments, directly to retirees. Widening this to entitlement programs in general, clears the way to a broader harmonization of money by a State freed of simulations conceivable even in the golden age. The State no longer is seen to be limited by taxation in its ability to distribute social credits.

Of course, the forces driving the bank oligopoly and their ancillaries are great. Indeed, there has been a titanic capital conversion of the State's own creation of money, the latter ever-more accumulation of debt ownership, not goods. Attempting to lift the yoke of the national debt solely through jettisoning the income tax alone therefore is likely doomed to failure.

A second proposal here then tied to the first is a novel and radical reconstituting of the central bank. In retrospect, perhaps the central failure of the Glass-Steagall regime was to not have strictly separated the central bank from the private banking oligopoly, intersecting the strict separation of commercial and investment banks.

The ambiguous nature of the Federal Reserve's legal status, and more concretely the oligopoly's domination of the Federal Reserve, was not guarded against, and in time that proved fatal. But what has not changed is that the bank-oligopoly's debt, owned by its depositors, is ultimately guaranteed by the State. This has enabled the financial system's transformation into the grand pyramid scheme it seems to be, crucial to the oligopoly's ability to sustain the system becoming *too big to fail.*

The proposal here, then, is that, instead of the State insuring deposits held by private banks, *the central bank should be reconstituted as a repository of household debit accounts* (as well as the Federal Government's Treasury account). On the other side of the coin, deposits in corporate banks would no longer be State-guaranteed.

The oligopoly would now be predominantly investment banks, one imagines anyway. Their depositors would now fully bear the burden of risks theses banks would be willing to take. The central bank, on the other hand, would now more or less provide the services of the golden-age commercial banks. The open-market operations monetary policy traditionally performed by the central bank of course would cease, so that the detachment of the central bank from the bank oligopoly would be virtually complete. This might be described as a revision of Glass-Steagall, separating the public's commodity credit altogether from corporate banking institutions. Of note, the very question of too big to fail *would disappear at once.*

To transform the central bank and with it the financial system in its entirety, and to eliminate Federal income taxes, naturally imply a sharp reversal of the path travelled by the sovereign currency economies over the past thirty-five years or so. It aims both at an all-but-forgotten attention to entitlements owed by the State to the public and to the need for a decompression of private capital.

In semiotic terms, these radical changes free the State to create and insure basic household entitlements and liquidity. At the same time, the massive endogenous expansion of speculative financial capital, underpinned by a bank oligopoly whose debt is insured by the State, would be at an end, the ability to take on great speculative risk having been largely removed. In particular, no banking corporation would any longer be attracting depositors via a State guarantee.

This could be done! But even the sympathetic reader must be expected to respond at this point, 'Yes, but it is never going to happen.' To this I say, in conclusion, once money and the State are looked at directly, or, if you prefer philosophically, they are reflected in a new mirror, then new objectives of the State, and therefore new means of achieving new objectives may suddenly appear.

CHAPTER 4

Archaic Money

Barter Exchange and Gift-giving

The discussion here rests on a central thesis of Walter Benjamin (and in the body of thought known as *dialogism*, a meme of Michael Bakhtin) articulated by Benjamin below:

> What is communicable in a mental entity is its logistic entity. Language communicates the linguistic being of things.
>
> A human communicates its own mental being in its language. However, the language of a human speaks in words. It is therefore the linguistic being of the human to name things. (p. 316–318, *Reflections*)
>
> To whom does the lamp communicate itself? Or the mountain? Or the fox? But here the answer is: to the human. This is not anthropomorphism. If the lamp and the mountain and the fox did not communicate themselves to us, how should we be able to name them?
>
> Does a human communicate its mental being by the names that it gives things? Or in them? The paradoxical nature of these lies in their answer. Anyone who believes that a human communicates its mental being *by names* cannot also assume that it is their mental being that it communicates, for this does not happen through the names of things, that is, through the words by which he denotes a thing. (p. 254, *Early Writings*)

The defining characteristic of *archaic money* is no word for it in the language spoken within the community exists. Rather, it is implicit in the observed practices as communication to observers outside them. The anthropologist Marcel Mauss, in his major work *The Gift* (1950) observes distinct practices of reciprocity between subjects, having in common a social object, the *commodity*, which as such, communicates itself to us in money. This in turn, helps provide a semiotic grounding of a political economy that uses archaic money in different forms.

Barter is a special case of the more general reciprocity type, being exchange of two things each of which is both a commodity and money. It is a distinct kind of exchange, but not as customarily thought because the exchange is un-mediated by money. Rather, to the contrary it consists of a pair of simultaneous movements of commodity and money.

In particular, then, barter is the purchase of a quantity of one commodity, C_2, by Party 1, who pays for it with a quantity of money in the form of a commodity, C_1; simultaneously it is a purchase of C_1 by Party 2, who pays for it with C_2. The archaic money the first party pays for C_2 is in natural units of C_1. C_2 thereby communicates itself in money: $M(C_1)$. And similarly, C_1 communicates itself in $M(C_2)$, which Party 2 pays for C_1.

Two-Party (Simultaneous) Barter-Exchange

$$M(C_1) \rightarrow C_2 \text{ [Party 1]//} M(C_2) \rightarrow C_1 \text{ [Party 2]}$$

$$M(C_1)/M(C_2) = P_2/P_1.$$

Two aspects of barter differentiating it from other forms of exchange are of note. First, globally, money takes as many forms as there are commodities bartered. This is true to some extent of gift-giving as well, and hence a word for archaic money as a single being is not apparent. Indeed, the use of the word *money* in a capitalist context may be for the same reason, but in reverse. It is the different monies, conceptually, are not apparent. Conceptually, money is only seen as unitary.

Mauss refers at one point to the archaic accounting method of the Trobriand Islanders with respect to the circulation of commodities as a "somewhat childish legal language which has given rise to a proliferation of distinctive names for all kinds of counter-services, according to the name of the service that is being compensated, the thing given, the occasion, etc" (p. 30). One sees here that such a method is not childish, but just the opposite. It is in line with the particular attribution of credit in its multi-dimensional form of money, associated both with barter and, gift-giving.

A second, aspect of a pure act of barter, the moneys disappear, each commodity having been transformed back into natural objects consumed by the respective parties. For this reason, it is an attenuated practice both in generalized exchange systems as well as in archaic production and distribution. Money does not naturally circulate, but rather ceases to exist in the act of exchange. Barter is thereby accidental.

The anthropologist Bronislaw Malinowski introduces in his book *Argonauts of the Western Pacific* (1922) a category he names "ceremonial barter" in taxonomy of reciprocities.

> In this class, we have to describe payments which are ceremonially offered and must be received and re-paid later on. The exchange is based

> on a permanent partnership, and the articles have to be roughly equivalent in value. (1922, 187)

Clearly, within gift-giving, some tribes are engaged in long-term exchanges where by lucky happenstance they are close at hand and produce complementary goods at different seasons (e.g., the fishers and the farmers). The prices of the commodities are in practice singular to the act of barter in space/times.

The anthropologist Raymond Firth, in an article of his in the book he edited, the name of each, the same, *Themes in Economic Anthropology* (1967):

> The fact that in many primitive (sic) economic systems there is no mechanism whereby goods and services can be consistently and regularly exchanged for one another in relatively free style has definite restrictive effects. It also raises a difficult problem for which no adequate solution has yet been found. In the absence of pervasive exchange, how can any system of evaluation of goods and services manifest itself? (p. 18)

In this context, the anthropologist Mary Douglas (1967) directly addresses the textbook narrative, whereby money generally originates in the practice of barter, a narrative that unites the broad theoretical models comprising classical and neoclassical economics. The latter are predicated upon a functionalist historical argument. A market directed system requires that, in the context of expanding barter, a single commodity that comes to circulate as money.

Douglas criticizes the premise, of neoclassical thought, in particular of a socially-accepted commodity transformed into money, serving to mediate exchange in general. She asserts that from observation such a thing was extremely unusual. That in turn, it would be functionally necessary for such a market system to exist.

Douglas, along with numerous other anthropologists, observes the existence of archaic societies that have systems of social credits. She sees that the experience of money as a language within exchange does not often occur, that that is a spreading of barter. Rather it is one of many archaic rationing systems, social credits that serve a safety net underneath the whole community.

Credit in the form of particular shells, for instance, is often claimed on specified goods serving *life-bases*. Hence, Douglas argues that the creation of social credits, i.e., *coupons*, in archaic societies, underlies quantitative communication of equivalence between commodities.

> Money may sometimes have emerged from the barter situation which is described in the first page of [economic] textbooks on money. On this

> familiar argument, the inconvenience of barter and the difficulty of arranging credit lead to the adoption of a medium of exchange. The only objection to this supposed historical sequence is that credit is never difficult in a primitive economy; credit exists before the market, and Adam Smith's tailor who wants to buy bread for his children should have no difficulty in arranging long-term credits with the baker for whom he has made a suit.
>
> In practice while I readily admit that money can arise in these circumstances of inhibited barter, the evidence for primitive money suggests that this is rare, while the origin of money in a type of primitive rationing system seems likely to be more widespread. I distinguish medium-of-exchange from *coupon-money* in primitive economies, and start by considering the conditions in which real money is likely to emerge.
>
> Karl Menger said that, where barter is going on, the commodity, which is the relatively most saleable, will tend to be used as a primitive medium of exchange. On this account, money emerges as the market develops. It implies that perfect money would be completely able to permeate any situation, for freely, be interchangeable with everything else, be more widely of primitive currencies whose purchasing power is so unrestricted. But in general, primitive currencies do not flow freely, they are acceptable only in limited situations, they are not highly saleable. (p. 1967: 121–122)

Menger is one of the founders of neoclassical economics, in the 1870s. Douglas refers to an article of his in the *Economic Journal*: On the Origin of Money, 1892 (pp. 249–250).

Gift-giving, a practice pervasive in archaic societies—is a reciprocal relationship distinct from exchange in general, and from barter in particular. Nonetheless, like exchange, it is a reciprocity in which the commodity communicates itself in money. Mauss quotes a much-cited passage from the works of the Maori sage, Tamati Ranaport, referring to the *hua* attached to the gift, and explains, its relationship to the commodity, which is called taonaga

> I will speak to you about the *hua*. The hua is not the wind that blows—not at all. Let us suppose that you possess a certain article (taonaga). You give it to me without setting a price on it. We strike no bargain about it. Now, I give this *taonaga* to a third person who, after a certain lapse of time decides to give me something as payment in return, *tutu*, to make a present to me of *taonaga*. Now, this *taonaga* given to me is the *hua* of the *taonaga* that I had received from you and that I had given to the

> other. The *taonaga* that I received for these *taonaga* (which came from you) must be returned to you. It would not be fair (tika) on my part to keep these *taonaga* for myself, whether they were desirable (*fawe*) or undesirable (*kino*). I must give them to you because they are a hua of the *taonaga* that you gave me. If I kept his other *taonaga* for myself, serious harm might befall me, even death. This is the nature of the *hua*, the *hua* of personal property, the hua of the *taonaga*, the *hua* of the forest. (p. 11)

One takes from this that the act of gift-giving is, by definition, unilateral. It is not founded upon a mutual agreement between parties that in turn would communicate the commodity in money: "We strike no bargain about the gift." In this sense, the reciprocity is not exchange (barter or otherwise), but mutual giving.

Malinowski:

> The main principle underlying the regulations of actual exchange is that the Kula consists in the bestowing of a ceremonial gift, which has to be repaid by an equivalent counter-gift after a lapse of time. But can never be exchanged from hand to hand, with the equivalence between the two objects discussed, bargained about and computed. The natives distinguish it from barter, which they practice extensively, of which they have a clear idea.
>
> The second very important principle is that the equivalence of the counter-gift is left to the giver. And it cannot be enforced by any kind of coercion. If the article given as counter-gift is not equivalent, the recipient will be disappointed and angry but has no direct means of redress. The Kula native loves to possess and therefore desires to acquire and dreads to lose, the social code of rules, with regard to give and take by far overrides the natural (sic) acquisitive tendency. (p. 95–96)

This kind of commodity circulation is more understandable when one realizes that gift-giving in archaic societies often involves the periodic hosting of grand prestations, within and across both kinship and tribal lines. In these contexts, the commodity communicates itself in a language that supersedes exchange, a language of giving. Here is a simple model.

Money, M(G), is the gift, carrying with it, to the recipient, the hua; the debt. The giver purchases debt-relief. In the pure case of a prestation, the gift (money) is consumed in the very act of transferring the hua from giver to recipient of the gift. This can be rendered as periodically alternating transfers of the hua, each party in turn attaining debt-relief by gift-giving. Hence the term, kula, meaning circle.

Pure Gift-giving

$$M(G) \rightarrow R1 \text{ [Party 1]}$$

$$M(G) \rightarrow R2 \text{ [Party 2]}$$

On the other hand, if the gift is a durable good, both the hua and the gift circulate. In this latter case the gift, for example highly-crafted items of jewelry are virtually experienced as money. Unfortunately, this phenomenon can be confused with barter. To avoid this, one must appreciate that the language of money is expressing things within the context of the gift-giving act that are opposed to those expressing the act of exchange.

Mauss, at the outset of *The Gift*, states a central problem he intends to address:

> What rule of legality and self-interest, in societies of an archaic type, compels the gift that has been received to be obligatorily reciprocated? What power resides in the object given that causes its recipient to pay it back? (p. 3)

As so posed the problem is not so much left unsolved by the remainder of the book as it is revealed to be misplaced. It presumes the gift is "obligatorily reciprocated," and so seeks to find what impels otherwise free subjects to act in this way. Rather, it may be the gift is the *transgredient* of the commodity, experienced by its giver as liberation of the self from the community. Hence, gift-giving is not an obligatory reciprocation in the sense of being experienced as an imposition. It is experienced as liberation from debt.

Firth (1967) articulates the broad position in this regard taken by Mauss:

> "What Mauss notes in essence is that giving is an extension of the self and hence the obligation to give is bound up with the notion of the self, its social bounds and social roles." (p. 10–11)

And Malinowski writes:

> The important point is that with them to possess is to give—and here those in the tribe differ from us notably. A person who owns a thing is naturally expected to share it, to distribute it, to be its trustee and dispenser. (p. 97)

Coming from what might be thought of as the other end of the circle, Mary Douglas argues that the nature of archaic money in relation to gift-giving is opposed to barter and therefore, like Mauss and Malinowski suggests that:

> It is well known that there are so-called primitive moneys which are rarely used as media of exchange, which are accepted for only a limited range of services and commodities and are transferable only to a limited range of persons. Their rates of exchange do not express a price system—or if there is one it is very insensitive. If these are money they do not expedite the transfer of goods and services as our money does.
>
> As I see it, money in its nature is essentially an instrument of freedom, rationing in its nature an instrument of control. Money represents general purchasing power over all marketed goods; coupons restrict and channel the purchasing power of money.
>
> Coupons are essentially instruments of control. In so far as they seek to contain and bar the use of money they are anti-market in intent, the tools of restriction. Money and coupons could only be more opposite in their beginnings and in their purposes. (p. 119–121)

Money in various forms is always being re-created within the movements of the individual of social Totality, including archaic money.

Corrupt Gift-giving

A sub-text of Mauss's attempt to grasp gift-giving as an obligatory reciprocity is his interest in, and even occasional alarm at practices which appear to embody a third reciprocity; neither gift-giving nor exchange. In his Introduction to *The Gift* (1950) Mauss expresses a great interest in tribes that practice a "highly developed" form of gift-giving, which he terms *potlatch*.

The latter is a feature of archaic societies in which gift-giving reciprocities are generalized, mediating production and distribution of food and land, and where, in the extreme, crises are brought on by an unstable bidding up of the (implicit) price of debt-relief.

> Everything—clans, marriages, initiations, Shamanist séances and meetings for the worship of the great gods, the totems or the collective or individual ancestors of the clan—is woven into an inextricable network of

> rites, of total legal and economic services, of assignment to political ranks in the society of men, in the tribe, and in the confederations of tribes, and even internationally. Yet what is noteworthy of these tribes is the principle of rivalry and hostility that prevails in all their practices. They go as far as to fight and kill chiefs and nobles. Moreover, they even go as far as to the purely sumptuary destruction of wealth that has been accumulated in order to outdo the rival chief. (p. 6)

Of note, where there is generalized gift-giving there is an extreme meshing of self and community. "Everything is woven into an inextricable network." This agrees with the notion that the giving of the gift is experienced as the purchase of debt-relief. It provides space for the self, absent the community. Hence one would expect in the midst of the potlatch an upward pressure at times on the size of the gift needed to acquire a certain degree of relief.

Mauss observes intrinsic asymmetry between reciprocating parties that is not characteristic either of barter or gift-giving. He refers to "fighting and killing" and "sumptuary destruction," suggesting that force separates the parties from the act.

> One can demonstrate that in the things exchanged during the potlatch, a power is present that forces gifts to be passed around, to be given, and returned. At least among the Kwakiutl and Tsimshian, the same distinction is made between the various kinds of property as made by the Romans, the Trobriand peoples and the Samoans. For these there exist, on the one hand the objects of consumption and for common sharing (I have found no trace of exchange). And on the other hand, there are the precious things belonging to the family, the various talismans, emblazoned copper objects, blankets made of skin or cloth bedecked with emblems. This latter type of object is passed on as solemnly as women hand over at marriage the privileges to their sons-in law, names and ranks to children and sons-in-law. It is even incorrect to speak in their case of transfer. They are loans rather than sales or rue abandonment of possession. (p. 43)

As described by Mauss, as well as Firth (1936) and Marshall Sahlins (1958), the reciprocal relations in the particular case of the potlatch are intra-tribal, between individual subjects, chiefs and clan leaders, for whom one might say the self effectively subsumes the social. It is especially found in the context of the Polynesian *ramified societies*, a single system of *overlapping stewardship* with unilineal kin groups functioning as political units. These are distinguished from descent-line systems, comprised of discrete localized common descent groups that function as an alliance of territorial political entities.

In the ramified societies, a chief oversees production and distribution across the entire tribe, and each leader oversees them within his clan. Chiefs and clan leaders, within their respective scope, have such (overlapping) powers, as: prohibiting land use, regulating planting arrangements, employing labor in and controlling communal craft production.

The last of these is of particular interest to us insofar as items such as highly-crafted jewelry, as we have seen, serve as highly-monetized gifts that circulate inter-tribally. It implies then that the chief, in particular, has some control over a money supply.

To the degree that clans retain group rights to the food produced (based on status within the ramage) then gift-giving is not generalized. With generalization, the chief receives as a gift from the clans, labor that produces the chief's household food, as well as requisite public goods, notably accumulation of stocks.

The chief's receipt of labor is passed from the clan leader down to the household level, and pressure is exerted on the clan leader from the opposite direction, that is by heads of households within the clan. Displacing group rights to some extent, then, the chief distributes food instead in the form of reciprocating gifts to the clans.

Mauss:

> An important kind of exchange takes on the form of exhibitions. Such are the *sagali,* distributions of food on a grand scale that are made on several occasions: at harvest time, at the building of the chief's hut or new boats, or at funeral festivals. These distributions are to groups that have performed some service for the chief or his clan, cultivation of land, the transporting the large tree trunks from which boats or beams are carved, and for services rendered at funerals by the members of the dead person's clan, etc. Generally, distributions seem to be due to group action, in so far as the personality of the chief does not make itself felt. Yet in addition to these group rights and this collective economy, already less resembling the kula, all individual relationships of exchange seem to us to be of this type. (p. 29–30)

With the potlatch in mind, corrupted gift-giving can be rendered as follows, where debt relief (R) is purchased with the clan leader's gift of labor M(L), on the one hand, and the chief's gift of food M(F) on the other.

Corrupted Gift-giving (three cycles)

$$M(L_1) \rightarrow R\ [\text{clanleader}]$$
$$M(F_1) \rightarrow R\ [\text{chief}]$$

$$M(L_1) \rightarrow R\ [\text{clanleader}]$$
$$M(F_2) \rightarrow R\ [\text{chief}]$$

$$M(L_2) \rightarrow R\ [\text{clanleader}]$$
$$M(F_3) \rightarrow R\ [\text{chief}]$$

$$M(F_2) > M(F_1).$$
$$M(F_3) > M(F_2).$$

To use a game theory term, where there is corrupted gift-giving, as described by Mauss, the chief has gained a *second-mover advantage*. The first move is the gift of labor from clans to the chief. The second is the chief's distribution of food to the clans, which—impinging upon group rights—has the social meaning of reciprocating the gift of labor. The chief can exact seigniorage, accumulations of food and crafts that require relatively little additional labor to produce. This can be added to the chief's reciprocating gifts to the clans. This pushes up the labor needed by the clans for debt-relief in the next cycle.

If a clan does not reciprocate, then a debt is owed and interest charged. The seigniorage enables further accumulation of the chief's stocks, insofar as the marginal labor to add to his gift is less than the additional product of the labor received as gift in the next cycle.

Gift-giving here is corrupted by the power relations of the chief and clan leaders, and the corruption naturally extends to intra-clan and ultimately intra-household life. The corruption is semiotic in that in isolation gift-giving is pure of the distinct forces each party exerts on the reciprocation. In its corrupted state commodity language is not replaced so much as hollowed out.

Much as the *state of exception* in contemporary times in which the Law exists but is not in force, in the potlatch the language of giving is spoken, but it is emptied of meaning. This helps account for the intensity of the potlatch that so intrigues Mauss, the actual killing of chiefs, as well as clan leaders presumably, amidst a frenzy of gift-giving that can lead to the actual destruction of objects of wealth as means of claiming debt-relief.

> The obligation to reciprocate constitutes the essence of the potlatch, in so far as it does not consist of pure destruction. These acts of destruction are very often sacrificial, and beneficial to the sprits. It would seem they need *not all* be reciprocated unconditionally. However, normally the potlatch must be reciprocated with interest, as must indeed every gift. Even if a subject receives a blanket from his chief for some service he has rendered, he will give two in return on the occasion of a marriage in the chief's family, of the enthronement of the chief's son, etc. It is true that the latter in his turn will give away all the goods that he obtains at future potlatches, when the opposing clans will heap benefits upon him.
>
> The punishment for failure to reciprocate is slavery for debt. It is an institution really comparable in nature and function to the *Roman nexum*.
>
> The individual unable to repay the loan or reciprocate the potlatch loses his rank and even his status as a free man. There is no need to point out the identical nature of this and the Roman expression (p. 21–42).

Nexum and *Mancipium*

Mauss's third and last section of *The Gift*, (not counting a concluding summary) is an attempt to give a brief philological overview of money. He connects archaic money in gift-giving, with the debt-relief of tokens in the archaic period of Rome.

> All the facts set out have been gathered in what we term the ethnographical field. Moreover, they concentrate on the societies that people the borders of the Pacific. They have general sociological value, since they allow us to understand a stage in social evolution. But there is more to them than this: they have also a hearing on social history. Institutions of this type have really provided the transition towards our own forms of law and economy. They can serve to explain historically our own societies. We believe that our systems of law and economies have emerged from institutions similar to those we describe. (p. 47)

Mauss identifies as a crucial element of that putative connection, the *nexum*, an area of common law in early antiquity, and relates it to the tribal societies.

> A comparison between these archaic laws and Roman laws that predates the Roman Empire era, somewhat earlier than before it really becomes historical, and Germanic law at the time when it does likewise, throws

> light on both types of law. In particular, it allows us to pose one of the most controversial questions in the history of law, the theory of the *nexum*. (p. 48)

The *nexum* generally is thought to be genealogically connected to the financial systems at the heart of capitalist economies, the latter first emerging some two millennia later. Mauss hypothesizes that the apparent "distinction" in this period of Roman law is between "obligations and services that are not given free, on the one hand, and gift-giving on the other." He then argues there must have existed reciprocity in a previous—unknown—phase that contained both.

Referring to social agents in this imagined phase, Mauss asks rhetorically: "Have they not in fact practiced these customs of the gift that is exchanged, in which persons and things merge." However, money as commodity language expresses different things with respect to reciprocities that are covered by the *nexum* and those associated with gift-giving. Thus, a synthesis of the reciprocities seems improbable.

The primary idea of *nexum*—as articulated by Edwin Charles Clark in his book *Early Roman Law: The Regal Period* (1872) is obligation, "affixed by law to the receipt of a nominal consideration" (p. 111). *Nexum* refers generically to a loan agreement as legal entity: oath, contract, bill, promissory note, bond, security, et al.

A subject borrows money, accounted for in tokens (e.g., copper). If the money is not repaid, as per the agreement, the subject is obligated by common law to provide the creditor labor, or more precisely the creditor has the legal right (among others) to force the debtor into servitude. The subject's relative freedom is then collateral on the loan.

Clark, citing Mucius and Varro, states that *nexa* referred specifically to the act of borrowing money. He attributes to Mucius the observation that the law imposes servitude on the seller (supplier) of the nexum; i.e., the borrower, in lieu of repayment.

Clark refers to Varro in this regard:

> This is the truer view the word in question itself shows; for the very thing which by balances becomes subject to obligation and not its own, is thence called *nexum*. The free man who owed his labour for servitude in consideration of certain money, until he should pay that money is called nexus, etc. The primary idea of *nexum* is obligation, affixed by law to the receipt of a nominal consideration. Some parallel may be found in the bargain and sale of our common law, by which a use was raised on the payment of any, even the smallest sum of money. If we consider

> *mancipium* as a conveyance then that *mancipium* was a species of *nexum*. The two original ideas of acquisition and obligation are so combined in the earliest form of *mancipium* that confusion between them was and is inevitable. But I cannot believe that the proper and primary signification of *nexum* was anything but bond or obligation. (p. 111)

Thus, the *nexum*, as reciprocity, was such that the acquirer of liquidity (the borrower) incurred debt. The social meaning of the *nexum* is the legal responsibility to repay the debt in money. Until a debt is repaid there is a *nexus* of the agreement. The servitude of the debtor, so long as the debt is not repaid by a third party, can extend the nexus indefinitely.

As opposed to the *nexum*, gift-giving, including corrupted gift-giving, is initiated by the giver of the gift. The giver acts to acquire debt-relief, as opposed to the creditor who acquires interest on a bond. Gift is not a transfer of credit, but rather of debt. The gift is a natural object of intrinsic worth. In the area of *the nexum*, by stark contrast, money speaks explicitly through tokens.

The latter takes the concrete form of an object expressly absent of intrinsic value save that of being a signifier of credit. In this light, then there may be less genealogical link of the sort Mauss imagines. Indeed, some degree of credit relations existed, in the form of coupons separate from gift-giving even in the archaic societies directly studied by Mauss

It bears mentioning that through much of Europe following the dissolution of the large-scale Roman slave trade, but prior to the revival of global trade around the twelfth century, money was to a large degree a language of giving, corrupted or otherwise, and as such was conceived of generally as treasure; an object of intrinsic worth.

Referring to this period, Michel Foucault writes in *The Order of Things* (1966):

> The problem of monetary substance is the distortion between the weights of cons and nominal; values. But these two series of problems were linked, since the metal appeared only as a sign, and as a sign for measuring wealth, in so far as it was itself of wealth. It possessed the power to signify because it was itself a real mark. And just as words had the same reality as what they said, as the marks of living beings were inscribed upon their bodies in the manner of visible and positive marks, similarly, the signs that indicated wealth and measured it were bound to carry the real mark in themselves. To represent prices, they themselves had to be precious. They had to be rare, useful, desirable.

> Moreover, all these qualities had to be stable if the mark they imprinted upon things was to be an authentic and universally legible signature. The two functions of money, as a common measure between commodities and as a substitute in the mechanism of exchange, are based upon its material reality (169)

Gold as treasure was somewhat akin to the highly-crafted jewelry that Mauss observes circulating between islands. Foucault indicates, however, that by the fifteenth and sixteenth centuries in Western Europe, the gift, turned into treasure, morphing into money, expressing the act of exchange now rooted in the *nexum*.

Along these lines, in a very broad reference to archaic (pre-feudal) peasant communities, Firth observes that across disparate regions of the world there are two separate credit systems at work, one of which he terms "social loans" and the other "economic loans." The former are effectively cycles of gift-giving: The accent is on the pattern of service as much as on the specific articles handed over. The act of giving obligates the recipient to give gifts.

The economic loans, on the other hand, point to the *nexum*. The initiator is the borrower who acquires liquidity by selling a bond, and is obligated in turn to repay a debt: "The accent is on the need for the actual good or overt service borrowed" (p. 30–31).

This suggests that, as Mary Douglas observes with respect to certain archaic tribal societies, there is a split between the reciprocities of gift-giving and the *nexum* that may well have existed in Europe before the archaic period of Rome.

The *nexum*, in its own right, is generally understood by historians to be one element of a set of reciprocities found in the common law—the *mancipium*—the latter being absorbed into overt Roman law at the end of the early period. The members of the set comprise the *mancipatio*. In its broadest sense, then, *mancipium* refers to things or property and the mode of moving and keeping things.

Clark dismisses as "remounting this hoar antiquity," the belief that the initial *mancipation* arose where land was not exchanged and literally applied instead to the legal right simply to take something and grasp it by the hand (p. 109). Buckland and McNair in their book *Roman Law and Common Law* (1936) emphasize that the legal importance of the *mancipium* resided in the figurative sense of taking something, laying claim to it, not the distinction literally between immoveables (e.g., land) on the one hand, and moveables (e.g., cattle and slaves) on the other.

This is to say, the broader issue here is the power of the subject to *possess* something or someone in the same sense that one possesses one's own self.

There is archaic ownership. The *mancipatio* covered large swatches of civil law: manumission, inheritance, marriage, adoption, and so forth. These included both property and exchange.

Clark singles out the latter as conceptually a key subset of the *mancipatio*—one which includes the *nexum*. He consciously uses the term, *mancipation*, for this sub-set which he contends post-dates the archaic period, strongly implying a genealogical connection looking forward in time.

According to Clark: *Manu capere* was the predecessor of *Mancipium*:

> *Manu capere* carried with it that peculiar idea of power and possession. This power and possession was asserted by the symbolical 'hand-seizure,' which, when accompanied by the formal words, the payment of the piece of copper to the seller, or its acceptance by him, all before the proper witnesses, operates as the original Roman conveyance. (p. 208)

Clark observes with respect to mancipation that the "taker" of the commodity acts to pay the seller and thereby seals the *conveyance*, in the sense of repayment moving back over time. In this context, the historian Theodor Mommsen, in his book *The History of Rome, vol. 1*, (1886), claims the term for the act of mancipation should be is "to purchase."

Clark's "repayment" though would seem more apt. While he emphasizes that the sense of "taking" in the context of *mancipation* becomes purchase, denoting payment of money, he nonetheless understands that the proto-act of mancipation was force of will, and ultimately enslavement. The basic legal issue addressed by *mancipation*, that is, concerns what the obligation is of the taker so as to balance, at least in theory, reciprocation of the ones that has been taken from.

Clark likens the reciprocation addressed by *mancipation* to what in English law was called bargain and sale: "a use is raised on the payment of any, even the smallest sum of money." He adds, parenthetically, "a use too, we may remember originated in the obligation on the conscience of the terre tenant" (p. 111).

Thus, he implicitly offers the example of *mancipation* with respect to peasant freeholders, who make and determine the use of land not statutorily owned by them. Direct exchange of money for commodity is thereby reduced to a limiting case of repayment of money for a taken commodity. Concerning the connection between *mancipation* and *nexum*, then, Clark is led to conclude:

> The old transaction out of which both *mancipation* and *nexum* grew, being a bargain and sale for value, where the article purchased is present property, absolutely transferred, the business would seem to be over, and

> the nexum, or bond between the parties, at an end; where anything is left to be done, i.e. where the article purchased includes, or is some future service, the *nexum* continues. Herein lies the important truth ably put by Mr. Maine, that in the original popular as well as in the professional view, a contract was regarded as an incomplete conveyance. (p. 112)

Mommsen writes of the initial migrations that constitute Roman pre-history: "The stern law of debt, by which one debtor was directly responsible with his person for the repayment of what he had received, is common to the Italians" (p. 50, Ch. 2). This suggests a conceptual basis of the *nexum* extant in the early archaic period and leads back to the previous imaginary phase pointed to by Mauss.

Buckland and McNair write of the general form of contracts as we know it in early archaic Rome, termed the *stipulatio*, i.e., oral promise, oath and so on. It applied to distinct reciprocities, social and economic loans within archaic peasant communities: "In most cases it may be a promise by way of gift. But more usually it will be a promise to pay for some service already rendered, or given in return for a counter-promise" (p. 271).

There is a mention by Buckland and McNair of a particular contract that was used, *contract literis, expensilatio*, a written promissory note, comprised of the two reciprocities of the more general *stipulatio*.

> In form, a unilateral transaction—contract *literis* is so unlike anything in our law that we need not say much of it. It is at least usually a *novation* [substitution] of some pre-existing dealing.
>
> It may be remarked that this contract, a statement of indebtedness entered by the creditor in his account book with the debtor's consent in the fictitious form of a loan to him, seems to be dispositive, in the sense that it was the contract and not mere evidence of it. It was however, obsolete so early and so little known of that we cannot be very certain of anything about it. (p. 271–272)

Buckland and McNair, in this matter, simply did not see on the horizon—established around the turn of 21st century, a predominant economic system, debt-capitalism, had become truly able to move the social Totality toward the precipice.

That it operated virtually the same way, back to the archaic period of Rome. The guaranteed US banks loan money (liquidity) to customers, which it deposits in a checking account for the borrowers and which can then be used by the banks to purchase additional debt ownership. Note that the new deposits can still leave a particular bank, as long as it enters another bank, because the reverse is happening too. As long as the banks altogether get larger the reciprocations as a whole, expands. The connection is astonishing of the 21st century and the earliest history of Rome.

Another aspect of the contract *literis* suggests a rather puzzling phenomenon. In the ancient formal acts of Roman private law, *inter vivos*, it is the person who is to benefit, who goes through the formal act. In this contract, the entry of indebtedness is made by creditors, in their own account books. In *mancipatio* it is the person who is acquiring who makes the formal declaration

What "puzzles" Buckland and McNair here is that unlike *mancipation*, wherein the debtor's act of borrowing money incurs the formal act of obligating a repayment, in the ancient law, instead, the creditor appears to be completing "some pre-existing dealing," insofar as "it is the person who is to benefit from repayment of the debt who goes through the formal act" (p. 272–273).

If, however, the reciprocity is understood in the language of giving, then interestingly enough the non-mancipation comes into focus. The giver of the gift is not a creditor and so the reciprocity referred to by the ancient law is not a purchase of liquidity. The giver is not substituting, but rather is relieving debt by re-circulating the gift. On the other side of the coin eventually the receiver possesses, acquiring liquidity in the form of a valuable gift.

Confirming the alternative hypothesis to that of Mauss, both Buckland and McNair remark that the ancient law "was obsolete so early and so little is known of it that we cannot be certain of anything about it." This suggests that in Roman history at least there may never have been a previous phase, as proposed by Mauss. As has been seen, gift-giving and mancipation are distinct experiences of the commodity such that their imagined unification is *aporetic*.

The former is founded upon a circular flow of debt (the kula), while the latter originates, conceptually, in an act of capture at a point in space/time. The act of repayment that completes the *nexus* is antithetical to the movement of the hua back to the giver. Hence it is not surprising that both in archaic tribal and peasant communities the two reciprocities are observed to have existed separately, applying to distinct sets of commodities or social relations, but there is no amalgam of the two that has been identified.

What seems more likely, then, is that these are two mostly unconnected genealogical branches of the commodity, what it communicates itself to be. From Buckland and McNair's assertion, it seems that gift-giving was already becoming less identifiable during the archaic period. Mancipation may be on the branch leading to the communication of the commodity in the context of generalized exchange.

In any case, if there is a division of this branch it is more likely to have been the one discerned by Clark, in writing: "The two original ideas of acquisition and obligation are so combined in the earliest form of mancipium that confusion between them was inevitable" (p. 111).

Wrapped in the *nexum* is the free act of making a purchase to acquire a commodity—exchange—but it also contains the obligation to pay back what you have taken, with loss of freedom (enslavement) being the consequence of not doing so.

CHAPTER 5

Life-needs and Money Sequences, Outside or Inside a Sealed Vessel

Value Reduction

Let us delve deeply into the relation of money to the product—commodity—in economic systems based on generalized exchange; i.e., where both consumer and investment products are produced for market exchange. The hypothesis is that money is the language of the commodity.

This seemingly odd assertion has its roots in the early writings of Walter Benjamin, notably his seminal piece, "On language as Such and on the Language of Man" (1916), as well as, contemporaneously the early works of the Russian founder of dialogism, notably Bakhtin. The premise is unusual perhaps because it is essentially semiotic.

Benjamin posits that thought is communicated in language: "We cannot imagine a total absence of language in anything." And from that he makes a central dialogistic inference. Since that which communicates itself in language is an idea (*awareness*), "It is obvious that the idea is *not* language itself, but something to be distinguished from it." (p. 315, On Language as Such and on the Language of Man, 1916).

The word "chair" is not an aspect of *a chair*, but rather a sound, or in the case of script a written shape. The word can only communicate *chair* in the context of dialogue. The word, and by extension spoken language in general, is essentially an inter-subjective experience of thereby necessarily *social* subjects.

The larger motivation of the present here then is to broaden dialogism by taking into it the realm of political economy. The object is to confirm that money is properly understood as the means by which the product communicates itself to social subjects, to show that much as an idea can only be heard in words, a commodity can only be heard in money.

At the outset, it is necessary to clarify further this surprising homology of spoken—inter-subjective—language and money. Benjamin observes that *language as such* is an awareness of the subject that is only communicated in its own being. This is to say, in the case of spoken language a set of sounds, understood as objects of nature experienced in dialogue, is not itself experienced as language, but rather as itself.

For example, one who wishes to understand a foreign language only has recourse to a translation from another spoken language that is already understood inter-subjectively, the conversion of one set of sounds into another set being sufficient. But there is no recourse to a language of any particular set of sounds as such, no language into which the sounds can be absorbed. Hence, what human language communicates itself in, as Benjamin states, is itself. The word "chair" refers inter-subjectively to any *chair*.

Homologous to spoken language, then, an accounting number in dollar units, to use an example, is the *transgredient* of credit, the latter communicating in dollars. Consider a 100-dollar bill, Federal Reserve Note, a particular holder of a number. It communicates the 100 dollars of credit through the act of exchange, reciprocated by the transfer of products.

The various 100 dollar sets of products available to the dollar-holder have in common only the *name* 100 dollars. They do not have in common, and the money does not represent the value of, a quantity in exchange, either in the natural units of gold or labor-time or a marginal rate of substitution, absent credit. To what does the 100-dollar number on the dollar bill refer to then? Like chair refers to a *chair*, "100-dollars of credit" refers to a purchase of 100 dollars of commodities.

It is necessary to interject that what is being said in commodity-language, the dialogue of reciprocation differs according to historical and/or geographic context. For instance, in archaic economies money as gift would seem to communicate debt-relief, not credit. Multiple communications simultaneously in money appear to be the norm as well. For example, the State money characteristic of contemporary capitalist economies communicates both credit, and debt ownership.

Here, then, the discussion is narrowed by specifying that it is limited to money solely as commodity-credit in the context of generalized exchange. This narrowing of scope does not necessarily weaken altogether the conclusions reached herein. Intuitively, constraints in the simplest models of generalized exchange and reproduction are likely to be less restrictive than those of expanded reproduction, and specifically of a capitalist system.

The key implication, however, of a semiotic notion of money is that it leaves no room for the belief that commodities (products), possess a homogeneous value represented by a number of dollars. A *value reduction* occurs with the awareness of money as language. The dollars are purely credits, homologous to words being purely ideas.

And just as the latter points to social subjects engaged in dialogue, so too does the former indicate *social subjects* engaged in commodity reciprocation via market exchange. *Value reduction* is the rejection of *commodity-primacy*, the latter being the belief that money emerges out of non-money commodity exchange, barter, and that the putative value of the commodity in units of gold, labor time, marginal utility or what have you, is that which the money reflects or expresses.

The question posed is, can commodity primacy as a principle be sustained? Can one, when the matter is looked at closely, find a silent commodity, one without money as identification. Or, is not this instead like searching for an idea without words to communicate it; (see Kafka's story *Investigation of a Dog*).

To go one step deeper into the homology of spoken language and money, certain central intra-language relations of word and idea are mirrored by money and commodity. The Prague School linguist Sergi Karcevskij advanced in 1929 the analogical principle that:

Every linguistic sign [word] potentially is a homonym and a synonym. It belongs simultaneously to a series of transposed meanings of a single sign, and to a series of analogous meanings, expressed by different signs.

This is to say, within spoken language, the elements of a set of words each of which refers roughly analogically to the same idea are synonyms: "different variants of the same phenomenological class." Transposing idea and word, elements of a set of ideas each of which has the same *name* are homonyms. The latter elements do not belong to a single phenomenological class but rather are purely abstract. Karcevskij contends that "homonymy and synonymy constitute the most important relational coordinates of spoken language because they are the most dynamic, flexible, and adequate to experience in open (*unfulfilled*) time" (p. 51).

The set of homonyms and that of synonyms is each infinite, and each synonym contains its own set of homonyms. Through synonymy, experience can be incorporated analogically into the existing set of words associated with an idea. And through homonymy new ideas do not require new names. A corollary is that an idea is necessarily contextual, indicating an inherently *pragmatic* aspect of semiosis.

Homologous to spoken language, synonymic and homonymic intra-language relations appear with respect to money and the commodity as well. Key to the value reduction is the fact that the elements of a set of commodities, each of which can be purchased with the same credits, are homonyms. The set is purely abstract. Hence, if commodities in a set are priced as 100 dollars, what is being communicated is that each commodity can be purchased for 100 dollars and no more.

The elements of a set of different monies, however, each of which purchases the same commodities are synonyms; *e.g.*, currencies traded in foreign exchange markets and contracts traded in future markets and financial markets. They are equivalent to different languages where one can be translated into another, and the set of synonyms are debts owned at any moment in various funds, best illustrated by the various categories of the money supply used by the US Federal Reserve.

To appreciate *value reduction* more fully then is to turn away from virtually all analytic schools of modern economic theory, going back to Mandeville and Smith, and thereby to reject the *value fundamentalism* of neoliberal thought, articulated as coherently as possible by members of the Austrian school, but are built into contemporary classical, including Marxists, Keynesian, and neoclassical economists of all types.

To illustrate value reduction, then, let us consider the seminal water/diamond *paradox of value*, famously introduced by Smith in *Wealth of Nations* (1776), although he never calls it a paradox, per se. He observes that water, which is so important to people, a matter of life and death, is so little valued in exchange relative to diamonds, even though diamonds are primarily ornamentation trivial objects by comparison.

Smith resolves this in the way that comes to mark classical political economy. Diamonds require much more labor per unit than water does, and labor is value. Neoclassical economists argue that, to the contrary, it is the relative scarcities of existing stocks that resolves the paradox.

The marginal rate of substitution—how many diamonds trade for a given quantity of water, on the margin—is such that scarce diamonds trade for quantities of plentiful water. It is concluded that for this reason the value of diamonds are indeed much greater than water in use, utility on the margin, and that this is confirmed by the observed rates of exchange between the two goods.

But the problem with the reasoning of both the classical and neoclassical schools is a failure to justify the putative observation that, in exchange diamonds possess more *value* than water. If this is thought to be observed, *a priori*, in the direct trade of commodities, the trade is not comparable to value equality.

For example, take 1 diamond for 1,000,000 gallons of water, also 1 gallon of water for .000001 diamonds. In the realm of value reduction, the price of diamonds is 1,000,000 gallons of water, and the price of 1 gallon of water is .000001 diamonds. The price of water is in units of diamonds and simultaneously the price of diamonds is in units of water. Thereby the prices are heterogeneous and hence there is no objective value comparison of the two commodities to be had. Rather, there is a fragmentation of money into diamonds and water.

Ironically, George Stigler, iconic University of Chicago theorist and neoliberal *par excellence,* speaks to this underlying heterogeneity, arguing on these very grounds that the classical approach, implicitly the appeal to labor as value being the solution to the paradox, actually renders any value comparisons nil, because labor is heterogeneous. Stigler is thus led to reprimand Smith for making a moral judgment, not allowing for the possibility that diamonds are indeed of more subjective value—marginal utility—than water to those who purchase them in an exchange. (1965)

> The paradox—that value in exchange may exceed or fall short of value in use—was strictly speaking a meaningless statement. Smith had no basis (i.e., no concept of marginal utility) on which he could compare such heterogeneous quantities. On any reasonable interpretation, moreover, Smith's statement that value in use could be less than value in exchange was clearly a moral judgment not shared by the possessors of diamonds (p. 65)

In the context of barter, Stigler's appeal to marginal utility runs up against the impossibility of making interpersonal comparisons of utility (whether total or marginal), a cornerstone of neoclassical subjective utility theory. Value reduction is not evaded, as Stigler would have it, through the homogenization of diamonds and water into common units of utility.

Stigler's heterogeneity critique of classical political economy can be traced back to one of the founding fathers of Austrian economic theory, Carl Menger, in his *Principles of Economics* (1871) although oddly enough Stigler makes no reference to Menger in this regard. At the outset of his discussion of prices, in the context of barter, Menger goes so far as to say that the basis of trade is the contrary, marginal utilities realized by the two parties must be different and hence marginal utilities cannot be homogenized into value (p. 191–194).

Menger finds this, however, to be irreconcilable with commodity-money, i.e. gold as value of products, and ultimately, unlike Austrian thought in general, he asserts toward the beginning of his much later chapter, *Money as Measure of Value*:

> In my discussion of price theory ... I have shown that equivalents of goods in the objective sense of the term cannot be observed anywhere in the economy of men (p. 193), and that the entire theory that presents money as *the 'measure of the exchange value' of goods disintegrates into nothingness*, since the basis of the theory is a fiction, an error (1871: 273)

This brings out that Stigler does not address homogenous labor, or labor of any kind, in criticizing Smith. In any case, the neo-Ricardian development of Smith's thought treats labor as only relative value expressed through an arbitrary (numeraire) commodity, much like the numeraire commodity of neoclassical general equilibrium theory.

Moreover, objective homogeneous labor does not escape value reduction either, due to the more important fact that the commodity quantities of diamonds to water in exchange are homonymic. They do not imply an equal quantity of labor, as revealed by the solutions to the transformation problem.

By assuming that relative prices can be determined by a system of equations, neoclassical theory does not take into account the problem of heterogeneity. Equations, in fact, can exist as relationships only between homogeneous magnitudes. Before the equations are solved, the magnitudes that enter them must be homogeneous. The result is their equalization and not their identity. If, as in the case of relative prices, these magnitudes are not homogeneous, they cannot even be related to each other. An operation is needed to reduce them to the same quality

The issue is confused by the fact that, outside exchange as barter, each of the analytic schools including contemporary Marxist theorists applying their general understanding of money to the paradox, implicitly presume that diamonds are more valuable than water directly in units of money; that is, via the mediation of a commodity exchanged at the completion of actual sale.

The difficulty is that the commodity quantities circulating as equal quantities of money, in their natural units, are homonymic, in the semiotic sense that nothing makes them numerically equal other than money; just like two words that sound the same but mean entirely different things. This includes the case of commodity-money, notably gold, since to the extent that it is a natural object it also has a homonymic relation to commodity quantities with which it exchanges.

5 diamonds for example are sold by one party to a second for 1,000,000 dollars. A third party sells 5,000,000 gallons of water to the first party for 1,000,000 dollars. Neither in terms of the (ordinal) measure of the marginal utility of the first party, or in a homogeneous measure of labor as social object, is there an equality of the two commodity quantities. All one can say is 1,000,000 dollars that is exchanged is equal to 1,000,000 dollars that is exchanged.

Addendum

By Marx:
Elementary and Simple Exchange Forms

Karl Marx's classic dialectic/historical/analytic account of the commodity, in relation to money, is found in the first 150 or so pages of his *Das Capital, vol. 1* (1867).

Marx's treatment of the commodity in Part 1, Commodities and money, stands as perhaps the most sophisticated treatment of early industrializing capitalism to have come out of eighteenth and nineteenth-century classical thought.

Commodities, first of all, enter into the process of exchange just as they are. The process then differentiates them into commodities and money, and thus produces an external opposition inherent in them, as being at once use-values and monetary values. Based on commodity primacy, Marx offers up an ontology of money, deriving it dialectically from an "elementary form" of exchange; elementary in the sense that it is prior to money altogether.

Marx renders this form as:

$$C_1 \rightarrow C_2$$

One party trades a quantity of commodity C_1 with a second party, from whom the original party gets a quantity of commodity C_2. The commodities are measured in natural units. Marx's example is 20 yards linen is exchanged with 1 coat. He asserts: "Whether the coat serves as the equivalent and the linen as relative value, or the linen as the equivalent and the coat as relative value, the magnitude of the coat's value is determined, independently of its value-form" (p. 55). More succinctly, exchange value is first an equation: 20 yards of linen = 1 coat.

Does this then, as commodity-primacy would have it, exemplify the fact that two heterogeneous quantities of the products can be apprehended as equal commodities independent of money? To the contrary, money here is the means by which each commodity is communicated in the other. As written by the Japanese economist Uno (1964): "Each owner of a commodity regards its value as the active agent of trade that fetches him other desired commodities" (p. 5).

The currency that the first party pays for C_2 is in natural units of C_1. C_2 thereby communicates itself in C_1, and C_1 communicates itself in C_2. Money is debited from the account of each party, and each has acquired a new good. Marx briefly remarks on this (1872: 48–49), but he does not explicitly link what he calls the "equivalent value" to money, *per se*. Marx's sense is of a commodity that is the equal of another insofar as is it can be apprehended as a "relative value": 20 yards of linen is *worth* 1 coat.

A more robust rendering of the elementary form is of two simultaneous movements.

Elementary Exchange

$$C_1 \rightarrow C_2 \text{ [Party 1]}$$
$$C_2 \rightarrow C_1 \text{ [Party 2]}$$

Or more precisely (remembering that M_1 and M_2 are in different units):

$$M_1 \rightarrow C_2 \text{ [Party 1]}$$
$$M_2 \rightarrow C_1 \text{ [Party 2]}$$

We see that the equality of the commodities inferred from the expression 20 yards of linen = 1 coat, cannot be apprehended outside the language of money. This is to say, the commodities must be communicating in money that the two commodity quantities are homonymic.

$$C_1 P_1 = C_2 P_2$$

Example:

Commodity Quantity	Price
20 yd linen (C_1)	05 coat per yd (P_1).
1 coat (C_2)	
20 yd per coat (P_2).	

So that,

$$\text{(20 yd linen)(.05 coat/yd)} = \text{1 coat}$$
$$\text{(1 coat)(20 yd/coat)} = \text{20 yd linen}$$

Outside the language of money the products 20 yards of linen and 1 coat—each strictly in its own natural units—have no discernable quantitative relationship. In short, barter exchange is comprised of two exchanges via two currencies of money and two commodities.

This conclusion, however, is compatible only with value reduction, since there are as many heterogeneous commodity monies as commodities bartered, each expressed in its own natural units. What Marx calls the "simple form" of exchange seems from this standpoint to be an effort to retain commodity-primacy by positing the emergence of money in the form of gold out of barter exchange.

Money as such is now inserted by him as a third entity into the elementary exchange form. It is conceived of as mediator of commodity exchange. He suggests that commodity relations thereby cease to be accidental: "The leap taken by value from the body of the commodity, into the body of gold, is the *salto mortale* of the commodity" (p. 106).

Marx renders the simple form virtually as a one-party movement:

$$C_1 \rightarrow M \rightarrow C_2$$

The principle of commodity-primacy that Marx first attaches to this form is articulated by David Levine (1977):

> Within a circuit, the movement of money is subordinated to the circulation of commodities, as the means to the end of the movement of commodities. The logic which underlies this movement is independent of the money, which is nothing more than the means to an end (p. 119–120).

There are a number of movements, however, not explicitly depicted in the simple form as rendered by Marx, but which are not entirely lost on him either. A more robust rendering shows that, indeed, the simple form does not achieve the closure of pure commodity exchange determining the mediation of money.

Simple Exchange

$$C_1 \rightarrow M_1//M_2 \rightarrow C_2 \text{ [Party 1]}$$
$$M_1 \rightarrow C_1 \text{ [Party 2]}$$
$$C_2 \rightarrow M_2 \text{ [Party 3]}$$

This makes explicit that while a first party exchanges C_1 to a second party and is credited M_1, a second party has purchased C_1 and been debited M_1. And there appears a separate movement. A third-party exchanges C_2 with the first party and is credited M_2, while the first party is debited M_2.

At first glance, looking at Marx's rendering of the simple form, the first and second players seem to have exchanged commodities, and money seems to be purely a mediator of commodity reciprocation, no different essentially from pure commodity exchange. There is an appearance of money disappearing in the mediation.

But this is because the movement of money from the second party, in the purchase of C_1, to the third party, in the sale of C_2, is masked. The second party begins with a quantity of money, M_1 and has had that debited, but the third party has acquired an additional credit of M_2 in exchange for C_2. Whether or not the commodities are consumed in the end, the quantity of money extant at the start is conserved at the end of the circuit.

Marx remarks upon this but does not confront directly the fact that in the end it contradicts commodity-primacy.

> The change of form C-M-C by which the circulation of the material products of labor is brought about, requires that a given value in the shape of a commodity shall begin the process, and shall, also in the shape of a commodity, end it. The movement of the commodity is therefore a circuit.
>
> On the other hand, the form of this movement precludes a circuit from being made by the money. The result is not the return of the money, but its removal further and away from its starting-point. So long as the seller sticks fast to the money, which is the transformed shape of his commodity, that commodity is still in the first phase of its metamorphosis, and has completed only half its course. But as soon as he completes the process, so soon as he supplements his sale by a purchase, money again leaves the hands of its possessor.
>
> Hence the movement directly imparted to money by the circulation of commodities takes the form of a constant motion away from its starting-point, of a course from the hands of one commodity-owner into those of another. This course constitutes its currency. The currency of money is the constant and monotonous repetition of the same process. The commodity is always in the hands of the seller: the money as a means of purchase, always in the hands of the buyer. And money serves as a means of purchase by realizing the price of the commodity (pp. 114–115).

Contemporary Banking & Finance

In the context of value reduction, the existing capitalist system provides *commodity-credits* held by households, and on the other hand, returns to debt-ownership of speculators, and money circulating within private corporate banking, ancillary private financial funds and equity firms of various sorts. Marx, in *Das Capital: volume 2* is virtually alone among classical and neoclassical theorists in perceiving that these differing communications systematically separated the parties engaged in exchanges, albeit in the context of the first-forming industrialization, mid-to late 19th century.

In contemporary *debt-economies* the social subject, generally the family, tries to sell labor, and conjointly to buy products Money thereby communicates commodities termed by John McMurtry as *Life-capital* (p. 1). For those who cannot buy enough commodities, much of the rest must be borrowed in money. To corporate owners of *product capital*, money creates debt ownership by lending to those whose income from employment is not sufficient life-capital.

The capital relations during the process of production arises only because it is inherent in the act of circulation, in the different fundamental economic conditions in which buyer and seller confront each other. It is not money which by its nature creates the relation. Rather it is the existence of this relation which permits the transformation of a money-function into a debt-function.

This dual communication of money is generally overlooked in conventional economic policy analysis. Nonetheless, when a basic harmony exists between money as commodity-credit and product capital, market economies have proven transformations in human production and distributions that have been wonderful. But the cost has been great, and in the future, it would seem to be considerably greater.

Such harmony is captured (apocryphally) by the industrial giant Henry Ford, who when asked "Why do you pay your workers so much," is said to have given the quintessential Keynesian response, "If I didn't who would buy my cars?"

Perhaps the most harmonious economic period of the modern era has been the *Golden-age* of industrializing capitalist economies, especially the US. It was founded on the New Deal programs of Roosevelt in the 1930s, and was added to by presidents Truman, Kennedy, Johnson, and Nixon in the post-WW II period. These programs were supported by a consistent application and coordination of fiscal and monetary policies rooted in Keynesian demand theory.

Under Glass-Steagall, the major bank regulatory bill of the 1930s the banks of the oligopoly were exclusively commercial banks whose purchase of debt was for the most part limited to long-term financing of product capital. And in that context the aspect of endogenous money creation likely helped to mitigate crowding-out effects of the expansion, and harmonization with increased production and employment.

However, beginning roughly with President Carter's advocacy of radical de-regulation of monopolistic industries, dissonant chords were being sounded. Eventually they became more and more frequent, loud and intrusive, among them a crescendo of crises; the savings and loan bank scandal of the late-1980s, the Southeast Asian banking collapse of 1997, a technology bubble—speculation-burst in the early-2000s and the Enron scandal of 2001. Of course, these have climaxed, for the moment, with huge housing and banking collapse of 2007/2008.

Underlying these crises has been a cancer-like growth of financial capital, virtually eradicating any harmony of product capital and commodity-credit of the sort articulated by Ford, and nurtured in the Golden-age. A key alteration in banking practices over the 1980s and 1990s, indeed a transformation of corporate culture, was led by the banking oligopoly and Presidents Reagan and Clinton.

At its pragmatic center, the sole responsibility of high-level corporate managers became maximizing short-run returns to shareholders thrust upon the corporate managers. Inside the law, at most, it became simply wrong to subsidize other stake-holders should it reduce shareholder returns from what it might have been; these are low-level corporate managers, employees, consumers, local communities and the State.

With the demise of the Glass-Steagall regime, the bank oligopoly became free to engage heavily in investment banking, while their checking account deposit loan service remained backed by Federal insurance.

The commercial loans had been a way for the public's holdings in checking accounts, pure liquidity, to lend without risk toward the industrializing of the economy for the sake of the public. Now they are a small percentage of the bank oligopoly's debt-purchases. The major industries to a large degree internally finance long-term projects now. In addition, given the short-run perspective of share-holders such projects are in certain areas simply not engaged in as before.

Further, the de-regulation opened up a can of worms known to the Keynesians of the 1920s and possibly as far back as common law of Roman contracts between 8th and 3rd BC. The debts purchased by the oligopoly provide new money to purchase more in: money markets, mutuals, stocks, hedges, securitized mortgage options, high-yield (aka *junk*) bonds are instruments among many others of circulation and with it new debt ownership.

This touches upon an aspect of the endogenous money-supply multiplier associated generally with Federal Reserve monetary policy. Under the Glass-Steagall regime—this aspect amounted to a kind of kiting, practiced during periods of rapid growth and with it accelerating product investment demand. The banks were thus enabled to make loans and meet reserve requirements by borrowing, primarily in money markets or the like, covering interest payments with the new deposits generated by the banks' loans.

A development that lay behind the transformation of a new oligopoly of less-regulated banks, opened the way to them financing into existence *equity firms*. As late as the Golden-age in their classic work *The Modern Corporation & Private Property* (1932) Berle and Means told themselves:

> The law's primary design was protecting individual attributes of individual relationships—their right to property, to free motion and locomotion, to protection of individual relationships entered into between them. The corporate management took its place in the picture alongside of agents, trustees, ship captains, partners, joint adventurers and other fiduciaries. The tendency of the law has been to stiffen its assertion of the rights of the security holder. The thing it has not been able to stiffen has been its

> regulation of the conduct of the business by the corporate management. (p. 296)

They were wrong. With the loosening of regulations in the 1970s the notion of the corporation as one that balances various stakeholders is no longer acceptable. The law is with the share-holders. The large investment banks are free to finance equity firms for a straight cut. These are speculators who with the help of the bank buy up a majority share of a corporation, which is treated in most cases as a short-term asset of the firm.

For example, the equity firm might immediately buy up all the existing shares and reduce drastically costs, notably employment. The corporation within a year is making large profits quarterly. It is the right time for the speculators to sells new shares for a very high price. The return to the equity firm can be astronomical and not bad for the bank as well.

The equity firm is emblematic of the domination of financialized institutions that accumulate debt ownership, and to do so must continually accumulate debtors. At the same time, the banks have ceased to finance purchases of debt by drawing added deposits from their own loans, thus creating new deposits that are then leveraged, adding further debt acquired by the banks altogether.

John McMurtry in his book: *Cancer Stage of Capitalism:*

> In a nutshell, credit debt and money creation have been silently expropriated from public purpose and the common interest to multiply private transnational *money-sequences*.
>
> How is it done? The primary mode is by creating even more bank money-demand by debt issue without legal tender to back it, and from there to demands for debt-servicing without end on every government and home. The complementary mode is intermediating and creating massive margin exchanges in ever new elaborations and extractions that never stop invading the real economy at every node. (216–217)

Culture of Liquidation

John McMurtry in his book *Cancer Stage of Capitalism*:

> In countless such ways the financial lifeblood of the public is poured out to grow the global corporate system at the same time as its natural and human *life-capital* bases are predated with no life-standards.

> Yet the essence of the mater remains unseen. Deregulated tides of so-called capital and investment are in fact private transnational money-sequence demand on real capital—especially public capital—to turn it into more private transnational money demand which is not productive capital providing goods.
>
> Least of all considered is that this globalization is driven by private transnational banking system that exponentially leverages and almost all the circulating money demand. (16–17)

Except during a crisis, the money being created by the bank oligopoly circulates almost exclusively as debt ownership. This has engendered a culture in which products, except as financial instruments, virtually disappear. The culture is contained in a sealed but elastic *social vessel*, ruled by the bank oligopoly in conjunction with the central banks globally. The vessel holds in it the private wealth of a selected few individuals in a world of many-billion.

The concentration of an enormous circuit of money-capital provides those in the vessel the ever-increasing wherewithal both to move prices in virtually any market, also to circulate within the vessel exclusive information in key markets, and of course the power to corrupt the State so as to tailor the Law to suit their desire, indeed literally the power to write the Law.

There is an important semiotic distinction between money communicating products on the one hand, and capital on the other. The former is in the first instance materialized only insofar as it buys products. Thus the answer to the question in popular language to: 'How much money do you make?' it translates into: 'What are the products you can afford to buy'.

Money cannot communicate capital in that way. Money as capital, on the other hand, is never materialized, it remains an *illusion*. It is a marker of self-expansion, captured both in its own rate of growth, by its base, debt-ownership. Capital, as such, never stops being in essence a rate. It must always be reverting to more money so as to mark the rate and to calculate the quantity of own debt.

In principle the creation of money by the banks is bounded by the requirement to meet its depositors' demand for commodity credit; *i.e.*, the acquisition of goods to meet certain wants rather than the expansion of money. Also, the forms of financial capital that constitute the oligopoly's debt ownership, *e.g.*, derivatives, ultimately are grounded in the flows of commodity-credit throughout the economy into and out of individual income.

In that sense the private contemporary financial system is much like a grand Ponzi scheme (aka Pyramid) scheme. And the virtually inevitable implosion of the scheme is when increasing debt no longer can generate added money capital. This then exposes that which is not seen from within the vessel until it is too late (like the iceberg and the officers on the *Titanic*): without individual incomes debt ownership is an allusion to capital, but as money capital alone it never materializes.

For example, the interest payments on sub-prime mortgages, and in turn the value of many mortgage-based securities, each disappeared when large numbers of those in residential housing did not have sufficient income, given their need for other products to make the payments on their mortgages. Along the same lines, the capital base, the residential housing stock, relies on the willingness of individuals to purchase houses to live in, *i.e.*, as goods.

Thus, the unfettered bidding up of housing prices via financial speculation eventually must eat away real demand, enough to cause a deflation of the housing stock, greatly accelerated by capital flight. What happened was fully-understandable, and indeed was quite predictable, and it was foreseen by many outside the vessel.

Yet it proved to be hidden from those inside it, notably those who ruled and continue to rule the bank oligopoly. The result of course has been massive disruptions, and a deepening fragility of existing financial systems in and between States.

This speaks to a dangerous myopia afflicting those in the sealed vessel, the culture of liquidity. One can appreciate the blindness to the obvious in what might kindly be described as the very odd testimony of arguably the highest officer of the US bank oligopoly before, during and since the crisis first occurred, Jamie Dimon.

It was revealed at the first hearing of the Financial Crisis Inquiry Commission (FCIC), January 2010. The following questioning of Dimon by a commissioner, Douglas Holtz-Eaken (former Director of the Congressional Budget Office under GW Bush), is especially telling. Dimon is asked, what the "biggest mistakes" were, made by the banks, leading to the crisis (FCIC, 2010: 60; 65–66; also see 11, 13–14).

DIMON:	In mortgage underwriting somehow we just missed, you know, that home prices don't go up forever and that it's not sufficient to have stated income in home prices.
HOLTZ-EAKEN:	If you've been doing—you have been doing stress tests prior to the crisis?
DIMON:	Yes.
HOLTZ-EAKEN:	Did you do a stress test that showed prices falling?
DIMON:	No I would say that was probably one of our biggest misses.
	…

HOLTZ-EAKEN: To close my time, I'd like to just ask Mr. Dimon to go back to the mortgage underwriting and your observations on how so many bad mortgages could be written in the U.S....

DIMON: Right. So, it's really not a mystery and it's kind of surprising. A high LTV [Loan To Value]. A long time ago you did 80% loan to value loans. With proper appraisals, it went up to 85%, 90, 95, 100%, even higher than that. Second is, in the old days you had to verify your income, show a tax return or pay stub and make sure the income was there. And there was more and more reliance leading up to the crisis on FICO scores and people saying "I earned this."

Observe that, referring to the banks' abandonment of the most obvious, fantastically elementary banking practices, looking out for a speculative bubble obviously requiring collateral on loans, and verifying income statements of the borrowers. Dimon seemingly to himself, says, "Right. So it's really not a mystery and it's kind of surprising." This contradiction gives one a glimpse into true myopic perplexity. Dimon's insight, if only for an instant is a flash of light in the darkness.

In Karen Ho's book *Liquidated: An Ethnography of Wall Street* (2009) is puzzlement over a peculiarity that she discovered concerning the social hierarchy of the banking liquidation culture. It proves to be not just an oddity, but a reflection of the myopia inside the vessel that is mightily pushing and moving the social Totality.

A basic division, Ho reports, is between *front-office workers*, whose areas are financial strategy—called corporate finance or investment banking—as well as sales and trading plus asset management, and on the other hand, *back-office workers*, those whose areas—referred to generally as staff support—include operations, account services, trade reconciliation, IT and so forth. The former clearly are the privileged class, lavished upon by the institution, while the latter are provided minimum support and little monetary reward in the form of income.

Exploring the basis of this Ho finds an answer that is itself hard to explain. Front-office workers—referred to as bank "officers"—are the most valued employees because they are understood to generate revenue for the company. Everyone else in the banks is back-office support a division that depletes money because of the refusal of investment banks to recognize or compute their contributions as part of revenue generation staff, and treated as a cost center.

What Ho characterizes as "a refusal of investment banks" can be understood as a reflection of the fact that communication in money within the culture of liquidity is an allusion; lacking Being. In the sealed vessel, the contributions of the back-office workers never literally bring in money, they generate no value-added in money.

The front office workers, by contrast, are seen as producing all the value-added in revenues so that by rights, or simply as an incentive, they are entitled to revenues, along with share-holders.

Ho points out that the back-office employees, however, do produce services, i.e., goods production. But it is that which is not being seen, because production here literally refers to *pure money-capital.*

If anything, then, the belief of the culture is that money syphoned from the back-office increases the returns in money. Making reference to the equity firm in its classic mode, this accounts for why there typically is an immediate plan to liquidate parts of the corporation, once under the equity firm's control.

Indeed, plunging a corporation into debt by borrowing money on its account, and/or collecting high fees in money from it is a usual practice. The thirst is literally for the expansion of money-capital alone, and hence corporate product—*aka* industrial—*capital* no longer exists in its own right. Rather it has become a vehicle of liquidation.

Ho refers to an interview in a Fortune magazine article in 2000 of a virtual CEO for various Silicon Valley corporations, Randy Komisar. As she points out, he captures in few words the enormous transformation that has occurred.

> "People walk into a VC (Venture) capitalist presentation and their first line is about exit strategy. They're not talking about the investors—they're talking about themselves. How will they cash out. And this raises a subtle point: These founders don't think of themselves as CEO of operating companies. They think of themselves as investors." [Ho]: If the CEO sees the company as a stock and he/she as simply another investor, it is not surprising that the notion of the company as an ongoing social organization, an institution with multiple stakeholders and roots in particular communities, falls by the wayside. (p. 124–125)

Ho poses a fundamental question, then, upon the basis of which the sustainability of such a financial system is called into serious doubt. What are the implications for traditional constituents of the corporations, such as the employee, if corporations are now conceptualized as components of individual and institutional stock portfolios governed by an ideology of instant convertibility into money that enters, metaphorically, a sealed vessel.

Enlarging upon Ho's ethnography, the current banking culture has proven to be a great force accumulating money capital, independent of commodity-credit. It is the force that draws money into the sealed vessel through the creation and ever-greater leveraging of money by the bank oligopoly.

What McMurtry describes as ungrounded and increasingly leveraged transnational money-sequencing, is conjoined to the relentless and more often than not successful drive to convert commodity-credit into money-capital and to resist the reverse. The effects of this on what one might call the culture of the State have been dramatic. In addition to extensive capital conversion of goods formerly provided directly by the State, in the US the State now typically contracts out large proportion of its own internal activities to corporations.

Through such capital conversion, then, quantities of money are guided into the vessel, money as commodity credit converted into pure money capital. This is a form of immiseration that generally is not understood because it requires treating money as language, communicating two different things, rather than as a measure of value. An amazing disparity has arisen in the US between the concentrated debt ownership, on the one hand, and on the other the miniscule flows of income into to life capital.

A measure of the disparity is impossible, leaving out the fact that one is a stock variable and the other a flow, the units each are qualitatively different. The money in the vessel being an allusion, a perennial circulation and expansion of debt ownership, a relatively tiny percentage of it leaks out in into the purchases of goods.

The connection between the two legs of the disparity is that money as commodity credit, unquestionably the life-blood of the modern market economy, is being squeezed out by the cancer-like growth of virtually pure money capital, which itself has little if any life-giving properties. To the contrary it sucks out those properties through capital conversion

And like a cancer it is spreading throughout the economies of the world, and if not reversed, like an organism, the economies will be destroyed along with it. The bitter irony is that what might cause the death of the market economy is a simple oversight. The fact is that pure money capital is a language whose words have no meaning. Or in the words of Jamie Dimon: "Right. So, it's really not a mystery and it's kind of surprising."

Addendum

Senator Elizabeth Warren, perhaps the most intelligent US political figure these days, surprised and perhaps momentarily puzzled members of a senate committee at a recent hearing a few years ago. She asserted that the health reform law was "a value statement" And she explained somewhat: "No one deserves to be bankrupted or shut out of the health system when they get sick."

Warren dares to imply—no matter how subtly—a meta-social condemnation of a global system that has formed in the post-Golden age. At an accelerating rate basic things that a family needs in order to live decently are less and less available to more people across almost all the leading nations. Particularly if one includes never-ending indebtedness.

We might infer from Warren that a necessary meta-social condition of a *good* system is one that immunizes itself from immiserating masses of people for the sake of a few. But it is taboo among those who identify themselves with the culture of liquidation to say the social system, rooted as it is in large-scale corporations serviced by the State is dangerously faulty.

Indeed, if you listen carefully to US politicians, whenever one of them—and it is rare—upholds the provision of a basic need in its own right, a monetary motive is nonetheless required to clinch the deal: Everyone deserves to have access to health care. And, more importantly, emergency-care cost reductions will more than make up for the expense. Even the word "deserve" used by Warren is at best empty of meaning. Are there any who can say with certainty who deserves to live well and who does not.

McMurtry:

> "None [of the world's cultures] are grounded in objective life-goods. For within the last thirty years there has been a great sea-change towards one system of transnational corporate market rule which is indifferent to this entire life-substructure of humanity and to the consequences of its life-blind rule system." (p. 1–2)

One sees here the amazing blindness of those inside the culture of liquidation, an inability to comprehend the real lives of others. The making of money, the equation money equals value, the corporatized capture of massive accumulation of money only a tiny fraction of which will ever be realized as *goods*. The global system is such that the blindness robs more and more the rights of people to pursue a decent life. To "follow your bliss."

There can be no doubt that this indifference to human life is systemic. Virtually no good, from the point of view of human entitlement, which includes life itself, is immune to the cancerous drive to expand money, effectively siphoning it off from money to use in support and enhancement of human life.

Drug companies commonly hide their own studies if they show a profitable new drug or device of theirs to have dangerous, even fatal effects. Gun-manufacturers fight tooth and nail requirements that would have them distinguish between buyers who are likely killers from those who are not.

The military-industrial complex puts enormous never-ending pressure on the State to demonize others around the world, and in so doing to generate never-ending warfare, ruining the lives of millions upon millions of people.

Even the health reform that Elizabeth Warren characterizes as a gesture toward human entitlement is based to a great extent on subsidizing the corporate health-insurance industry, enabling it, one hopes to at best provide more affordable insurance in the private market.

The onset of the corporation as essentially a financial asset, a creature born to the culture of liquidation, is a shift away from the common conception of capitalist economies, encompassing Marx's thought as well as both classical and neoclassical schools of thought.

McMurtry's critique in the context of what he terms the current cancer stage of capitalism goes deeper than the Marxist one of the Golden-age. It dates back as far as the late 19th century in the writings of Cournot and Marshall, contesting the neoclassical faith in an efficiency of competitive markets.

It has long been clear to Marxists that since industrialized capitalism established, markets have been dominated by corporate oligopolies. The latter strategically set prices in conjunction with production levels aided of course by mass marketing, collusion, political corruption and so forth. Hence *perfect competition*, which gives life to the invisible hand—or as expressed in 1705 by Mandeville, private vices bring public benefits—is invalidated.

Deeper critique, however, aimed at Marxist thought, has been little less than classical or neoclassical concerning an assumption so basic to each school that it is seldom made explicit. Ricardo in the chapter, "On Profits and Interest," in *Principles of Political Economy and Taxation* (1821) obliquely but succinctly articulated it however:

> The rate of interest, though *ultimately and permanently governed by the rate of profit* is however subject to temporary variations from other causes. When the market prices of goods fall from an abundant supply, for example from a diminished demand a manufacturer naturally accumulates an unusual quantity of finished goods. To meet his ordinary payments for which he used to depend on the sale of his goods, he now endeavors to borrow on credit. This, however is but of temporary duration. If by the abuses of banking the quantity of money be greatly increased there is probably always an interval during which some effect is produced on the rate of interest. (p. 349–50)

Marx, casts a faint shadow over the assumption which, like Ricardo, he agrees that "This is but a temporary duration." And yet, in *Das Capital vol. 2*, he writes

> Industrial capital is the only mode of existence of capital in which not only the appropriation of surplus product but simultaneously its creation is a function of capital. Money-capital and commodity-capital are nothing but modes of existence of the different function forms now assumed, now discarded by industrial capital in the sphere of circulation—modes which due to social division of labor have attained independent existence and been developed one-sidedly.
>
> The circuit M ... M' on the one hand intermingles with the general circulation of commodities, proceeds from it and flows back into it, is a part of it. On the other hand, it forms an independent movement of the capital value for the individual capitalist, a movement on its own which takes place partly within the general circulation of commodities, partly outside of it, but which always preserves its independent character. (p. 55)

Further in the text, where Marx is now discussing the three circuits together—money, production, and commodity—the shadow over the money circuit again seems to be lifted. But then the same uncertainty returns:

> Since every one of these circuits is considered a special form of the movement in which various individual industrial capitals are engaged, this difference always exists only as an individual one. But in reality, every individual industrial capital is simultaneously in all three circuits. So long as the purchases M-C (L plus MP) are made, the entire capital exists and functions only as money-capital. (p. 101)

In short, there has been a strong belief about modern capitalist economies. A necessary vehicle by which owners expand money is profit-motivated production, an assumption of the dominance of *product capitalists*. Money now, however, is continually accumulated within a financial system that can generate money internally, independent of product capitalists. It forms a vast web of money circuits that control industrial capital as an asset, and not in the traditional sense of a flow of products let alone *goods*.

McMurtry:

> Even the world's leading productive-capital formations have moved to this unmediated system of decoupled money-capital growth. General Motors and General Electric, for example, both made more profits in 1994 from their financial subsidiaries lending credit-money at compound interest than they did from all their production of automotive and electrical manufacturers put together.

> This pattern began with the Rockefeller fortune which reproduced and grew from oil to banks (for example First National Bank, Citibank, Chase Manhattan). But it was not until recent years when the money-to-more money sequence became autonomously self-multiplying and that productively-coded enterprises switched their dominant pathways of growth to the non-contributing circuit of money-profit appropriation. (p. 175)

It is a sign that an historic change in the nature of the capitalist economy is the self-identification of securitized, financialized corporations, institutions truly owned by share-holders. The object becomes to leverage flows of money coming into the corporation whether through sales or by taking it out of the corporation itself via junk bonds, equity firms and so forth.

The cost of generating these flows of money is of course minimized. But this is in order to maximize net revenues, not profits per se. In particular cases the self-multiplication of leveraged revenues are maximized with there being no profit from production at all, even losses, but nonetheless creating enormous share value, e.g., Amazon.

Costa Lapavitsas' *Profiting Without Production*

The difficulty that Marxist theorists have in going beyond the contextual limitations of Marx's thought is epitomized by Costa Lapavitsas's recent work; *Profiting without Producing*: *How Finance Exploits Us All* (2013). This is not to say that Lapavitsas has nothing of interest to tell. Quite the contrary, certain of his insights into the meaning of money and the empirical evidences of the culture of liquidation are very sharp and well-worth reading. In addition, the writing is remarkably clear, helpful to those less schooled in these things.

However, the reality of a malignant culture of liquidation—a cancer as John McMurtry conceives of it that metastasized around the 1980s—never comes to the surface of Lapavitsas's book. And, on the other side of the coin, the clarity of the writing makes it all the more painful to read vast tracts searching out writings of Marx for answers to the mysteries of a different capitalist economic system.

The mechanization of the 19th century that transformed the capitalist economy is an empirical and theoretical foundation of Marxist thought: oligopolistic profit-driven industries comprised of *publically-owned corporations*, financing production in part by the issuance of debt sold to the public in the form of shares. And to give Marx his dues, his thought proved to be the most powerful means of analyzing capitalist systems in his own lifetime, the mid-19th century.

For roughly the last fifty years the mechanized profit-driven oligopolies have been digitalized. And in that new context, the corporations have been financialized. With this has come the domination of the industrial oligopolies by private, but government-protected, digitalized banks and ancillary private funds that leverage at great multiples ownership of debt. These banking institutions thereby create ongoing accumulation and transferring of money, termed by McMurtry as money sequences. These are held tightly in a vessel inside of which is the *culture of liquidity*.

In the key chapter of his book, "The conundrum of financial profit," Lapavitsas's comes back to important points he'd made previously, in reference to money, but now addresses what he terms financialized capitalism.

> The simplest primary form of financial profit is earned by making loans: receiving interest. Analytic insight into financial profit could be gained by focusing more closely on interest as a share in surplus value for loans among capitalists.
>
> There are two strains to Marx's work in this regard: the first assumes that the lender is a money-capitalist who owns capital for lending; the second assumes that loanable money-capital is created out of idle money generated by the circuit of capital. Both approaches assume that the borrower is a functioning capitalist (*typically an industrialist*) who obtains the capital necessary for the project on hand and proceeds to generate surplus value.
>
> Marx related this qualitative distinction to the putative division of the capitalist class into the 'monied'—aka money-capital—and the functioning fractions that are presumably in opposition to each other over the division of total profit.
>
> This is not a persuasive argument especially in conditions of financialized capitalism. To be specific the relationship between borrower and lender is not simply a zero-sum game corresponding to a tug of war between the money and the functioning capitalist and involves more than a straight forward opposition between borrower and lender. (p. 151–152)

But faced with the challenge of confronting debt-capitalism for what it is, and therefore going beyond it, Lapavitsas doubles back. The reader is presented unfortunately with a common principal-agent model based on a slightly more moderate opposition of agent and principal, but otherwise one that retains the same basic class separation of money-capitalists from, as he uses the term "functioning capitalists" as if it were the days of the 1930s through the post-WWII Golden age.

> For the purpose of analyzing the conceptual content of financial profit, most prominent feature of joint-stock capital [aka publicly-owned enterprises] is the separation of ownership from control. This is a direct result of enterprise organization that relies on pro-rata, tradable, limited liability ownership combined with a corporatist internal bureaucracy. Marxist economics was quick to notice the separation of ownership from control.
>
> It took longer for mainstream economics to appreciate the importance of separating ownership from control, though in recent years the separation has become a standard feature of microeconomic analysis under the guise of the opposition between principal (owner) and agent (manager). This view lies at the heart of the ideology of *shareholder value*, which has characterized the rise of financialization. This is evidently an appropriate ideological shroud for financialization of non-financial enterprises.
>
> Shareholders can be thought of as economic agents committing money-capital or plain idle to acquire property rights over the enterprise and thus over future flows of surplus value. The money-capital committed by shareholders could be loanable capital mobilized through the financial system; but shareholders differ from lenders insofar as they commit potential loanable capital or idle money indefinitely rather than for given period of time. (p. 157–158)

This conception of the corporation generally is associated with the well-known book *The Modern Corporation and Private Property* (1932), written by two who definitely were not Marxists, Adolph Berle and Gardiner Means. But as Lapavitsas observes it was introduced by Rudolf Hilferding in a major work of Marxist theory, *Finance Capital*, published in 1910.

Lapavitsas bases his model on a premise that effectively denies the financialization of the corporation as it now exists, where for example an entry firm that buys majority stock is not one to be committing potential money capital indefinitely; to the contrary. There has been a clean break from the independent control of the corporate manager, and the passive owners having no dominant share-holders. Now debt ownership of major shareholders is both principal and agent, as such.

And the reader of the book cannot help feeling deeper in the mud from a previous introduction of the above.

> The equity market corresponds to publically-owned corporations—to the leading form of organization of capital (productive, merchant and

> banking) in mature capitalism. The corporation is a long standing historical form of large capitalist enterprises, but has become dominant only since the emergence of monopoly capitalism in the late nineteenth century. The period of financialization has been stamped by the supremacy of the corporations, and the global economy is dominated by large multinational enterprises. Accordingly, publically-owned enterprises function on the basis of pro-rata ownership of both the corporation and its profits and could be traded in stock markets. Ownership of capital becomes impersonal, delimited from other personal property, and easily transferable. (p. 156)

In a passage of her must-read book, *Liquidated: An Ethnography of Wall Street* (2009), Karen Ho points to the crucial roles of culture and context in confronting the late-twentieth century transformation from mechanized production to digitalized finance.

> Shareholder value has been, on the one hand, largely ignored by anthropologists as a powerful explanatory tool, and on the other, decontextualized, naturalized, and globalized by institutional financial interests and many economists. A historical and localized understanding of shareholder value is crucial to understanding the extent to which corporate values and mainstream economic assumptions have changed since the mid-twentieth century.
>
> In the 1990s during an historic economic boom, workers in the US suffered massive downsizings. I argue that the notion of a jobless recovery is only a quandary if social scientists are still trying to explain today's social economy using the terms and assumptions of the post-Second World era. In other words, if shareholder value, not welfare capitalism, is the ideal then the jobless recovery makes perfect sense for stock prices (which spike because of downsizing), not jobs, are the focus and the measure of corporate health and success. (153)

The purpose here is not to downgrade *Profiting Without Producing*. To the contrary, Lapavitsas's work locates a key theoretical cusp, one side of which is Marxist thought, and on the other side the Beyond. And implicitly tied to this, Lapavitsas taps into a commonality within Marxist thought shared by virtually all orthodox thinkers. Beginning with, among others, Bernard Mandeville, James Steuart along with Adam Smith, these precepts have continued into the present, some three hundred years later, in the writings of Kenneth Arrow, Gerard Debreu, Gary Becker and so many others.

Lapavitsas points in a direct connection of Marx to Steuart, contemporary of Adam Smith, and by most accounts as highly regarded as Smith in their lifetimes.

> Marx deployed Steuart's concept of profit [as] *expropriation* in his work, though not extensively and often in analysis of financial transactions relating to personal income of workers. Exploitation occurring in financial transactions is qualitatively distinct from exploitation in production. To be specific, exploitation in financial transactions amounts to a direct transfer of value from the income of workers to lenders—that is it stands for a re-division of money revenue streams, typically taking the form of interest. The more standard form of exploitation in production, on the other hand, amounts to creating a fresh flow of value out of unpaid labor. It follows that profit as expropriation that arises from lending to workers represents a form of exploitation which is independent of surplus value. (p. 143–144)

And Lapavitsas observes throughout the book that most significant corporations have been financialized to some extent over the last thirty to forty years or so. And yet, he does not seriously confront the ramifications of such a monumental change. To take an example, a question—one of special interest to Marxists—arises. In the present context, what is the corporation's motivation with respect to those who need to work to attain money to buy things that are what McMurtry calls *life-needs*?

In the contemporary world, debt is created to the degree that wages are driven near or below the money required to fulfill life-needs. Such debt then, with the deregulation, has invited usurious interest rates, fees, seizers of property, collection agencies and so on.

Perhaps Lapavitsas does a good deed for readers of *Profit Without Production*, if they are led to take a look at a few but long passages in *Das Capital volume 3* where he tries mightily to convince himself that in the end there is no M ... M' without a M—C—M'.

The fact is that the culture of liquidation has tapped into rich expanding sources of money-capital. This practice, but in a radically different context, was known to Marx back in the 19th century. However, he dismissed it as atavistic, as it certainly appeared to be at the onset of mechanization. He implicitly makes it clear the Ricardian conceptualization of capitalism basic to his own, rules out such creation of debt ownership—i.e., independent of goods production—via poverty wages.

Here is, in part, one of Marx's passages in volume 3 of *Das Capital* in which his inner struggle cannot be missed.

Money as money is potentially self-expanding value and is loaned out as such—which is the form of a safe for his singular commodity. It becomes a property of money to generate value and yield interest. The actually functioning capital presents itself in such a light, that it seem to yield interest, not as a functioning capital, but as capital in itself, as money-capital.

This, too, becomes distorted. While interest is only a portion of the profit which the functioning capitalist squeezes out of the laborer, it appears now, on the contrary, as though interest were the typical product of capital the primary matter, and profit, in the shape of profit of enterprise, were a mere accessory and by-product of the process of reproduction.

Thus we get the fetish form of capital and the conception of fetish capital. In M—M' we have the meaningless form of capital, the perversion and objectification of production relations in their highest degree, the interest-bearing form, the simple form of capital, in which it antecedes its own process of reproduction. It is the capacity of money, or of a commodity, to expand its own value independently of reproduction—which is a mystification of capital in its most flagrant form.

For vulgar political economy, which seeks to represent capital as an independent source of value, of value creation, this form is naturally a veritable find, a form in which the source of profit is no longer discernible, and in which the result of the capitalist process of production—divorced from the process—acquires an independent existence

As interest-bearing capital, it assumes its pure fetish form, M—M', being the subject. In the reproduction process of capital, the money-form is but a mere point of transit. But in the money-capital market capital always exists in this form. The surplus-value produced by, here again in the form of money, appears as an interest part of it.

In interest-bearing capital, the movement of capital is contracted. Money is now pregnant. As soon as it is loaned out, or invested in the reproduction process, interest grows, no matter whether awake or asleep, at home or abroad, by day or by night. Thus interest-bearing, money-capital fulfills the most fervent wish of the hoarder. (Ch. XXVI: pp. 391–399)

Atavistic Critique

Two passages in the second volume of *Das Capital* point to the last remnant of *industrializing*, when looked at in the context of the contemporary economy, fading into an atavistic Marxist critique.

> The circuit M—M' on the one hand intermingles with the general circulation of commodities proceeds from it and flows back into it, is a part of it. On the other hand, it forms an independent movement of the capital-value for the individual capitalist, a movement of its own which takes place partly within the general, circulation of commodities, partly outside of it, but which always preserves its independent character.
>
> The form of circulation M—M', the initial and terminal points of which are real money express most graphically the compelling motive of capitalist production—money making. The process of production appears merely as an unavoidable intermediate link, as a necessary evil. All nations with a capitalist mode of production are therefore seized periodically by a feverish attempt to make money without the intervention of the process of production. (p. 55–56)

It has become apparent that the course of the leading contemporary economies are not primarily directed anymore by a clash of product capitalists, and wage-laborers within, at the time, a burgeoning Taylorism and for that matter Leninist industrial organization. Marx himself, by the 1860's and 70's was not blind to the fact that growing credit markets—and therefore concentrations of debt ownership—were arising out of industrializing. If a market can be cornered in one way or another, money can serve spectacularly as speculative capital, i.e., independent of product capital.

Marx's argument however is that surplus-making products remain the long-term basis of meeting any payment of interest, even if it is the debt-owner, not the corporate executives that absorb the surplus. At the near end of *Das Capital: third vol.*, under the heading "The trinity formula"; capital, land, and wage laborer:

> The land on the one hand and labor on the other are two elements of the real labor-process common to all modes of production and have nothing to do with its social form. Capital, land and labor appear respectively as sources of interest (instead of profit), ground-rent, and wages, as their products, or fruit; the former [the elements of the real labor process] are the basis, the latter, interest, ground-rent and wages, the consequence. (p. 816)

Speculative capital alone, without production-capital, is thus seen as little more than a form of gambling, much like merchant capital in the mercantile period. And indeed, from the 1950's to roughly the mid-70s—the years of the Golden-age—short term speculative purchases and sales were severely limited to the US stock market. Early on, at least, with the exception of future markets, there were few derivatives or investment banks. Beyond that even the returns on stocks in that period primarily were in the form of dividends, based on long-term shares of specific sets of industries and corporations.

But, when Marx disclaims "feverish attempts to make money without the intervention of the process of production," he falls prey to not knowing what one does not know. In this case, digitalization at the disposal of an already enormous military-industrial complex by the end of the 1950s topped with, in the 1980's and 90's, money creation by the banking oligopoly.

Over the last four decades or so, there have been constant, all-encompassing social forces that squeeze product capital. It comes from within the contemporary corporate culture of liquidation now including the State.

Along lines that go beyond Marx, these social forces have rapidly torn apart tethers that have kept together industrializing capitalism for much of the 20th century; in particular the bloody years of WWI, and then the Depression of the 30's, through the Golden-age.

Crucial in the change from the late-1970's and since, has been the disconnection of money-capital from a conception of laboring activity as a significant source of money-capital (what Marx means by surplus value). And conjointly, there is a disconnection of employee income as money, on the one hand, and the cost of sufficient goods needed by a family on the other.

This is to say, it is as if the payment for employment is like any other commodity, not to be seen in the context of life-needs. . The speculative capitalists are those—directly or indirectly—who then accumulate debt ownership within money-capital circuits that must be always churning debt into new money.

The social forces of the post-Golden age have triggered a recursive dominance of speculative capital. It has transformed corporations into short-term financial assets. And the corporation is not, as such, seen by its owners as any more or less than a form of debt ownership

One might not need to note, perhaps, that many nations did not by their own nature industrialize. Some still have not to a large degree. And many of these—from the end of WWI to the present—have been bereft of robust normal populations so to speak. These many States have been all the while debtors, without an effective military globally, and trapped on the inside by a corrupt military supported by industrializing States—the US at the head—who own their debt.

The social forces within the industrialized nations have gone through various stages from the end of WWI, up to the 1980s. Looking back the inter-war period adumbrated the dominance of debt ownership over product capital in the present. Of course, there was a response to that during the Depression of the 30s that led to great advances in the provision of life-needs to families in the industrializing nations.

Then was the blossoming of the Golden-age of industrializing product-capital economy, the welfare States in their prime, termed in the introductory undergraduate textbooks of the time as mixed economies. There was nationalization of important industries, or, more common in the US than Western Europe publicly-regulated industries, as well as Federal financing of independent non-profit enterprises.

The previous problem of lack of growth coupled with great unemployment was relatively successfully in the Golden-age, following as it did Keynesian macroeconomic demand policies, along the lines of Henry Ford.

In those immediate post-WWII years there was a near-symmetry of corporation and unions in relation to the State, the latter moving far in the direction of playing the part of neutral arbitrator of the two. During those years the social forces moved the Totality toward greater distributions of income, wealth and opportunities, as well as the stated if fleeting objective of the US nation in the sixties of eliminating all poverty.

This is the junction of classical, neoclassical, and Marxist thought. In the context of product capitalism, Labor—marginal labor in the neoclassical models—is seen to be the necessary agent to generate the revenue of the corporation without which there would be no profit and hence no interest payments.

To the speculative capitalist, the employee—unlike the capital stock or land—is not an asset with a money value. Rather, it is outside the culture of liquidation. The contemporary debt corporations rid themselves of labor to push up share-value, Labor is seen as a costly short-term necessity. Thus, there is a strong push toward more and more extensive digitalization of production, and more unskilled families who are unemployed or paid less than enough to satisfy life-needs.

Maurizio Lazzarato's *Making of the Indebted Man*

Maurizio Lazzarato, in his important book, *The Making of the Indebted Man* (2012):

> We have moved from Fordist regulation, which privileged the industrial and debtor side, to financial regulation, which prioritizes the financial and creditor side. Credit or debt and their creditor-debtor relationship

> constitute specific relations of power that entail specific forms of production and control of subjectivity—a particular form of *homo economicus*, the "indebted man." (p. 30)

Lazzarato explores the core of the existing political economy, which he terms *debt-capitalism*. The latter is rapidly encompassing social life to a point that may perhaps match the industrializing of the previous century.

> The condition of the indebted man now occupies the totality of public space. Consumer, beneficiary, worker, entrepreneur, unemployed, tourist, etc. are now invested by the subjective figure of the indebted man, which transforms them into indebted consumers, indebted welfare users, and finally as was in the case with Greece, indebted citizens.
>
> It is debt and the creditor-debtor relationship that make up the subjective paradigm of modern-day capitalism, in which economic activity and the ethico-political activity of producing the subject go hand in hand. Debt breeds, subdues, manufactures, adapts, and shapes subjectivity. With what kind of machinery does debt produce the subject? (p. 38)

By the turn of the millennium an awareness of deep change was being felt across the major capitalist nations, planted as they were in the industrial revolution. They were not prepared for such a social transformation and were in denial until the crisis of 2007/2008.

Unseen for the most part, the economy built on product capital had been coming apart as early as the 1970's, the post-WW II Golden age of a functioning capitalist economy coming to an end. In the 1990's debt capitalism blossomed, coming up between cracks in the concrete, and contributing heavily to the crumbling of the industrial foundation underneath.

In the place of industrializing capitalism becomes the constant buzz of parasitic loan-contracts dominating the lives of a growing population of young debtors, while turning debt ownership into a State-guaranteed scheme of accumulating liquidity, leveraged to create new debt ownership, and to turn it into more liquidity. As such, debt-capitalism is ruled by the empty but seductively discursive relation: Money is power and power is money.

As Marx would have had it, referring to industrializing capitalism, interest incomes are dependent on product capital. In the realm of debt-capitalism, production is a stage of liquidation, a Nietzschian way to close open time; stealing away the Gods' right to be Messianic.

Lazzarato:

> Whereas in the Middle Ages time belonged to God and God alone, today, as possibility, creation, choice, and decision, it is the primary object of capitalist expropriation/appropriation. What are the enormous quantities of money concentrated in banks, insurance, pension funds, etc., manipulated by finance but potentialities, immense concentration of possibilities? Finance sees to it that the only choices and the only possible decisions are those of the tautology of money making money, of production for the sake of production.
>
> Whereas in industrial societies there still existed an open time—in the form of progress or revolution—today, the future and its possibilities, quashed by the huge sums of money mobilized by finance, seems to be frozen. For debt simply neutralizes time, time as the creation of new possibilities, that is to say, the raw material of all political, social or esthetic change. Debt harnesses and excises the power of destruction/creation, the owner of choice and decision. (p. 48–49)

A telling example is the financing, through long-term credit, of what is a very expensive university education in the US. Connected to this, more than ever, is a university degree, which is considered a near-necessity (not sufficiency of course) for entrance into an occupation paying a robust income and in which employment is by and large secure.

These two powerful forces pull many families into enormous debt that can easily grow rather than ever being paid back. It means a tight harness of money owed regularly for decades, whether or not in looking back it was ever worth the price. Compounding this in the US is the exceptional case where there is no right to go into bankruptcy with regard to student loans. The effect is millions in the population whose young-adult years (and possible lifetime) are to be lived in cages of debt.

It is of some interest that as seen by Polanyi, the great transformation to industrializing capitalism was centered in the lifting of the Speenhamland Laws in 1834, which are said to have reached a cul-de-sac:

Polanyi:

> Under Speenhamland society was rent by two opposing influences, the one emanating from paternalism and protecting labor from the dangers of the market system; the other organizing the elements of production, including land, under a market system, and thus divesting the common

people of their former status, compelling them to gain a living by offering their labor for sale. The right to live was abolished.

Lazzarato:

Debt ignores boundaries and nationalities; at the level of the world-economy, it knows only creditors and debtors. For the same reasons it forces us to shift our perspective from labor and employment in order to conceive a politics at the level of Capital as 'Universal Creditor'. Debt surpasses the division between employment, or non-employment, working and non-writing, productive and assisted, precarious and non-precarious, divisions on which the Left has based its categories of thought and action.

The figure of indebted man cuts across the whole of society and calls for new solidarities and new cooperation. We must also take into account how it pervades nature and culture, our debt to the planet, as well as to ourselves as living beings. The negative that debt institutes informs the historical conditions from which struggle turns away to invent new forms of subjectivity and new possibilities of life. Still, these conditions are indeed at each instance, historical, unique, and specific. And today they come together in debt.

Chelsea Hotel no. 2

I remember you well in the Chelsea Hotel
You were talkin' so brave and so sweet
Givin' me head on the unmade bed
While the limousines wait in the street

Those were the reasons
That was New York
We were runnin' for the money and the flesh
And that was called love for the workers in song
Probably still is for those of them left

Ah but you got away didn't you babe?
You just turned your back on the crowd
You got away
And never once heard you say

I need you
I don't need you
I need you
I don't need you
And all of that jivin' around

I remember you well
In the Chelsea Hotel
You were famous your heart was a legend
You told me again, you preferred handsome men
But for me you would make an exception

And clenching your fist
For the ones like us
Who are oppressed by the figures of beauty
You fixed yourself and said
"Well never mind
We are ugly but we have the music"

And then you got away yeah didn't you babe?
You just turned your back on the crowd
You got away I never once heard you say
I need you
I don't need you
I need you
I don't need you
And all of that jivin' around

I don't mean to suggest
That I loved you the best
I can't keep track of each fallen robin
I remember you well in the Chelsea Hotel
That's all. I don't even think of you that often...

Words and music: Leonard Cohen
CD Leonard Cohen I'm your Man, sung *by Rufus Wainwright*

CHAPTER 6

Life as a Baby Boomer

Red Diaper Baby

At the outset of the classic 60's film *Yellow Submarine*, a cartoon Ringo Starr, heads down, hands in his pockets, walking across the screen muttering over and over to himself in a sad resigned voice *nothing ever happens to me ... nothing ever happens to me...*

That was me. At least it was a part of me that I was conscious of and I distinctly remember it even now, many years since. It was before the Beatles, including Ringo, the 1950's had ended and the sixties had literally begun, 1960, 1961,1962, and I and was getting impatient to get on with it, go to high school.

The huge fins growing out of ever-longer and longer automobiles were becoming passé, and the custom of buying a brand-new car every single year, trading in of course the old one, was being replaced by an exodus to the suburbs where cars properly belonged. A decade before, the automobile had already pushed out the trolleys in Newark, where I grew up, so that I only knew their obsolete tracks, the way our 1952 green Desoto skidded when we drove on Clinton Avenue.

I was born in 1949 the quintessential early baby boomer, now entering the early years of the baby boomers' grand entry into Medicare and Social Security. It will go on for the next several decades until there are no more to enter, no one left alive born before 1965.

One of my first memories is sitting in front of a TV at a neighbor's house, the one on my block among the first to buy a TV set, it being heavily marketed immediately in the New York area. Not that I knew anything about that. The next memory of mine is getting up early in the morning, the rest of the family asleep, a pioneer in growing up watching TV. I remember absorbing in wonder and confusion, at the age of 3 or 4, an odd stew of shows, though I didn't realize it at the time.

Most of those shows are virtually unknown to anyone else now so I'll name a number of them: the elegant New York sit coms, My Little Margie, Topper and Private Secretary (The Anne Southern Show); the creepy Andy Devine Show, incongruously containing within it a film-like series of adventures of a boy and his elephant in the jungle; Flash Gordon, an adumbration of Star Trek, which for some reason I found very disturbing; and the heart-warming I

Remember Mamma. These were my first experiences of television. And it was an experience that not just new to me—of course, little more than a baby—but a new experience really to everybody around me.

What is especially of interest to me of these days, and those to follow, is that the life of the baby boom generation has continued in that way, to contain within it the life of the world. And as it grows older, to me—for what it's worth—it is hard not to see that we are dying of cancer.

In most respects, my family life and friendships as a child fitted the norms of the 1950s (A film that creates an uncannily accurate feeling of life in the 50's I think is Terrence Malik's *Tree of Life*). In one respect, however I was a member of an extremely tiny subset of baby boomers, apart from the rest, in the way our parents looked at the world.

We were known—as I was only to find out many years later—as "red-diaper babies," an affectionate term mostly used within the tribe. My father had been in the American Communist Party during the 30s leading up to the War. Like many others who had been in the Party, he severed ties with it when the Hitler-Stalin Pact was signed in 1939.

He had a tight circle of friends, primarily, like him, high school teachers in the Newark public school system, his closest ones having been in the Party like him. And they loved to talk politics. Oh, they loved to talk. They would gather at each other's houses for Saturday night dinner parties, with their spouses, and there would be a lot of arguing, but never in real anger. And all along it was the things they didn't argue about that really mattered.

A few in the circle and many that they knew in the Newark School systems at large had lost their jobs due to the red-scare led by Joseph McCarthy. One of my father's closest friends, Bob Lowenstein, a French teacher who taught at Weequahic high school was fired and did not teach all during my childhood. Later a court ruled that due to tenure his firing was unwarranted and he received back pay for all those years.

I soaked it all up. I have memories of sitting on the carpeted staircase leading up to my bedroom dead tired but unable to break away from their arguments. Often as I got older I took sides in my mind, not always siding with my father, but most of the time. And by the age of around 10 or 11 I would use what I heard from my father and others to make unusual pronouncements, and get into long arguments with my elementary school classmates: challenging unquestioned matters such as the threat of the Soviet Union, the Cuban revolution, and supposed freedom in America. I still remember how I told my class-mates Khrushchev wasn't crazy for taking off a shoe and pounding it on his desk because he was so mad. It's just the way Russians clap, a cultural thing I said. I had heard it somewhere.

In the end, what came from my childhood, for better or worse, a genuine detachment from presumed social agreement. It left me comfortable on the other side of the line. And more importantly perhaps, I loved dialogue, argument you might say. Dialogue for me is the source of insight into the reality of social life, as suggested by the social philosopher (if you will) John McMurtry.

> When people come to explain any way of life in the world, they are conditioned not to expose their own social order to the same critical eye with which they view a different or opposed social order. This is because the identity with their own way of life as normality, and thus the other as abnormality. If the other is not only different also opposed to the home order, then to abnormality is added the offence of enmity.
>
> The twentieth century has come to be known as the Age of Massacre, but the mind-bias at work in blocking out one side of the massacre has been repressed from view. There is not only a rule against recognizing the monstrous in one's own social system, but a ruse against recognizing that there is such a rule. This mind-lock is as old as civilization itself (p. 87).
>
> In the second half of the twentieth century, social thought seemed to be moving beyond the systematic repression by which it had traditionally been confined. The knell of the old imprisoned social consciousness seemed to have been laid. The foundation of a liberated social self-criticism seemed to have been laid.
>
> In the brief era of unlimited social interrogation which emerged between 1965 and the early 1970s, humanity witnessed the most fundamental far-reaching and transcultural questioning of the social-structural given in human history. (p. 96)

Such was the future of this red-diaper boy. Of course, Ringo's complaint is miraculously answered. He stumbles into a wondrous world animated by the Beatles, the yellow submarine, which we lived in for a while.

McMurtry's description of the Sixties is an extremely apt and insightful one. It was an historic moment in which the uniquely cruel appraisal of parents, the nation, the world by their adolescent child, had galvanized into a living generational critique, a loud rejection of the silently evolving culture they had grown up in, hence the infamous *generation gap*.

At the heart of the mid-fifties and early sixties was a struggle by the baby boomers on-masse to free themselves from what was broadly referred to then as *commercialization*. Rooted in the Beatniks—many like Ginsberg and Ferlinghetti remained prominent figures throughout the Sixties—there was an instinctive urge to shed the weight of corporations, to somehow render them harmless, to create a truer life-road than pursuit of money and obeisance to power.

Writer/singer Leonard Cohen, himself a unique figure of the Sixties, expresses this in his *Chelsea Hotel no. 2*, about a brief affair he had with the iconic Janis Joplin:

> *I remember you well in the Chelsea Hotel // you were famous, your heart was a legend // You told me again you preferred handsome men // but for me you would make an exception. // And clenching your fist for the ones like us // who are oppressed by the figures of beauty, // fixing yourself you said, "well never mind, // we may be ugly but we got the music."*

It is also seen in very personal everyday aspects and customs of life in the sixties that have been forgotten. For example, with respect to women, only during the Sixties—not before or after, and more or less just among baby boomers—did it become acceptable (and for a few it still is) to not regularly, if at all, do things like shaving your legs and under -arms, using deodorants, putting on lipstick and nail polish, wearing stockings or high-heeled shoes.

Along the same lines it was relatively unusual in the Sixties, and not before or after, for there to be formal paid weddings. Rather the typical wedding was at the home, often not catered. It was simply a large party with a ceremony of the bride and groom's own making, and often without the bride wearing a formal wedding dress or the groom a tuxedo and without bridesmaids and such.

My own experience of the Sixties was one in which adolescence and the Sixties were inseparable. In 1965, I was a junior in high school and my life changed. Toward the beginning of my senior year I was suspended from school for wearing blue jeans. By the end of the year the school abandoned their dress code except, if I remember, limiting how short mini-skirts could be.

The Beatles of course entered the pop cultural scene around 1964 and transformed it (the day the music died). I was transformed in 1965.

That one year I discovered Bee Bop, flowering then—John Coletrane, Miles Davis, Eric Dolphy, etc., etc.—along with traditional Mississippi and Chicago blues from the fifties and early sixties, Bill Broonzy, Howlin' Wolf, John Lee Hooker, Lightning Hopkins, whose careers were being revived. These were the first LPs I owned, along with all three Bob Dylan albums and a few of Joan Baez (all the records still monophonic). And I had my first hi fi system, which I brought with me to college.

By 1966 I was smoking grass. I was sexually active and had a girlfriend who wore miniskirts. My hair was almost down to my shoulders. My parents were beside themselves.

One thing that set me apart was the consequence of being a red-diaper baby. I adopted the critical view of "big business" from my father and his circle of friends at a young age. I'd argued all through elementary school that nobody went without food in the Soviet Union and that advertising made us buy things that we really didn't need. I had grown up on the wrong side of the argument and I took it to heart.

Therefore, I never questioned the sudden unexpected appearance of the yellow submarine, a grand flight under the sea escaping commercialization. Indeed, like Mohamed and the mountain, social reality seemed in my adolescent self to be coming to me rather than me to it. To me it was very different from the feeling of being confused, in doubt, forced up a mountain to see the view that was experienced by many of the baby boomers. Like Ringo I eagerly welcomed the submarine with open arms and got right in the sea.

The Loves of Dobie Gillis

The Sixties are a black swan. McMurtry raises the nature of its uniqueness but sees its heart to be from 1965 to the early 1970s (p. 96). I suggest that the time-span is misshapen, if one takes the uniqueness of the era as the spontaneous rejection of almost an entire culture from within, and not, in the first instance, a political movement or an organized rebellion against an existing authority or something of that sort. In short, identifying the Sixties with the Vietnam War, as McMurtry implicitly does, is far too narrow.

It can be argued that the counter-culture began with the *beatniks,* a radical, artistic sub-culture that arose in the 50's. Poets, playwrights, painters, musicians, writers and intellectuals, free spirits, Gnostics of various faiths, Buddhism, Hinduism, Gurdjieff, all pacifists, all, you need is love. It formed a creative counter to the seeming triumph of post-World War II consumerism and power. It even tore open the existing culture, its rigid adhesion to a century of industrialization.

A telling aspect of the beatniks is that they blended into the bee-bop jazz scene, which set the stage for the popularization of pot, and eventually the wide use of psychedelics, and of course, from that, electrifying rock. The latter was to be a life-blood of the counter-culture rising up.

The emergence of the beatniks in the fifties signaled a most unusual cultural phenomenon as the baby boomers made their way into adolescence, at which point in unheard of numbers they would soon join an historic flood of students filling up the leading colleges and universities across the country, giving the counter-culture an incomparable space to create and live in, to expand into and far from the universities, into multiple pursuits, each outside of the existing culture.

I myself was 10 years old in 1959 when without of course thinking much about it I was drawn to a new TV program for that season entitled *The Loves of Dobie Gillis*. It had something that intrigued me, for a little while anyway: the Maynard G Krebs character (Krebs becomes better known later as Gilligan). Maynard was a humorous caricature of a beatnik, a thing not seen before on TV.

I knew what a beatnik really was already, enough to be amused—in the way of a 10-year-old—by how Maynard was completely isolated, no other beatniks to be found. How did he know how to be a beatnik? How did he know the lingo? All the other characters were always dressed up, very neat, extremely 50's TV types of teenagers. They made a point of it from time to time, especially the inane Dobie, who on occasion is rightly lectured by Maynard for his frivolous, meaningless, unrelenting, and uncaring flirtations with *girls*.

Looking back at it now, it is uncanny how basic differentiating characteristics given to Maynard G, Krebs the *beatnik* in 1959, show that already the seeds that came into bloom in the 1960's, were being planted as early as the mid-50's. Maynard wears one outfit all the time, a plain sweatshirt, jeans and sneakers, a sailor's hat and a goatee (the latter commonly associated with beatniks). Thereby Maynard presents himself always as indifferent to either appearance or wealth.

Moreover, Maynard gives the impression of being in his own world. The others treat him on the one hand as a child whom they never listen to—but whom they do try to take advantage of, but are usually outsmarted by him—and, on the other hand, simply an alien being. But he is the one to have bought a hand-held *radio* complete with ear phones. The others just laugh at it, but Maynard doesn't particularly care. He takes it into class, shuts his eyes and just enjoys bee-bop in his ears until of course he's caught by the teacher.

The beginnings of the Sixties—the appearance of the black swan—coalesced then at the outset of a singular ten to twelve-year period in the US, 1955–1965, a rare decade indeed. For all ten years the US was not in overtly (declared) war with any other nations.

Along with that, unlike any other time, with the exception perhaps of the decade after World War I, the US was a monopolistic supplier of production and financial capital to the entire industrialized world. At the same time, domestically the US was functioning under fairly, protective labor laws, ones that legitimized strong, but extremely narrow-minded unions. There were as well strict financial regulations of commercial banks. Both were first being established in the years of the 20s and 30s.

The effect of this on the social whole of the US during the Golden Age has no equivalent to any other years of US industrialization. The income distribution was meaningfully progressive (90% top marginal tax rates for instance) even as real incomes on average were increasing at a significant rate, and unemployment on average was low until the 70s.

As a culture, then, the explosion of baby boomers coincided with a relatively safe world that we grew up in and took for granted, of course, at the time. It invited us to self-liberation rather than simply survival.

Of course, there was real fear of nuclear war, during this time, which was tied of course to the newly unshakable cold war with the Soviet Union. But nonetheless in open time for me as an early baby boomer—for whom such dangers were scary at times, but at the same time too abstract. In closed time it is the most tranquil and promising years of my life.

I clearly remember when friends of my parents came back from a rare trip to England or France, how they inevitably voiced their shock at the lack of central heating, lack of toilet paper, tiny cars, not much good food and so forth. One could not ignore being privileged. A widespread appeal to my sister and me to finish our meals—*there are people starving in India*—was something I thought about. Still, it did not stop me from leaving food I did not like on my plate.

World War II, my father fought in and never wanted to talk about. He was held in a German prison camp for over a year. But those days lived in by my parents, before I was born, seemed to me at the time light-years away. In fact, the distance from my father's world and mine, itself, contributed to an ingrained security I felt. The black and white films of German concentration camps, limbless bodies being thrown into mass graves, were shown to us by the Hebrew school I went to when I was also about 10. I went to Hebrew school after my regular school, twice a week. However, you know, the more horrendous the sight of the camp became the more that it seemed to, thankfully, have been conquered, to never come back again.

The effect was a cultural gap separating many baby boomers, including me, from their parents, at an early age, transferring daily life to a culture of peers. But unlike an immigrant child who adopts a new nation's culture, here baby boomers like me experienced ways of adopting a culture forming from within. This became known popularly as the *generation gap* when the early baby boomers first reaching adolescence, late-50's and early 60's. By 1965, when I was still in high school, the sixties were well underway, and indeed the Vietnam War ended those years of relative peace, that never have come back.

Herman Hesse's *Steppenwolf* Revisited

It's been my habit for several years now to go back, every once in a while to some book that I tried to read when I was much younger, but the experience was, let us say, unsuccessful at the time. The books that I've gone back to are only the few that while abandoning them in the moment nonetheless that I remain puzzled by, to the point where at a certain age, or because of a random circumstance, I decide to see what if anything I had missed out on it, been perhaps the wrong time to read it. But as we were taught at my alma mater St. John's College: Upon being confronted by a great work that leaves you cold, ask yourself the question, To what flaw in me, do I owe this lack of appreciation.

Maybe it was recent thoughts of the 60s that put it in my head not long ago to revisit a novel by Hermann Hesse, *Steppenwolf*. In my last year of high school, and then into my college years, I avidly read Hesse's novels. It was a time when elements of the Beatniks of the late-50s had melted into Hippies of the early sixties, and more generally a cultural/political stew was bubbling in the pot. Hesse's poetic writings were nice spices thrown into the brew. With one true exception, *Steppenwolf*, each of his novels approached a closed narrative prose poem, similar to the works of Novalis a century or so earlier, an elegantly spun spiritual tale.

Hesse's novels aligned easily with the peace/love missive of the hippies and with the attraction of non-Western philosophies in reaction to the consumerism of the 50s. And it was toward the end of 1966, around Thanksgiving (the beginning of my high school senior year), that out of nowhere I entered what I experienced as the most exotic, exciting mysterious, liberating and encompassing transformation of who I was in my life up until then, and ever after. I was ushered into a new world by two brand new high school companions: my first never to be forgotten love, and a best friend of hers and soon a best friend of mine.

One of their initial gifts to me was an introduction to Hesse's novel *Demian*, first published at the end of WW I in 1919; the same year that Hesse settled in Switzerland (away from Germany). He lived a secluded life there, continuing to write until his death in 1962, at the age of eighty-five.

Thomas Mann in 1947 wrote of *Demian*, as quoted in a later editiont:

> The electrifying influence exercised on a whole generation just after the First World War, by *Demian* is unforgettable. With uncanny accuracy this poetic work struck the nerve of the times and called forth grateful rapture from a whole youthful generation who believed that an interpreter of their innermost life had risen from their own midst—whereas it

> was a man already forty-two years old who gave them what they sought. (p. IX–X)

Four leading novels of Hesse's were newly issued in paperback during the sixties. In addition to *Demian* (1919) the book racks contained *Sidartha* (1922), *Steppenwolf* (1927) and *The Glass Bead Game* (1945). Also available in paperback at that time was *Journey to the East*, Hesse's last book. It was first published in 1956 in paperback and had been available as such in the interim.

Accustomed in 1967 to, and entranced by, Hesse's poetic writing, I see now, having re-read *Steppenwolf*, why I was unable to grasp large segments of the various inter-woven narratives of which it is composed. I found them, unlike in any other of the books by Hesse, tedious at best and at worst verging on the reduction of sentences to pure sound.

I see now that I was indeed blind along a certain crucial dimension of the work. *Steppenwolf* is an unusual but not unique case of an author writing an anti-novel, here directed at, among other things, the genre of Hesse's own novels. Mann, in the same passage as above comments along these lines:

As an experimental novel, Steppenwolf is no less daring than *Ulysses* and *The Counterfeiters*.

What I missed in 1967 was that I, the reader, was experiencing Hesse himself, as he is writing it, a man about to turn fifty, in the midst of a deep mid-life crisis. At the heart of the novel is a painful self-mockery of Hesse's spiritual tales, a condemnation of his personal failure to live life in the moment. This is expressed by the attempt to turn the closed time of his tales inside out. *Steppenwolf* is struggling throughout to live in open time. And in the end Hesse has him wearily concluding, hardly the inspiration to 1960s adolescents at the threshold of a cultural explosion:

> I knew that all the hundred thousand pieces of life's game were in my pocket. A glimpse of its meaning had stirred my reason and I was determined to begin the game afresh. One day I would be a better hand at the game. (p. 245–6)

However, along another dimension there is a social critique within *Steppenwolf*, particularly the first few narratives. And indeed, I remember being absorbed in those early pieces of arts, and some of the images it created never left me since. In this respect the anti-novel in betraying poetic writing, allows Hesse, perhaps for the only time, to openly contextualize contemporary culture as he sees it, via the fictional imagining of which he was, of course, a master.

Reading the novel now, brings back to me something that fueled strong desire for an alternative culture on the part of so many baby boomers as they entered adolescence and young adulthood in the 60's. This, even as the economic golden age in the US was at its peak. Partly it was an adolescent's rebellion against fearful parents, the silent generation. But it was a deeper critique on a macro level of a society whose being was to be mechanized, and whose wants were to become exclusively that of money.

> A wild longing for strong emotions and sensations seethes in me, a rage against this toneless, flat, normal and sterile life. For what I always hated and detested and cursed above all things was this contentment, this healthiness and comfort, this carefully preserved optimism of the middle classes, this fat and prosperous brood of mediocrity. (p. 28–29)
>
> You are right, Steppenwolf and yet you must perish. You are too exacting and hungry for this simple easy-going contented world of today. Whoever wants music instead of noise, joy instead of pleasure, soul instead of gold, creative work instead of business, passion instead of foolery, finds no home in this trivial world of ours. (p. 170)
>
> The modern man has lost the love of inanimate objects. He does not even love his most sacred object, his motor car, but is ever hoping to exchange it as soon as he can for a later model. (p. 180)

It is striking that these words of Hesse's, written in the roaring 1920s, now can be read as an uncanny echo, in reverse, of the 60s, amazingly with the same effect on adolescent readers. For this reason perhaps *Steppenwolf* is the most-known of all his novels. Hesse, in *Steppenwolf*, explicitly contextualizes his own generation, between the European enlightenment of the 17th and 18th centuries, on one side, and on the other the industrialization through the 19th and into the last decades of the 20th on the other.

> There are times when a whole generation is caught in this way between two ages, between two modes of life and thus loses the feeling for its self, for the self-evident, for all morals, for being safe and innocent. (p. 23)

Hesse sees colliding ages. Masses of individuals are left to suffer from it. They have no social anchor to keep their very identities in tow. This was the interwar periods. Economic theory—Marxist, Neoclassical, and Keynesian—have been and still are virtually monolithic, insofar as being blind to a deep irrelevance of the imaginary self-regulating competitive capitalist economic system. Even if in some form or another it ever existed, it surely has been gone for some two hundred years.

Steppenwolf writes:

> I dress to go out to visit without really wanting to at all, so it is with the majority of men day by day and hour by hour in their daily lives and affairs, without wanting to at all. They sit out their hours at desks and on office chairs; and it is all compulsory, mechanical and against the grain, and it could all be done or left undone just as well by machines; and indeed, it is this never-ceasing machinery that prevents their being like me, critics of their own lives and recognizing the stupidity and shallowness, the hopeless tragedy and waste of the lives they lead, and the awful ambiguity grinning over it all. (86)

It is the baby-boom generation—who grew up during the golden age but for whom much of their adulthood has been the post-golden—to whom the Sixties are a shadow in closed time, and in open time, to cite Benjamin on such a matter, solely an idea. And yes, Hesse is right. Many growing older are experiencing confusion, loss of feeling for whom we are and whom the other, and for that which is self-evident, moral, and safe and innocent.

Counterculture of Walter Benjamin

Walter Benjamin in a (much-disputed) interpretation of Klee's famous painting, *Angelus Novus*, sees in it the modern time of history; i.e., *Progress.* It is found in what is perhaps the final piece ever written by Benjamin, "Thesis on the philosophy of history," (1940). It eerily hearkens back to his early writings some twenty-five years before. In the fall of 1940, at least according to the current consensus, being in great danger of capture by German Nazis Benjamin committed suicide.

> The painting shows an angel looking as though it is about to move away from something he is fixedly contemplating. ... This is how one pictures the angel of history. The angel's face is turned toward the past. Where we perceive a chain of events, the angel sees one single catastrophe which keeps piling wreckage upon wreckage and hurls it in front of the angel's feet. The angel would like to stay, awaken the dead, and make whole what has been smashed. But a storm is blowing from Paradise, it has got caught in the angel's wings with such violence that the angel can no longer close

> them. This storm irresistibly propels the angel into the future to which its back is turned, while the pile of debris before it grows skyward. This storm is what we call progress. (p. 257)

The lawfulness of closed time does not exist in open time: By the turn of the 20th century a clean separation of social control of production has been attained. Capitalists within corporate institutions now exclusively design and direct mechanized production processes. And production, in principle, is carried out on behalf of capital-ownership mostly in the form of stock.

Benjamin, born in 1892, the last years of peace, and in the years leading up to WW I was a college student active in the German youth movement. In his initial writings, he envisages a radically-reformed German approach to education, in which students are key participants in dialogic learning, existing as it does in an expansive open time, i.e., in the moment, in addition to the closed-time of reading.

With the coming of 1914 and through the years of the war and then the rest of his life beyond—the inter-war years—Benjamin's insight widens and deepens. Capitalists in the context of industrializing capitalism are seen clearly to him to be the threat of a storm propelling the social Totality in an unimaginable direction.

In particular, the production and sale of military weapons, including for the first time the dropping of explosives out of the sky, capable of wreaking massive death and destruction. This, when the very capability of great profits is seen created out capital invested in War. And sadly, the angel of history, back turned, sees the carnage, but not the direction of the storm propelling it forward or back.

In, To the Planetarium, a section of the larger piece, One-Way Street. written between 1923 and 1926, Benjamin masterfully analogizes technology with education in the context of the relation of industrializing capitalism and the natural world.

> Because the lust for profit of the ruling class sought satisfaction through it technology betrayed man and turned the bridal bed into a bloodbath. The mastery of nature (so the imperialists teach) is the purpose of all technology. But who would trust a cane wielder who proclaimed the mastery of children by adults to be the purpose of education? Is not education, above all, the indispensable ordering of the relationship between generations and therefore mastery of that relationship and not of children? And, likewise, technology is the mastery of not nature but of the relation between nature and man. In technology, a *physis* is being

> organized through which mankind's contact with the cosmos takes a new and different form from that which it had in nations and families. (p. 487)

As the extreme hardships of the 1920's progressed in Germany, Benjamin—and small groups of others scattered around Europe—both conceptually and subjectively sought out a kind of counter-culture of the self, an inner resistance of being sucked into the storm of industrializing capitalism. He did it through writing and the use of psychedelics, notably hashish (i.e., cannabis) and opium. He succinctly expresses the nature of this counter-culture in a transparently autobiographical, albeit fictional piece published in 1930: "Marseilles: Story of a Hashish Trance" in his book *On Hashish*:

> Never before had I felt myself so at home in the community of cognoscenti whose records of their experience—from Baudelaire *Paradis artificiels* to Hermann Hesse's *Steppenwolf*—were perfectly familiar to me. I lay on my bed and smoked. Through the window opposite me I could see one of the narrow black streets of the port district of Marseilles that intersect the body of the city like the marks of a knife. I was thus able to enjoy the absolute certainty that I could surrender to my dreams, quite undisturbed in this city of hundreds of thousands of which not a single soul knows of my existence. But the expected effects failed to appear. Three-quarters of an hour had already passed, and I began to feel suspicious about the quality of the drug. (p. 109–110)

The identification with psychedelics here is a revealing adumbration of the counter-culture of the Sixties. However, Benjamin—along with the likes of Baudelaire, Coleridge, Hesse and Ernst Bloch a tiny set trapped in the jaws of the great industrial transformation, each looking for how to live life inwardly as a way out.

Benjamin—having first experienced the industrializing war in his youth and then again in his thirties when WWII was ever-creeping up on him—makes it prophetically clear in the above passage (written in his early 30s), that for him and the others of his ilk there would be in the end no escaping the immense force going against them.

The experiences of the baby boomers in the years leading up to the counter-culture of the Sixties were quite different, unique of its kind in 20th century, as befits an historic black swan. By and large even the early baby boomers in the US (I myself was born only four years after WW II ended) had little real experience of the second war growing up, and virtually none of the first.

The wars were way back in the past. They had little to do with us. At our youngest stage, soldiers were toys we played with among ourselves, and later in school the threat of an *atom bomb* was for most, a bell ringing and in a straight line going to the corridor, standing facing the wall until the bell sounded again.

The fact is, in the US in particular, most of us as children during the fifties and into the sixties did not feel any obvious consequences of the wars. Our parents (the *silent* generation) did not as a rule want to rehash their experiences of the war anyway. To the contrary if anything they wished to put it out of their own minds. Therefore, one heard over time a stock of anecdotes, not much more. If the baby boomers in the US learned anything it was, "the good guys won and the evil guys lost, thank God, and now everything is pretty great."

In the sixties, then, the psychedelics, which included LSD, in addition to marijuana (cannabis), were being smoked by many in the population, well beyond small sets of intellectuals and jazz musicians. Also unlike the interwar period, use of psychedelics was now discovery in the moment as a rule, rather than finding subjective effects through quasi-scientific experimentation.

Beginning with the expansion of the universities, bringing together large numbers baby boomers in constant dialogue and reading, the Sixties recursively generated counter-culture socialization on a wide scale, involving a variety of institutional/collective structures and introducing new social behaviors, in all cases, independent of commercial considerations.

And there was a child-like comic aspect to the counter-culture absent from Benjamin's adumbration, a sense of laughing at itself, or perhaps laughing at how easily it all seemed to have happened. For example, the emergence of Abby Hoffman and the yippees, disrupting the 1968 Democratic convention in Chicago and becoming the mocking defendants in the famous trial of the Chicago seven.

Psychedelics, then, were not used in the sixties as a way out as much as a desire for an unparalleled freedom of *human subjectivity* that became available to virtually any baby boomer who sought it out. That same freedom is seen in other ways, of course, as well. Of note, the pursuit of various ancient philosophies and practices during the sixties opened up worlds for many within.

Three of the most common books read in the sixties, within the counter-culture, were the *Bhagavad Gita*, the *I Ch'ing*, and *The Meditations* of Marcus Aurelius. And along with Hesse's early twentieth century works, the teachings of contemporaries of his, Khal Gibran and Georges Gurdjieff for example were also deeply studied. These inner explorations of the mind, and control over the places one's mind inhabits, were the prerogative of each individual subject, as has never been known before, and even more so, perhaps, since.

George Orwell's *1984*

In the midst of a seminar course of mine this last semester I had occasion to look at Benjamin's early writings on the shapes of time, and out of the blue I found myself having a mysterious yen to re-read George Orwell's *1984*, first published in 1949.

It was only after the semester ended, and my second reading of *1984*, that multiple shapes of time along crucial social dimensions were visible, shapes in which I presently live. In *non-ergodic* fashion the other me that first read *1984* was just turning fourteen years old. I remember because it was a few months before the Kennedy assassination, November of 1963. It was in turn connected to my reading of Aldous Huxley's *Brave New World* around the same time, and it stuck with me that it was reported at the time, as an aside, that Huxley died on the same day.

My first reading was spiced by the single specific year title, particularly a year that hadn't yet occurred—at the time—but still was easily within my lifetime unless some unforeseen happenstance cut it short. It caused me, even if I was not wholly conscious of it, to enter closed time, calculating how long 20 years was to me in relation to what the social Totality might have changed to. But really I didn't get much further than a hazy picture of going to college. After that, was vaguely the rest of my life ending in my death. A similar but less ominous effect occurred soon thereafter, the Beatles' lyric: *When you're sixty-four*.

There was an eerie otherness of the social Totality the first time I read *1984* that touched me. But reading it again, I realized that Orwell's attempt to sew into the world-fabric of the work a love story suited for a post-WWII romance film starring Barbara Stanwick must have been lost to me in the moment. It was all new to me now, and now I see it was a major contribution to an utterly failed ending of the story from a literary point of view.

As a red diaper baby then, I still remember now, that reading it in 1963 Orwell's implicit prediction of the future had to my mind already been proven wrong, taking the air out of the novel's balloon very quickly. The Stalin regime—which in almost all its characteristics serves as a template of the ruling *Brotherhood* of State, Oceana, in *1984*—was officially being rejected by Khrushchev. Among other things Kennedy and Khrushchev were negotiating reduced stocks of nuclear weapons and limiting future developments of them.

As it happened, I was drawn to read in that same period the Russian novel *One Day in the Life of Ivan Denisovich* by Alexander Solzhenitsyn. He was to be one of the leading Soviet Russian dissidents in post-WWII. It was originally published in the Soviet Union in November 1962, in Russian of course, and the print was sold out in the first day. It came out in translation (and in paperback) published and distributed in the US and Britain in early 1963, and was equally popular in the West, including with me. It masterfully communicates what the normal day felt like being in a labor prison under Stalin, as Solzhenitsyn was in for about ten years, Siberia.

Solzhenitsyn remained extremely critical of the Soviet Union throughout the remainder of his life. He found himself equal to, if not more critical of US capitalism and culture however. He lived a rather solitary life for several years in Vermont, but eventually returned to his native land in southern Russia. *One Day in the Life* was followed by four major novels of his over the next two decades and numerous essays. He was awarded the Nobel Prize in 1970.

At 14 years old, marking the non-ending ending of the Korean War around 1954, I had lived the last ten years up to that point, with no open US war underway, at least officially. What *One Day in the Life* meant to me, influenced by my father and his circle of friends, was a significant opening up of the two great powers. It seemed an indication that the Cold War actually was melting into peace.

Khrushchev's explanation to the Congress of the Communist Party of his decision to allow publication of the book affected me at the time.

> It is our duty to gain a thorough and comprehensive understanding of the nature of the matters related to the abuse of power. Time will pass and we shall die, we are all mortal, but so long as we work we can and must clear up many points and tell the truth to the Party and to the people. This we must do so that such things never happen again. (p. 5–11)

To add one more thing to my quick dismissal of *1984* at the age of fourteen, the early baby boomers like me grew up in the dark shadow of WWII. For young Jews such as me the war was much more powerful than Orwell's novel. It was made *real*. I saw actual videos of Nazi concentration camps shown to us in Hebrew School long before I was fourteen. Black and white old-looking film of naked skeletal bodies piled up and being shoveled in huge pits.

I remember that on a number of occasions during my childhood came an internal sigh of relief that World War II was over before I was born, and we won. In the progressive spirit of the time, I was assured that the concentration camps like that would never be seen again. In that sense, *1984* was quite pale in comparison.

Reading *1984* the second time the imagined world of Orwell's is still, strikingly, a literary picture of the Stalinist regime. But the imagination is seen by me in much greater detail. Unknown to Orwell, who died in 1950, Stalin's influence on the Soviet Union lingered on in the post-War fifties and early sixties.

For instance, main character Winston Smith has a job changing history in various ways. One of them is associated with Stalin's well-known practice of taking an individual in the State bureaucracy out of photographs, and any other official references as part of the process of *disappearing them* by the State.

Another example is the encouragement of the populace by the Brotherhood to be informants for the State. This was extreme in East Germany during the Cold War and was common in the Soviet Union itself, especially but not only under Stalin. In the case of The Brotherhood, the State is so powerful its children are encouraged at a very young age to inform on their parents.

A telling aspect of Orwell's imagined world is its economic structure. The *proles*—i.e., the proletariat—are kept socially separated from those in the State bureaucracy. The proles are not chief subjects disappeared by the State. As far as one can tell the system of production and distribution does not have markets in its foundation. As described vaguely by Orwell, it is much like the economy of the Soviet Union built by Stalin, except the novel leaves out altogether the crucial place of agricultural workers.

In both the Stalinist Soviet Union and The Brotherhood there is a scarcity of consumer goods relative to demand, causing a lack of availability, particularly regarding the proles, but to those in the State bureaucracy as well. Even those at the highest levels of power in *1984* are seen to not be fabulously wealthy, at least absolutely, for instance compared to industrialists in the gilded age, or dictatorships around the real world.

Moreover, the leaders of the Brotherhood are subtly of a mind the same as many of those that were high up in the Stalinist Communist Party. A declaration made by one of the Brotherhood to Winston is: "We are interested solely in power. Not wealth or luxury or long life or happiness, only power, pure power" (p. 275).

By the same token the provision of basic life-necessities—food, shelter, health—were generally provided to the end financed primarily by the Soviet State, enough produced for the entire urban population. But at the same time, while life was livable, the fulfillment of life for most was minimal. Talking to an elderly prole at a bar, Winston cites a central Soviet communist critique of capitalism voiced throughout the Cold War. Orwell puts forward the basis—by the account of the Brotherhood—of the *Revolution* by which it came to power.

> The history books say that life before the Revolution was completely different from what it is now. There was the most terrible oppression, injustice, poverty—worse than anything we can imagine. Here in London, the great mass of the people never had enough to eat from birth to death. Half of them hadn't even boots on their feet. They worked twelve hours a

> day, they left school at nine they slept 10 in a room. And at the same time there were a very few people, only a few thousand—the capitalists, they were called—who were *rich and powerful.* They owned everything that there was to own. (p. 93)

The expansion during the golden-age of the US's capitalist economy lasted from the mid-fifties into the mid-seventies and was marked by an acceleration of new technologies and products beyond necessities or one might say of many, which became new necessities. Recessions were shallow and short, and real wages were increasing for many, unemployment being relatively low.

It might seem that one can dismiss Orwell on grounds that he was right about a Revolution, and he was only about five years off when it happened (1989–1991), but it was not the *communist-state*, it was the *capitalist-state* that prevailed. *1984* seen in 2016 caused in me an eerie otherness of the world to come. And unlike that fourteen-year-old's world in 1963, his world in 2016 is entering a true dystopia, going further and further into it as the 21st century proceeds.

The greater power of *1984* now is Orwell's sense of social Totality as actual dystopia. One that as the Brotherhood claims has created its own human endlessness. In addition, strangely enough Orwell's atavism with respect to the Stalinist Soviet Union brings to light the revolution inside the US instead.

It took hold in the 1990s. The US was no longer being forced into a global dialogue with communist enemies who subsidized their proles. The establishment of *debt-capitalism* comes into robust being in the wake of the defeat of the Soviet Union and the freeing of Soviet hold on to the Eastern Europe States. In the course of the first two decades of the 21st century the outcome of debt-capitalism has coincided with the history books read by Winston: "The rich and powerful capitalists own everything that there is to own."

Winston eventually falls into the hands of the Brotherhood, and in the process of being disappeared, he engages in a dialogue of a sort with his superior in the bureaucracy, O'Brien. The latter was involved in trapping Winston into revealing himself (and his lover) as dissidents. Winston is now completely in his control.

> **O'Brien:** "You understand well enough how the Party maintains itself in power. Now tell me why we [the Brotherhood] cling to power? What is our motive? Why should we want power? Go on, speak."
>
> *Winston remains silent until...*

> **Winston:** "You are ruling over us for our own good. You believe that humans are not fit to govern themselves, and therefore..."
>
> A pang of pain shoots through Winston's body. O'Brien pushes the lever of the dial up to thirty-five.
>
> **O'Brien:** "That was stupid, Winston, stupid! You should know better than to say a thing like that."
>
> *He pulls the lever back and continues:*
>
> **O'Brien:** "Now I will tell you the answer to my question. The Party seeks power entirely for its own sake. We are not interested in the good of others, we are interested in only power. Not wealth or luxury or happiness only pure power. The German Nazis and the Russian Communists came very close to us in their methods, but they never had the courage to recognize their own motives. Power is not a means, it is an end. One does not establish a dictatorship in order to safeguard a revolution; one makes the revolution in order to establish the dictatorship. The object of persecution is persecution. The object of torture is torture. The object of power is power." (p. 274–276)

O'Brien ends the dialogue addressing the being of power:

> **O'Brien:** "It is time for you to gather some idea of what power means. The first thing is that *power is collective*. The individual only has power in so far as he ceases to be an individual. You know the Party slogan "Freedom is Slavery." Has it ever occurred to you that it is reversible? Slavery is freedom. Alone—free—the human being is always defeated. It must be so, because every human being is doomed to die, which is the greatest of all failures. But if he can make complete, utter submission, if he can escape from his identity, if he can merge himself in the Party so that he *is* the Party, then he is all-powerful and immortal. The second thing is that *power is power over human beings.*" (p. 276–277)

The US Revolution—Orwell's error—has ridden on a *neoliberal ideology*, ironically falling back often on pre-industrial 18th century notions of contemporary capitalist systems. The ideological backbone of neo-liberalism is The Individual. *Product capitalism*, the jewel of the industrial revolution, was glittering in the post-War period, the economic golden-age, centered especially in the US.

Its central institution, the modern corporation is described by Berle and Means as late as 1991—the last edition of their classic *Modern Corporation & Private Property*—at the very time of the Revolution by which debt-capitalism was taking over the US economy.

> To Adam Smith, private enterprise meant an individual or few partners actively engaged and relying in large part on their own labor their immediate direction. The great associations are so different as to make the concept of private enterprise an ineffective instrument of analysis. It must be replaced with the concept of corporate enterprise, enterprise which is *the organized activity of vast bodies of individuals, workers, consumers and suppliers of capital,* under the leadership of the dictators of industry control. (p. 306)

Concentrated ownership of debt converts corporations into financial assets, held by the monetary value of the asset it represents. Debt ownership is individual and its power is the ability to claim any money in the future or to cut off new credits owed on debt not met. That can include private and public institutions as well as individuals, and on a large scale, municipalities and entire States.

Guattari identifies in *The Three Ecologies* (1989) "the dominant modes of valorizing human activities" in a neo-liberal model:

> 1. A global market that puts on the same plane of equivalence: material assets, cultural assets, wildlife areas, etc.
> 2. All social and international relations are under the control of police and military machinery.

And Guattari adds:

> Trapped in this double pincer movement, the nation states see their traditional role of mediation being reduced more and more, and they are frequently put in the combined service of the authorities of the global marketplace and of military-industrial complexes. (p. 20–21)

The years after the Cold War, then, have seen an ongoing conversion of the capitalist States, led by the US, into *ungovernable space* and toward a dystopia ever-further from Orwell's imaginary triumph of Stalinist communism. Rather, a dystopia that is truly real. Toward a world where, to twist O'Brien's words: The State only has power in so far as it ceases to be a State.

In writing this I can't help finally going back once more to my days before the return to unending wars, reading George Orwell's *1984*. I'm reminded of an episode of Rod Sterling's *Twilight Zone* (originally on the air from 1959 to 1964). The humans of the world are getting hotter and hotter and hotter, and the sun brighter day and night, dripping with sweat, without anything that can be done about it. The earth has fallen out of its orbit around the sun, to which it is now getting closer and closer. Soon all humans will be burnt to death.

The episode ends when one of the characters we see is dreaming and is now coming out of her sleep. She is shivering in the cold and it is darker than it's ever been in the morning. The earth has fallen out of its orbit around the sun from which it is getting farther and farther away. Soon all humans will be frozen to death.

Gulf of Tonkin Resolution

By signing in August of 1964 the *Gulf of Tonkin Resolution* the US declared an undeclared war in Vietnam. It was almost immediately confirmed by the Congress. The US yet again, but after a hiatus of over ten years, was rearing up to large-sale engagement in industrialized war, this time against a non-industrializing foe.

In April of 1967 Martin Luther King announced to the public a decision he had come to over the previous two years or so; a shift toward widening the scope of the civil rights movement. In a speech at the Riverside church entitled *Beyond Vietnam* he pointed a finger directly at the US military industrial complex, the enormous institutional force opposing the kinds of commitments made by John Kennedy in his 1960 campaign and then over again by Lyndon Johnson in 1964.

It was Johnson that coined the fitting name *War on Poverty*, the object being to significantly improve both financially and institutionally the lives of families whose basic needs were barely being met or worse, including those not able to support themselves by circumstance: the elderly poor, children in poor or incapable families, the disabled, the otherwise unemployed or unemployable and so forth.

More generally the government was addressing the failure of the life-ends of so many within the existing social system. Epitomized early on after the Second World War, for instance in Arthur Miller's *Death of a Salesman* (1949). The object of capital, the infinite expansion of money and power, as such, was to be seen as purely instrumental means without end in itself. And in some respects the major reforms of the banking system in the 1930's allowed the federal government to take much of the profit-motive out of the means of fulfilling basic life-needs of the family.

What King perceived happening with the entry into Vietnam was a lasting fixture of a war industry in the US and hence globally, generating a recursive function of military-industry profit and industrial warfare abroad. Thus, the social Totality was to become more and more continuously prey to, and obsessed by death and destruction.

King's prophetic understanding was expressed in speeches like *Beyond Vietnam* over the rest of 1967 and into 1968. He saw that that identity politics on the part of the leadership of the non-violent civil rights movement—notably the NAACP—not to say the blossoming violent black-power movement, precluded any possibility for a truly popular movement against the war. Given the vociferous anti-war movement which in 1967 was becoming quite loud, if King had been successful things might have turned out differently.

Instead, King in 1967 knew already that an historic social achievement, a purposeful elimination of poverty and need in the US, was being lost. The price paid for this is that the US (then and now) is a nation that represents the interests of privately-owned military-industrial capital. As such it fails to meet the *life-needs* let alone *life-ends* of people, globally as well as nationally.

King's hope in 1965 had been to galvanize a populace with the power to cut off the war, one that would dismantle the military industrial complex over time. Of course the latter had firmly planted itself in the US following WWII, and unlike ever before, it had of course become at the same time the repository of nuclear weapons,

The shocking election of Richard Nixon, I can still feel the impossibility of it—the first of many—less than a year after King's assassination, made it clear that the Vietnam War was escalating and indeed was expanding beyond all previous bounds. With the vast draft of college-age males, and their deaths and those of the supposed enemy, the war on poverty in a flash had ended. It didn't take long for Nixon to show his disdain for it, declaring a war on drugs. And it has not come back in almost fifty years now.

In these fifty years an unimaginable scale, a state of permanent industrialized warfare around the world is being reached. As of now it has been sustained into its third decade with no end at all in sight. Since the Civil War and then in the late-nineteenth century with a sharp expansion leading up to WWI–the military industry has been growing, accelerating after the fall of the Soviet Union. It is a hub now of ever-expanding global munition markets, along with their enormous ancillary industries and an uncountable loss of lives in so many ways.

Looking back, prior to the Gulf of Tonkin resolution having firmly set in, the years between the election of Kennedy in 1960 and Nixon's in 1968 stand apart. They were an historic black swan. They were years of freedom to find new places of the mind, new insights into the relation between industrialization and the natural world, triggered by Rachel Carson's *The Silent Spring* published in 1960. And, the new social subject within the US was reflected in one of the first tangible acts of John Kennedy's presidency, in 1961, the establishment of the *Peace Corps,* whose purposes read "To promote world peace and friendships."

Johnson's War on Poverty referred to major governmental actions at a federal level of legislation, addressing a spectrum of *life-needs.*

1) After a three-year pilot, in 1964 food-stamps (*coupons*) were federally financed in the *Stamp Act,* making available to the poor food in stores across the nation.
2) In 1965, health insurance, also financed federally, was legislated to cover the elderly, *Medicare,* and poor families with no insurance, *Medicaid.*
3) Also in 1965, creation of new public housing was legislated—the *Housing and Urban Development* (*HUD*) *Act*—federally subsidizing poor families and the needy (elderly and disabled).
4) Access of children of the poor to pre-school, *Head Start,* was piloted in the summer of 1965 in large urban areas, and was fully begun, financed federally, in 1966.

The importance of these laws is that they conceptually bring the various racially repressed groups into the larger fold of economically and culturally-repressed others. This is a theme of a speech by King at Stanford in 1967, entitled *The Other America,* which he gave shortly after the one given at the Riverside church.

> There is another America. This other America has a daily ugliness about it that constantly transforms the ebullience of hope into the fatigue of despair. In this America people are poor by the millions. And as we look at this other America, we see it as an arena of blasted hopes and shattered dreams. Many people of various backgrounds live in this other America. Some are Mexican-Americans, some are Puerto Ricans, some are Indians, some happen to be from other groups. Millions of them are Appalachian whites. But probably the largest group in this other America is the American Negro.

> But it is a fact now that Negroes and whites are tied together, and we need each other. The Negro needs the white man to save him from his fear. The white man needs the Negro to save him from his guilt. We are tied together in so many ways; our language, our music, our cultural patterns, our material prosperity, and even our food are an amalgam of black and white. And so there can be no separate black path to power and fulfillment that does not intersect white groups. There can be no separate path to power and fulfillment short of social disaster.

The ascendancy of Kennedy to the presidency meant for many, both pro and con, the natural continuation along the federalizing lines of Franklin Roosevelt begun in the 1930s. It was merely interrupted by WWII. To a degree continuation of the 1930s reforms were raised again by Truman in the late 1940s, but that also was interrupted, first by the Korean War, and then Dwight Eisenhower's passivity, particularly when it came to domestic policy.

The full-grown black swan, the Sixties, made a test appearance in the years of 1958 and '59. As if pre-figuring Kennedy, there was a yearning for resolution of the Cold War on the part of a broader counter-culture than just the baby boomers, many of their *liberal* elders having lived through the 20th century wars, and prayed that at some point industrialized wars would cease to break out.

Toward the end of his presidency Eisenhower arranged negotiations of an invitation from the highest levels of the US government and those representing Khrushchev, for the famous Russian Bolshoi Ballet to tour the US in the spring of 1959.

The lead article on the front page of the *NY Times* (April 29th, 1959) captures the mood of the Bolshoi's opening evening performance, in New York's Metropolitan Opera; the beauty of music and dance, or even simply the gift of its bringing an experience of the one and the other together in peace.

> Russia's Bolshoi Ballet opened in an international atmosphere of thrills, glamour and excitement such as New York has seldom seen in this century. Few artistic spectacles of the present era have generated the interest which has attended the first visit to America of Soviet Russia's finest dance ensembles.

In February 1968, King announced specific demands on the Johnson government: $30 billion for antipoverty, full employment, guaranteed income, and the annual construction of 500,000 affordable residences. Such demands were ignored then, and have never been seriously raised again, almost fifty years later.

Evaporation of the Sixties

Recently, on TV, I ran across the tape of an old speech by Ron Dellums, a well-respected and influential black radical of the Sixties who from 1971 to 1998 represented a section of Oakland, California in the House of Representatives.

Where I came in he was talking about the evaporation of the sixties. When and why did it become lost in the atmosphere engulfing the social Totality? As I listened Dellums pointed to Martin Luther King's crucial speech given in Riverside Church in New York, April 4, 1967. Riots in many of the urban ghettos were in the offing by 1968, fueled to some degree by black power counter-forces, but more directly by incidents of brutal treatment of blacks in the ghettos by police and authorities in general.

In that context, Martin Luther King announced that the civil rights movement needed at that historic moment to become much wider in its concern. There must be concerted non-violent action aimed at the ending of the Vietnam War in the short-run and in the long-run the dismantling of the military-industrial complex. No more Vietnams.

King was assassinated exactly one year later, April 4, 1968. And Nixon was elected that November. For me, the years from 1969 to 1972—my last years of college—were bleak, the most difficult and lonely years of my life. Looking back at it, the thing that was so awful to me was not just the evaporation of the Sixties, but rather, as subject, the movement away from what had been my social Totality as far back as the mid-1950s, the days of beatniks and the seeming triumph of racial integration included.

Dellums in the tape opines that it was the failure of a mass movement to take up what King, like Moses in the desert, envisaged, but would not be reachable himself. Instead, tragically, with King's death one felt the life going out of the sixties. From 1968 to 1972 some 25,000 US soldiers were being killed (half the total in the war altogether) along with countless Vietnamese, as well as Laotians and Cambodians due to Nixon and Kissinger's ruthless bombing campaign.

Nixon was allowed to delay the inevitable ending of the war, avoiding a sign of surrender, until he (safely?) was re-elected in 1972. Signifying the evaporation of the Sixties, Nixon wins by a landslide over George McGovern in 1972, a landslide equaled only to Johnson's over Barry Goldwater a mere eight years earlier in 1964.

The significance given by Dellums to Martin Luther King resonates in the soul of many early boomers, especially those who either participated in the civil rights marches, or like me were too young for that, but old enough to understand what was going on. I watched on the news, roughly from the ages of

11 to 13 sometimes for many months in a row, the struggle in the deep south to end segregation.

And I'd heard King's constant declaration of the basic principle of the movement, *non-violent action*, enough to have become a pacifist in my own mind around that time of my life, a belief from which I've never swerved.

The water hoses used on the marchers by the state police forces coupled with the hesitance of President Kennedy to step in made it all the more uplifting when the civil rights movement in open time seemingly won. King had proven himself to be one of the very few great leaders in US history. Kennedy finally brought the National Guard in and the southern governors, as well as court judges and legislators, were eventually overcome. The latter were epitomized by George Wallace, who sooner than any of the others made sincere apologizes for the positions and actions he took in those years.

But that was not all. Major federal programs, developed initially under Kennedy, were put into law under Johnson. The aim was to raise the economic living standard of the poor: federally financed food stamps, health-care insurance for the retired and the poor respectively (Medicare and Medicaid), new preschool education (Head Start), newly subsidized low-income housing, and so on.

I was, as it happens, a teacher-assistant in a brand-new Head-Start class, the summer of 1965. The first initial pilot included Newark, where I grew up. I was sixteen and it was my first real encounter with children so young and good-hearted and excited by the experience, or for that matter my first encounter with teaching, and I have to say my own experience of it is still deep inside of me.

These major reforms were viewed by many at the time as a natural extension of the social reforms, instituted in the 1930's: e.g., Social Security and the Glass Steagall act. There had been a push for national single-payer health-care in the late-forties, but it was rejected by the slimmest of margin in the congress. These reforms were set aside what with Harry Truman's Korean war and then Eisenhower's federal passivity, and thus his criticism of the military-industrial complex only in the moment of his leaving office.

Little did the early baby boomers like me know that for the rest of our lives there would be no experience again like the authentic attempt, from roughly 1960 to 1967, to rid the US of human want, years in which the social Totality in a significant way was living up to its own being.

However, in August of 1964 the Gulf of Tonkin Resolution was passed by Congress in a flash, okaying Johnson's immediate decision to go to war with the North Vietnamese, without having to *declare war*. At the time, and then confirmed over and over again in the next fifty years or so, the immediate cause of the war, a supposed attack on a US ship in the Gulf of Tonkin, was fraudulent, much like war on Iraq was.

In his 1967 speech, King sets out several bases of a radical shift in the civil rights movement toward focused opposition of the Vietnam War. The very first reason he gives, goes directly to the historic that the black swan was doomed, a truly tragic ending. As Dellums suggests, King saw the fork in the road, though he did not have the chance to lead us along in a direction left not untaken:

> A few years ago, there was a shining moment in [our] struggle. It seemed as if there was a real promise of hope for the poor, both black and white, through the poverty program. There were experiments, hopes, new beginnings. Then came the buildup in Vietnam, and I watched this program broken and eviscerated as if it were some idle political plaything of a society gone mad on war. And I knew that *America would never invest the necessary funds or energies in rehabilitation of its poor so long as adventures like Vietnam continued to draw men and skills and money like some demonic, destructive suction tube.* So, I was increasingly compelled to see the war as an enemy of the poor and to attack it as such.

CHAPTER 7

Financialization of the Universities

Nicholas Kristof on Knowledge and Deep Learning

Nicolas Kristof, a few week ago, devoted his column in the *Times* to lamenting the decline of the *public intellectual,* a term that itself is virtually absent from the vocabulary. Entitled "Professors, We Need You!"—February 15, 2014—the piece scolds we who are university professors and administrators.

Among other things, Kristof complains of their using languages that only those among them (*specialists*) understand, and criticize them for "relying on quantitative models or developing theoretical constructs." The consequences are that professors thus exclude themselves from the public debate and (implicitly) thereby render themselves unable to educate the public.

As to research, one of several letters to the editor published in response to Kristof (February 16th, 2014 [Steinberger]) makes the salient point that "Such criticism [that of Kristof] simply denies the possibility that many important questions are in fact enormously difficult, inherently technical and deeply complex in ways that require modes of analysis and forms of discourse that are equivalently difficult, technical and complex."

Coming to grips with mathematical models, for instance, and articulating the foundations of existing theoretical approaches, in various disciplines, is in its own right a valuable aspect of studying at a university. It fosters the ability and even the need both to identify and to question one's own ideas through formalized dialogue with others.

Strangely, perhaps, Kristof does not realize that a crucial contribution of higher education is in fact the great opportunity to master languages of the specialists: philosophy, mathematics, physics, economics, history, semiotics, literary criticism, the fine and performance arts et al. The new meanings contained in these languages are sources of real transformation of the subject (the I) at an age for most college students when one is in the real development or discovery of a consciousness of subjective identity.

Thus, a university education can be and often is at once a boring, strenuous, intense, exciting, and fulfilling experience. It will also be an experience for many, like late-adolescence itself, never to be repeated again. Enabling the university to provide students such a rich experience is a great contribution made by academic professors and administrators alike. Sadly, absent in Kristof's conception of the university, like that of others, is the transformative center of higher education, an intrinsic value internal to the dialogue between student and professor and framed by the wisdom of contemporary thinkers as well as those of the past.

To the extent that it becomes an instrumentality, however, the experience changes and the intrinsic value are liable to become secondary, if not to disappear altogether. Of course, acquiring mastery of these languages, the ones that Kristof is so critical of, ultimately is what connects higher-income employment to higher education. The embedding of professional schools within the university—usually along-side a liberal arts college that serves them on an undergraduate level—is understandable on that ground. And this structure has long been the norm in the US.

A notable exception is schools, some of the oldest ones in the U.S. that are solely liberal arts colleges. The share of these peaked during the 1960s and early 70s. Nonetheless they are still a significant element of undergraduate education in the US.

As exemplified by my own alma mater, St. John's College, they cater to an indomitable set of students for whom the object of education is the intrinsic value of the formalized dialogue. In addition, however, these institutions typify the fact that a conflict exists between that value and economic want. Such schools implicitly ask of students that they follow Joseph Campbell's famous rule of the inner-life: Follow your bliss and don't be afraid, and doors will open where you didn't know they were going to be.

The professional element within the universities became intertwined with the GI Bill after WW II, lending a patina of universality to *going to college*. This added to the subsequent explosion of university enrollment since the mid-1960s, and as of the early 80s in the post-golden age period, the stature of a university degree has grown to that which is *needed* to guarantee a job, be paid paying a decent income. And in the current crisis especially, the stature seems to be that which is needed to get a job at all. Thus, even the liberal arts colleges are under great pressure to prove their instrumental bona fides.

In this context, Kristof is unfortunately oblivious to what is actually happening. University professors are coming face to face with the *culture of liquidation,* in the context of the corporatization of the university.

The corporatization of the university first blossomed in the 1950s. And, despite being put on the defensive by mass student resistance in the mid-1960s into the early 70s, it had become by the 80s deeply rooted. in an oligopoly of leading state universities, *e.g.,* UC Berkeley Texas, and Michigan and leading private ones e.g. Columbia, MIT, Stanford,

Harvard. It occurred in the science departments and schools within the university specializing in technical fields of engineering, computer science and the like. By the waning years of the Golden-age, graduate work in these areas was and continues to be generally guided by professors and programs connected to particular industries. Through a relatively small number of extremely large, and, in the case of many, extremely wealthy institutions, higher education was firmly entrenched in the *military-industrial complex* and its many ancillaries. And it expanded to other industrial complexes rapidly with the advent of the post-Golden age.

Advanced work in physics, chemistry, biology and even psychology—not to mention the queen of the *social sciences*, economics—became and continue to be molded to fit the needs of corporations, undergirded now by digitalization, and with it an ever-burgeoning ability to do complicated mathematical modeling. In turn, professional schools, notably law and medicine, became and continue to be fitted to suit corporate purposes as well.

In this way corporate profit came to dominate the province of practical knowledge. Expertise produced knowledge through mediation of graduate work is now tailored to the armament industries, the agri-businesses, pharmaceutical and private health insurance industries, fossil-fuel and nuclear-power industries etc., etc.

Kristof of course is not alone in appearing oblivious to the subordination of scientific endeavor, within the university to suit corporate profits, and with expected and unexpected social effects. It has contributed mightily to such major forces bearing upon life since the end of WWII as increasingly destructive weapons of war, reduced nutritious food due to processing and myriad untested chemicals including pesticides; dangerous pharmaceutical drugs and medical practices; more and more exploration and use of fossil fuels, despite the possible mega-effect of destroying the natural ecologies needed to support human life and others.

Failure to perceive the symbiosis formed between major universities and the corporate oligopolies leaves Kristof with little insight either, into higher education in the post-Golden age. That is, when the *culture of liquidation* is spreading wildly on a global scale. Within this culture there is no conception of the university as essentially an institution of deep learning, ideally occasioning a transformative experience of intrinsic value.

Very few corporate leaders or contemporary political leaders, almost all of whom share the same culture, evince even the slightest grasp of deep-learning. This is precisely because a transformative experience is an intrinsic value; a gnostic spirit one might say, inside, and changes subjectivity during the years in the university and for some the rest of their lives, and most perhaps in between.

In particular deeper-learning is the dialectic experience of reading, talking, and writing, between professor and students in what is essentially a formal study of ideas; ideas held by deep-thinkers historically and by contemporaries who participate in study of social entities.

As far as I know, there is not one US president in the post-War period that has anything beyond a mediocre academic record. Whether Woodrow Wilson was any better is questionable, however he's the last true president who comes out of academia. Neither is there references made by any of them as to what they got out of their college education other than high positions in student government, political apprenticeships with one of the major parties, making political connections.

Building on the symbiosis established with certain major universities, the culture of liquidation now seeks to eliminate aspects of all universities that are not instrumental, indeed which are in fact seen to be detrimental to the corporations.

Now money purchases power by buying debt in the form initially of gift-giving. Power in the culture of liquidation commands money not by buying debt but by selling expansion of the physical structures of the universities and a basis for the University to accumulate money capital in its endowment. The freeing up of this recursive connection through gift-giving blossomed in the 1980s and 90s.

The universities are an important case of so many others, institutions that we are witnessing a tiny coterie of asocial subjects spread throughout the globe, their unchecked buying and selling of debt threatening whole social and ecological systems to collapse. These individuals themselves it seems are oblivious, and/or have very extremely short time horizons.

They live in a walled-in vessel of their own, in which virtually all others, whether individuals, the State or the University or even the corporation as a generic institution are each purely instrumentalities. Their objective is itself, paradoxically, instrumental: an accelerating accumulation of money that remain at all points of time numbers of capital-money and which create power in the hands of individuals so as to use it to accumulate more capital-money.

Homer captures the essence of the *asocial subject* in his description of the high and mighty Cyclops, one-eyed giants on whose land Odysseus unwittingly trespasses on during his journey back home from the war:

> From there we sailed on, our spirit now at a low ebb, and reached the land of the high and mighty Cyclops. Lawless brutes, who trust so to the everlasting gods they never plant with their own hands or plow the soil.
>
> Unsewn unplowed, the earth teems with all they need, wheat, barley and vines, swelled by the rains of Zeus to yield a big full body wine from clustered grapes. They have no meeting place for council, no laws either,

> up on the mountain peaks they live in arching caverns—each a law to himself, ruling his wives and children, not a care in the world for any neighbor. (p. 214–215)

Due to the empowerment of asocial subjects, the corporatization of higher education, over the last decade or so, has gone well beyond the large elite research institutions. It has clearly been moving into relatively small universities like my own, Adelphi, that generally speaking service undergraduates, offering selected graduate programs for the most part in professional fields.

Such institutions—and a vast number of US undergraduates go to those institutions—are not financed to a significant degree research contracts or endowments. Rather, they depend a great deal on tuitions, and in the case of public universities, of course, government funds.

The nature of this movement is honestly observed in an interview of one Chris Hunt, an expert on search firms that structure and otherwise advise universities in the process of a Presidential hire.

> The game has stayed much the same over the years, but the players have changed. It used to be that the president of the university came right out of academia. It would be a former president of another university or someone who might be in no. 2 position, like a provost at another university. Recently it is important to bring in leaders from other industries, who bring in a fresh skill set into the mix. Many colleges are run like companies. They are big, big operations, and you need to have someone who has those skills. (Fox, 2014)

He correctly observes that colleges are not corporations, but they are being run like corporations. In particular Boards of Trustees are dominated by individuals engaged in the buying and selling of debt on an enormous scale, and as Hunt suggests, more and more university presidents are the same. He then asserts, however, that the college must have someone who has those skills. But those skills exist, as such, in the context of a culture of liquidation. They are the skills of playing money and power games at the highest of levels. As such the object of the game and hence the skill at the game, has no purpose outside the money and power needed by the detached individuals.

There has been in recent years a huge incursion of university presidents being hired, who are in the culture of liquidation and therefore have almost no understanding of the academics of a *deep-learning* institution. There again is a recursive movement, universities presidents are appointed by boards of trustees who are in the culture, and the president then appoints members of the board who come from the same culture. This has the effect of strengthening a wall that is growing up between the academic aspects of the university and its treatment of it as an asset that can function as money-capital. Often in the form of the construction of lavish buildings so as to isolate their offices and conference rooms, attaching underground garages reserved for their cars and so forth.

The center of the university is in its essence as analogical and dialogical. On one side of the wall I think that that is still alive. The faculty that primarily teach undergraduate courses, almost all of whom have PhDs, are especially immersed in an academic culture which is not easily taken from them. At the same time, it is a culture that will ever be a mystery to those caught in endless pursuit of money and power signifying nothing.

A Brief History of Adelphi

I arrived at Adelphi University in 1981 just as the golden-age of the post-War capitalist economies out of nowhere it seemed in open time, came completely to an end. At the center of the thirty-six years of my life as a professor at Adelphi have been of truly intellectual interactions primarily in class with students roughly between the ages of 18 to 22, with a few exceptions, a fair number of them from outside the US, with almost always a small stream in my classes taking courses of mine in each semester over 2, 3 or 4 years.

At the same time over these 36 years of teaching and publishing I have felt inside that Adelphi could be so much more as an institution of learning if only those who spoke and acted in its name—and those like Kristof who wish it to go in the opposite direction—took the university seriously as an institution of deep-learning.

For the first four years I was there the president was Timothy Costello, a well-known New York politician, the deputy mayor under John Lindsay, a New York City liberal of that era. He had been the president of Adelphi since 1972. Earlier he taught at NYU doing research in psychology. Under Costello, the academic decisions were for most part done by the faculty within departments and through governance rights of the faculty within different schools and the institution as a whole. The rights were set out into the faculty contract negotiated by the AAUP union.

The Board of Trustees at that time was for the most part from local corporations, including a few bankers but mostly in production, along with some political figures like Costello and of course alumnae. As in the *Golden-age*, although there are no shares of stock, the relationship of the President and the Board was that of control and "ownership," in the sense that the Board was solely responsible for the non-profit well-being of the institution. At that time, the President was the highest level of control over the university, but with the understanding at that time that Deans of the various schools, and department Chairs and finally full-time professors need to have a major say in academic decisions.

The president for the next 12 years was very colorful and controversial Peter Diamandopolous. In a sense he went against the grain of both Costello and the culture liquidation. Eventually he was forced to resign for stealing, but that is for elsewhere. In his role as president he was more deeply in the academy, a much respected by some as a classical philosopher and who moved up from Harvard until he left the presidency of Sonoma College to come to Adelphi.

Unlike Costello, Diamandopolous pushed the faculty toward programs and new faculty, intellectuals for one or two years teaching and such. It was met from the larger wind of universities toward the instrumentality of a Degree. It also angered many of the faculty because the president and the provost in particular seemed they were dictating to the faculty. It should be said that under Diamandopolous some of our best professors in terms of research are still at their prime here; also, there was a significant increase in high-level students due to the creation of an outstanding Honors school.

On the other hand, for whatever reason Diamandopolous did it for, he made negotiations over the faculty contract intense—causing the union to strike early on. It was the Glass-Steagall repeal moment at Adelphi that occurred in the early nineties. The faculty's priority in the governance of academic realms, as was written in the faculty contract, was fought in negotiations by the President and Board until finally the faculty union gave in, agreeing to its publication as a separate document. They gave up governance control in other words in the contract. In retrospect once he was gone, and as the years have gone by, the very notion of faculty control of certain academic decisions—outside to some extent their classes—has pretty much disappeared.

After three years a new president after Diamandopolous (for one year Goldstein) was Robert Scott. His career has been deep in academia for his whole life. He had done some time as a professor and continues to be interested in anthropology and sociology. In the fifteen years before Adelphi he was the President of Ramapo. He was then president of Adelphi from 2000 to 2015.

Unlike Diamandopolous, Scott did not push for new academic programs of any significance, based on improving scholarship and such at Adelphi. He himself in his Adelphi profile gives as his main contribution of Adelphi a common symptom of the culture of liquidation: the *edifice complex*.

> During his presidency at Adelphi University, more than 300 new faculty were appointed and dozens of new academic programs were added; the first new residence hall in 36 years was completed to accommodate growing student demand, with another added in 2011, and 500,000 square feet of new and renovated space was added, including the Adele and Herbert J. Klapper Center for Fine Arts for sculpture, ceramics, painting and print-making, the Alice Brown Early Learning Center, the Center for Recreation and Sports and related fields and courts, the Performing Arts Center and a 320-car garage below Motamed Field. Nearly 120,000 square-feet of construction received LEED certification. The Nexus Building and Welcome Center—the new home of the College of Nursing and Public Health as well as a number of student and alumni services—begun under Dr. Scott's leadership will open in fall 2015.

Scott along with the Board of Trustees have free reign to make academic decisions, notably when it comes to tenure decisions (not to say renewals of non-tenured faculty contracts and sabbaticals). Hence, more than ever the conception of the institution as a corporation pervades Adelphi, although it is far, far, away from a for-profit university.

While I myself only later vaguely remembered noting in 2005 that Adelphi had awarded Robert Willumstad of all people an honorary degree, and moreover that he'd been elected to the Board of Trustees, I still didn't think much about it. I missed altogether his rise in 2007 to Vice-Chairman of the Board.

My awakening occurred in 2009. An announcement joyously swept the Adelphi campus. Robert Willumstad has given a 9.5 million-dollar gift to the Adelphi School of Business. It would now have his name on the business-school building, which was now named after him; an exchange of gifts?

Robert Willumstad is a former president and COO of Citigroup and, briefly CEO of AIG just before among other things becoming chairman of the Adelphi Board of Trustees? He was a major contributor of the full-service bank that was developing in the Clinton presidency of the 1990s, climaxing in 1999 when Clinton signed the bill repealing completely the Glass-Steagall bill of 1933. Thus, it is necessary in the first instance to take into account Willumstad's significant role in the economic crisis of 2007/2008.

Having said that, what matters more perhaps is the role Willumstad currently plays within the powerful private financial sector and how that motivates him with regard to a university like Adelphi. In that regard Willumstad dropped out of Adelphi when he went to college many years ago and he left after two years, never to graduate there or anywhere else. He has no serious experience of a university.

Nonetheless, Willumstad was also elected as Chairman of the Adelphi Board of Trustees; a second gift? And as such in turn seems to have helped in the financing (how much debt accrued is not readily known) of a huge building that President Scott thinks will be the contribution of his to Adelphi that will always be there:

> The Nexus Building and Welcome Center—the new home of the College of Nursing and Public Health as well as a number of student and alumni services—begun under Dr. Scott's leadership will open in fall 2015.

President Scott retired in 2015. Willumstad clearly was leading the school from the time he had become Chair. He was in charge of the committee deciding the new president. The new president of Adelphi was Christine Riordan. The faculty had no say whatsoever.

From her profile on Linked-in and her Resume, Dr. Riordan's entire career before Adelphi, is steeped in the culture of liquidation. There is virtually no intellectual connection she has to ideas that are not instrumental.

Dr. Riordan's higher education is a BA from an institute of technology and both an MA and PhD from a College of Business. Her career starts with a ten-year stint at a College of Business, a professor from 1995 to 2000 and then 5 years as a director of a business leadership institute.

Business leadership is also the central theme of her published articles.

From there she was an Associate Dean and Chair of Leadership at a different School of Business for three years, followed by an appointment as Dean at yet another College of Business for 5 more years. For the last year (2013/2014) she was the Provost of Kentucky University.

A biology professor at KU commented on her performance as Provost, "not enough time for her to get any traction." And concerning her move to Adelphi: "I think this is a great opportunity for her. Dr. Riordan's business background will serve her very well."

But will it serve Adelphi, an *institution of deep-learning*? One can surmise from her own words, as well as her *job experience* over the past sixteen years, who it was that appointed Dr. Riordan, and why.

Like Robert Willumstad, there is little doubt that Dr. Riordan inhabits the enclosure of the culture of liquidation, cutting it off from, among other things intellectual and critical dialogue, the very heart of a university.

Continually, universally, and in open time, within the bubble purchases of debt ownership are ever-being turned into ever-more money, liquid capital, that money accruing in the moment to ever-more powerful winners inside the bubble. There is no closed time in which one steps out of the bubble. To do so is a cultural taboo.

As described at the top of her resume (to be found on-line), Dr. Riordan's chief quality is that of a leader. One reads that she is: "Effective at determining specific strategies and operational tactics to advance organizations from a variety of industries." Underneath she has bullets of specific areas of expertise, 18 of them altogether. None make any references to any thought or academic work that is not instrumental; not even a word about the nature of non-profit institutions in general.

Three of the bullets, however, go further, sending signs of coming from behind the wall.

- Revenue optimization
- Branding and marketing
- Multiple industry experience

Dr. Riordan clearly conceives of Adelphi as a corporation, and moreover one that is controlled by the owners of its debt, not by those who would hold the school itself in trust. To those engaged in academia the presidency is not one of "specific strategies and operational tactics." It certainly is not guided by "revenue optimization," a particular sign of debt ownership. We are guided by the motto: *The Truth will make us free*, at Adelphi. Thus expert leadership in *branding and marketing* does not serve us well.

Finally, there is a concrete sign of how Dr. Riordan views the presidency, the fact that her prime job experience for now 16 years has been serving on multiple Boards, experiencing, as she puts it, "a variety of industries" so as to "advance organizations."

Within the last few years alone, Dr. Riordan has served on:

Central Bank Lexington
Advisory Board (2014-present).

Georgia Institute of Technology
President's Advisory Council (2013-present).

AACSB
Board of Directors (2013–2014).

Colorado Society of CPAS
Board of Trustees (2012).

Mile High United Way
Board of Trustees (210–2013).

Rocky Mountain Junior Achievement
Board of Directors (2008–2013).

Beta Gamma Sigma
Board of Directors (2012–2013).

It is difficult not to come to the conclusion that Dr. Riordan suits the needs of Robert Willumstad, but is dangerous to Adelphi. Her expertise provides him a President of Adelphi who can help to use the institution as a financial vehicle generating at not much cost debt ownership that can continually be advanced to financial institutions within the bubble where it will be turned into ever-more money; this, with the knowledge that Adelphi in the doing is liable ultimately to be liquidated or destroyed.

Addendum

TABLE 1 *Key Executives for Adelphi University*

Name	Board Relationships	Title	Age
Robert A. Scott	52 Relationships	President	74
Timothy P. Burton	No Relationships	Chief Financial Officer and Vice President of Finance and Treasurer	–
Robert L. DeCarlo	No Relationships	Associate Vice President of Finance and Co-Treasurer	–
Gayle D. Insler	No Relationships	Senior Vice President for Academic Affairs	–
Laura J. Newman	No Relationships	Principal of The Alleghany Avenue Elementary School	–

SOURCE: BLOOMBERG BUSINESS WEEK. COMPANY OVERVIEW OF ADELPHI UNIVERSITY, 2017

TABLE 2 *Adelphi University Board Members*

Name	Board Relationships	Primary Company	Age
Robert B. Willumstad	80 Relationships	Commercial International Bank (Egypt) S.A.E.	67
Leon M. Polack	42 Relationships	Lazard Funds Inc.—Lazard U.S. Small-Mid Cap Equity Portfolio	72
Carol A. Ammon	56 Relationships	Endo Health Solutions Inc.	61
Steven N. Fisher	49 Relationships	Mechanical Technology, Incorporated	69

SOURCE: BLOOMBERG BUSINESS WEEK. COMPANY OVERVIEW OF ADELPHI UNIVERSITY, 2017

The Edifice Complex

A clearly wealthy woman is in conversation with a brief acquaintance concerning her luxury apartment on the East-side of Manhattan. She has been completely occupied with re-doing it ever since she bought it, she is telling the acquaintance, and finally "It is exactly, exactly the way I wanted it, it is finally perfect, nothing, nothing can make it more perfect," she says. And then there is a gleam from her eyes visible to the perplexed acquaintance, and she says with conviction: "And now I just know it is time to sell!"

Until recently I had trouble answering to myself an obvious question concerning universities like Adelphi is largely an undergraduate institution, along with professional majors that also graduate programs, very few give PhDs. Why then are so many within the culture of liquidation moved to take over a private, non-profit institution?

A necessary condition, given the nature of the culture there must be something that these institutions are thought relatively reliable sources of money-capital leveraging flows of money into the circuit of money capital: money markets, derivative markets, hedge funds, investment banks including equity firms (Willumstad) and so forth.

I do not pretend to have knowledge with any true sense of certainty how this necessary condition is met. The obvious belief held, however, is that liquidation is doable. And it does fit the fact that the relatively small private liberal arts schools were pretty-much left alone until the 1990s or so; that is, until the coming of the post-golden age. And the spreading of the culture inside these schools have greatly accelerated in the last 10 to 15 years or so, coinciding with the widening spread of debt capitalism.

At the same time, there are obvious gaps between the corporation and a liberal arts institution. Leaving out for-profit universities—that *are* corporations—universities of any sort, colleges will be included in this term, are not owned by shareholders and/or other holders of debt. Therefore these universities cannot be directly captured and liquidated in the typical way it is done to corporations, or to the large institutions. The latter are liable to being captured by equity firms in link with investment banks, including the full-service bank oligopoly.

Also, there are not any tight ties binding corporations to liberal arts schools. It is true that private universities especially are financed primarily by their students. The financial ability of many would-be students prevents going to college and for some from graduate or professional school. In that way the university is no different insofar as life-ends are not provided within existing societies, with perhaps a few exceptions.

By contrast, research universities are heavily financed by contracts with corporations and the government. And to a great extent the same is true of publicly-financed research universities. The latter are subject to stiff oversight and exploitation by *corporatized state-governments*.

Just recently Wisconsin and North Carolina at Chapel Hill, respectively, had their budgets cut for obviously-political reasons by their state legislators in league with the respective governors. Paraphrasing Governor Scott Walker, the mission of the University of Wisconsin should be changed from finding the truth to preparing students for good jobs in the future.

Despite such gaps there is an odd but observable clue that I think goes toward an explanation of how a university like Adelphi might well be a considerable source of money-capital. Moreover it suggests an easier and less risky method of liquidation than that done to corporations, although the latter it would seem can yield a much higher money return on the upside. On the other hand, the consequence to a school like Adelphi is liable to be not very different from that visited upon many a corporation; the parasite might ultimately destroy the host.

The clue is what is often called the *edifice complex*, a seeming compulsion to build buildings, adding to and around the campus. It is a strikingly common feature over the past twenty years, seen especially on university campuses, which seem to lend itself to it. The complex was common in the US in the early 20th century, especially in the inter-war period.

If one looks more closely, the liberal arts schools are members of a broader sub-set of non-profit institutions. The corporatization discussed here is a cancer that has spread over wide areas of intellectual and artistic life, classical orchestras, opera companies, museums are prominent examples. They have proved vulnerable to corporatization. And, interestingly this is a sign of it happening in each of these institutions as they are all are obsessed with putting up majestic buildings; that is to say that common to those in the culture of liquidation the edifice complex may be a lot simpler than thought.

The joke intrinsic to the name *edifice complex* subtly implies a belief that it is a psychological obsession with building buildings. It is no secret that the Willumstads of the world tend to love having their names on buildings, proclaiming how great their acquisition of debt ownership is through the concrete representation of it. Big solid buildings may indeed be a Freudian symbol of a life devoted to limitless accumulation of money to expand power and limitless power to accumulate money.

On the other hand, however, the very heart of the culture of liquidation is the absolute belief in money as measure of everything, the value of value. Or to put it another way, without money there is no power, and there is not a good deed done without buying ownership of a debt.

In 2013 there was a seemingly obscure intervention into the Dobb-Frank federal regulatory reform bill of 2011. It had to do with legal responsibilities of non-profit university boards of trustees. The Association of Governance Boards [AGB]—of which almost all university boards in the US are members (including Adelphi)—still has on-line its 2013 press release announcing a Security Exchange Committee agreement on a particular rule, one clearly of interest to university boards.

PRESS RELEASE
SEC Approves Registration Rules for Municipal Advisors
FOR IMMEDIATE RELEASE 2013–185
Washington D.C., Sept. 18

The Securities and Exchange Commission today voted unanimously to adopt rules establishing a permanent registration regime for municipal advisers as required by the Dodd-Frank Act.

> State and local governments that issue municipal bonds frequently rely on advisers to help them decide how and when to issue the securities and how to invest proceeds from the sales. These advisers receive fees for the services they provide. Prior to passage of the Dodd-Frank Act, municipal advisers were not required to register with the SEC like other market intermediaries. This left many municipalities relying on advice from unregulated advisers, and they were often unaware of any conflicts of interest a municipal adviser may have had.

> ...
>
> *The new rule approved by the SEC requires a municipal adviser to permanently register with the SEC if it provides advice on the issuance of municipal securities or about certain "investment strategies" or municipal derivatives.*
>
> "In the wake of the financial crisis, many municipalities suffered significant losses from complex derivatives and other financial transactions, and their investors were left largely unprotected from these risks," said SEC Chair Mary Jo White. "These rules set forth clear, workable requirements and guidance for municipal advisors and other market participants, which will provide needed protections for investors in the municipal securities markets."

Reading the release, the rule certainly appears to coincide with what someone in the know concerning Adelphi finance had told me when I first was looking into this whole question. He said it was legally impossible for Adelphi money to be leveraged through funds controlled privately by a board member.

However, there is an AGB *fact sheet* on-line along with the press release. And the fact is that university board members, in their role of making financial decisions for the institution, *are exempted*—along with municipal employees—from the rule being applied to advisers.

> Public Officials and Employees: Public officials do not have to register to the extent that they are acting within the scope of their official capacity. This exemption addresses an unintended consequence of the original proposal that generated significant public comment and created the impression that public officials and municipal employees would be covered if they provide "internal" advice. This exemption covers people serving as members of a governing body, an advisory board, a committee, or acting in a similar official capacity as an official of a municipal entity or an "obligated person." For instance, it covers:
>
> Members of a city council, whether elected or appointed, who act in their official capacity.
>
> Members of a board of trustees of a public or private non-profit university acting in their official capacity, where the university is an obligated person by virtue of borrowing proceeds of municipal bonds issued by a state governmental educational authority.
>
> Similarly, this exemption covers employees of a municipal entity or an obligated person to the extent that they act within the scope of their employment.

This is in effect a carte blanche given to high-end financial speculators who can buy their way onto university boards of trustees. Once there, a free path to leveraging substantial government loans taken out by the university can be paved. What's more, responsibility for the loan, in the first instance, is specifically that of the university as an institution and not of individual trustees.

Under the circumstances, i.e. almost no oversight, it would not be hard for money borrowed by the institution to turn into substantial flows of pure money-capital. From the financial inter-relations of leading Adelphi trustees including Willumstad, one can infer the very reason given in the press-release as to why being an adviser to municipalities must be regulated, then the same logic should apply to the trustees.

Prior to passage of the Dodd-Frank Act, municipal advisers were not required to register with the SEC like other market intermediaries. This left many municipalities relying on advice from unregulated advisers, and they were often unaware of any conflicts of interest a municipal adviser may have had.

What are these loans then used for in the first place? The university borrows large amount of money that is then deposited it in chosen banks? The creation of money-capital is through leveraging the deposits. At the same time, with the exception in Dodd-Frank Act large purchases of debt can be made, while on the other side of the coin, members of the board involved in the decision-making around the loan, nonetheless are not responsible if the university cannot pay back the loan. The edifice complex may perhaps be more accurately called simply: How to make money out of money at the expense of buildings.

CHAPTER 8

Identity Politics

Working Families Party: Is It the Moment? (May 2014)

The sinking of the *Titanic* started as little punctures along the starboard of the front of the ship, from scraping the iceberg it was trying to avoid. The holes covered a mere 12.5 square feet or so of the titanic ship. So too there are tiny holes in the side of the seemingly invincible culture of liquidation, the huge oligopolies, homes of the global corporations in which the culture thrives.

Frankenstein monsters of the post-Golden age brought to life by presidents Reagan and Clinton via the revamping of the US and in turn the European financial systems. In the still-nascent struggle of people to regain some control over these institutions, there are faint signs that the culture of liquidation may be pricked enough to eventually be opened up. And perhaps, amazingly, the monsters as we now know them will suddenly sink into the darkness of the sea, like the unfortunate *Titanic*.

Right now, one of those tiny but precious punctures could be made by New York State (NYS) in the coming months. It may mark the beginning finally of a break in the two-party stranglehold on the political system in one of the leading states in the US. The Republican and Democratic parties, increasingly seeped as they both are in the *culture of liquidation*, challenged by a third party, one that publicly stands for those victimized—the *99%*—by that very culture.

Not incidental to pricking the corporations' protective skin is the clear repudiation of Michael Bloomberg in the recent nomination and then election of Bill de Blasio as New York City (NYC) mayor. Bloomberg himself could not run again, having already violated once the NYC 2-term mayoralty restriction. But when his would-be successor, Christine Quinn, was defeated handedly by de Blasio it became obvious that New Yorkers had had enough of being ruled by a mayor from the 1%, or even just sympathetic to it.

It was a rejection of Bloomberg's uncompassionate attitude toward the poor, his unthinking drive to corporatize primary and high school education, his police department's racist treatment of the community, his unyielding stance in refusing to negotiate with public worker unions, and in general Bloomberg's pronounced social isolation, characteristic of the culture.

The Working Families Party (WFP) has been for a long time a major supporter of de Blasio, and in various states along with NYS it is strongly allied with the labor union movement writ large. It is the most established political party on the Left in New York, which itself of course is a very blue state.

Like other minor political parties in New York in relation to one or the other of the major parties WFP often nominates Democratic nominees. In those cases, therefore, the candidate appears twice on the ballot, the voter choosing the party supported. As a result, especially in the NYC area WFP receives a significant number of votes attributed to Democratic candidates, particularly in races for the higher-level state and city offices. This affords an important segment of the NYC public and that of certain other localities in the state as well, the ability to be unaffiliated with both of the major parties without effectively benefitting Republican candidates.

The question being raised now, however, by the WFP leadership is: Is this the time to move decisively toward transforming WFP into a third major party in New York? This is to say, not nominating Andrew Cuomo, but rather one of putting forward a well-established candidate roughly the same political stripe as de Blasio.

WFP has written to its members that there is much debate about who the party will endorse at their state convention in late May and that in a Siena college poll, 24% of New Yorkers support a progressive WFP candidate for Governor—just 15 points behind Governor Cuomo. Given with the election of de Blasio such a decision seems feasible because Cuomo has been caught in clumsy—and at this point obvious—Clintonesque triangulations in wake of the mayoral election. Like a boxer who throws a punch with his head arched up, Cuomo's chin has certainly been exposed to a knockout counter.

Right after the mayoralty election Cuomo voiced his disapproval of a tax increase to be paid by the richest of the rich, a popular proposal de Blasio had put forward in his campaign as means of financing universal pre-kindergarten classes. This opposition was coupled with Cuomo's executive budget in January, which set a cap of 2% growth of state-government expenditures, so as to produce projected surpluses, while pronouncing myriad corporate, business and property-tax extensions and cuts.

In a similar fashion, but in even starker opposition to de Blasio, Cuomo has quickly proved to be, like Bloomberg, an unabashed backer of the charter-school movement in New York, putting him in line nationally with the push toward corporatization, and ultimately financialization of public education.

The quality of the city's schools of course is a local issue of great concern to parents and children.

Cuomo not only has opposed de Blasio's popular call for charter schools to pay rent on their use of public school space if they are operated privately. He's gone further, cutting a deal (as is done in Albany) by which State legislation was passed giving charter schools in the city much wider protections from local government requirements than it currently had. Among these was that the charter schools cannot be denied free space in public buildings.

On a more national scale, de Blasio announced in his State of the City speech in February that he would ask the NYS Legislature for permission to raise considerably the NYC minimum wage. Cuomo immediately dismissed this as a matter for the state, and create chaos. His chin in the air, he seems oblivious to the growing movement of progressive city and state governments toward enactment of a *living wage*. The latter is contained within a truly transformative policy principle a guaranteed *livable income* for each.

Could there be then, a more opportune moment for creating a truly competitive three-way race for governor of one of largest and most influential states in the US? An opportunity to alter the fault-line that heretofore, since 1968, separates the Democratic and Republican parties. It is the politics of identity, and not life-needs.

At this moment, the divide is that of WFP and the Democratic Party, the latter is at one with the Republicans in so many areas. In this way, Cuomo personifies the Clintons' rule over the Democratic Party for over two decades now. It is time to move toward the Green Party.

It cannot be emphasized enough that while the Reagan administration set the plate for the coup carried out by the commercial bank oligopoly, ending for good the Golden-age, it was under Clinton that Rubin, Summers, Greenspan, et.al ushered in the world of junk bonds, equity firms, hedge funds, the primacy of shareholder value, proprietary trading and ultimately the straight-out repeal of Glass-Steagall.

The same Democratic Party under Clinton, and now Obama that has played their part in weakening the Federal entitlement programs, replacing them in large part with grants to the state, while allowing the minimum wage rate to decline sharply. Still, the same Democratic Party champions global treaties that allow unfettered foreign investment, both finance and production without protection of workers, nor any internalizing the cost of corporate externalities.

WFP is a unique party in its own right. On the heels of de Blasio's election victory, the consequent ramifications of a governor that will team up with rather than being an opponent of de Blasio is too good not to pursue. There is a promising candidate, a law professor, likely to run in the gubernatorial Democratic nominating election, Zephyr Teachout.

Addendum

Looking back at the facts in closed time:

2014

1. WFO leadership chooses by a slim margin to support Cuomo.
2. Zephyr Teachout runs in the Democratic nominating election and loses to Andrew Cuomo. She emphasizes the corruption of both major parties, but endorses Cuomo in the general election. She receives a surprising 35% of the vote.

2016

3. WFO leadership has an open vote of all its members as to whom to endorse, if any, in the Democratic presidential primaries. Bernie Sanders is chosen by a large margin over Hillary Clinton.
4. Zephyr wins the Democratic nomination for seat in the House of Representative, and is Quickly endorsed by Bernie, and she, him. Zephyr loses to a Republican, John Fasso, by about 10%. Zephyr and Bernie, each almost upon losing, whole-heartedly back Hillary Clinton. Sanders openly snubs Jill Stein and the Green Party, who in fact are more in sync with his than are the leaders of the Democratic Party.

Resistance on All Sides (September 2014)

The extent to which US health-care reform is aimed at wider private insurance coverage is being resisted from all sides. But it reveals, once again, the rarely-faced fact that the US body politic is under attack from powerful elements within it. And these are now reaching a point at which there is a threat of them devouring ever-larger chunks of the State; a cancerous growth that may well prove terminal, both nationally and even globally, and not just terminal for humans, but for the planet itself and a multitude of other living beings on it.

President Obama made clear from the beginning—as did the Clintons in their presidency–that single payer was off the table. A fusion of the parties, perhaps, beyond the never-ending wars, seem in sight. The argument is made that the extreme measures taken up in opposition to the health-care reform indicates that the Republicans are no longer members of a stupid party, they have become a crazy party that is out of control.

The main Democratic figures in the legislature, such as Charles Schumer and Nancy Pelosi, look back to Republicans that never used to go to such extremes. The conclusion is that such extreme behavior was bound to happen because Republican elites, going all the way back to Nixon's infamous southern strategy, have become amazingly cynical. They'll do anything at this point to get what is wanted of them.

Thus there has been substitute name-calling for a serious deciphering of what and who actually is motivating health-care extortion. This exemplifies the general state of denial throughout the public discourse in these very trying times.

John McMurtry; *Cancer Stage of Capitalism:*

> While the self-multiplying money to more *money-sequences* with no *life-function* are carcinogenic in their nature, they take man years to bypass reproduction inhibitors and immune suppressors even at the cellular level. Yet once the cancer has become aggressively invasive, the rapidly growing cancer is blocked out by the life-host at every turn on the social as well as individual plane. That is how the cancer spread, masking itself every move at both levels. Uncontrolled money-sequence multiplication and invasive growth into organic, social and ecological *life-hosts* is undeniable once the dots are joined. But joining the dots at the social level of life-organization is heretical knowing what is wrong with the accepted surrounding rule of daily life is ancient, but in this case is globally fatal. (p. 31)

Two opposing things suggest that the ultimate life-need is thereby the fortune to be had out of health-care extortion. The rapidly growing *culture of liquidation* requires the secret not be spread too widely that there is no affordability constraint on the US government's ability to pay for medical care, and not at all the public. No more than, let us say, the whole destruction of Iraq.

At the heart of the matter, with reference to each of these is a simple observation. The resistance to the health-care reform is at one with a wide attack throughout the post-golden age period on State-insured provision of goods, services and income to the public. The attack has been intense, cutting across Social Security, employer and public pensions, decent minimum wage rates, public guaranteed maternity benefits and universal child-care including pre-K education and the state universities, unemployment benefits, publically provided subsidized low-income housing, and of course insuring health-care to all, as the US state does directly only the elderly and the very poor—Medicare and Medicaid—as well as emergency hospital care.

Indeed, even as financing government operations and then the backing of its securities are both being held hostage right now in order to stop health-care reform, the US Farm Bill is being held hostage to a massive reduction of food stamps issued to the very poor.

The culture of liquidation essentially is a money cult. Inside the vessel the only things of worth are those that command money. It is opposed to Aristotle's understanding that money only has worth if it can command a true good. The cult of money has increasingly moved to re-route existing flows of money away from the State's provision of goods to the public. Leading the money, instead, into the flows of the private financial money sequences, money that thereby multiply without end but never have attained actual value.

The creation of a private health insurance industry in the US took off in the late sixties, and among similar countries it is unique. It was an early triumph of a budding culture of liquidation, and has been equaled perhaps only by the US private prison industry. For this reason health-care reform at this juncture may have hit a particular nerve, although of course the reform being put forward—as was the one that Hillary Clinton—does not in fact do away with private health insurance.

The culture of liquidation is extremely sensitive to the State's ability to create money at will, even if neo-Liberals hide the absence of an affordability constraint, hiding it under a pile of Austrian gold. Given the crucial State's guarantee of deposits, now held by the bank oligopoly, control of the Federal Reserve outside the culture of liquidation, and hence reigning it in—getting it into the heads of people, that health-care can very well be insured completely by the State—is quite a task.

More importantly, there is likely to be a deeper sensitivity in the culture of liquidation to movements toward a State that is willing to guarantee basic conditions of a decent life altogether. Should such a movement be set off, then the bare fact that the culture of liquidation is a culture of death will become easily evident.

Because I Am a Neurosurgeon

An op. ed. column of Charles Blow's in the *NY Times* (August 9, 2015) hits upon an internal contradiction in *identity politics*. It appears in the midst of a Republican presidential primary debate. Blow focusses on racial issues raised in the debate, especially a question the Fox moderator, Megyn Kelly posed to candidate Ben Carson, the question roughly: How would you deal with racial relations, in light of "how divided we seem right now"?

As quoted by Blow, Carson first provides a prelude to the question itself. The racial division Kelly refers to is akin to "pieces divided up in a game of chess, the whites and the blacks." And he further says:

> The framing of the state of race relations as a divide to my mind creates a false impression, an equivalency. It suggests a lateral-ness. But this discussion is about hierarchy.

Carson then answers Kelly's question directly:

> You know, I was asked by an NPR reporter once, why don't I talk about race that often. I said it's because I'm a neurosurgeon. And she thought that was a strange response. And I said, you see, when I take someone to the operating room, I'm actually operating on the thing that makes them who they are. *The skin doesn't make them who they are. The hair doesn't make them who they are. And it's time for us to move beyond that.*

A parallel to Carson's "I'm a neurosurgeon," one which goes directly to identity politics is found in an article in the *Times* on June 27, 2015; the day after equal same-sex marriage rights became federal law in the US. Andrew Sullivan, a well-known figure in the movement for gay rights is quoted in it saying, with some tongue-in-cheek maybe, "What do gay men have in common now when they don't have oppression?" And John Waters is quoted exhorting gay students at a commencement ceremony: "Refuse to isolate yourself. Separation is for losers. Gay is not enough anymore."

Self-identity is hidden from some people behind a curtain of struggles for equal rights over sexual preferences, women and men, transgender and so-called race. To the degree that institutions treat all equally, then self-identities of these sorts are seen to not identify an individual at all.

Blow first characterizes Carson's answer to Kelly: "An eloquent exposition of the *absurdity of race* as a biological construct"; the absence, that is, of any inherently natural linkage of individuals according to skin-tone or anything related to it, much like hair color, the size of noses, and other bodily features. In reality, there are no human races anymore, only humans.

But then Blow attacks Carson's answer on another ground. Having praised his biological exposition, within a sentence he severely criticizes him:

> It is an absurdly elementary avoidance of racism as a *very real social construct.* I wish it were that people could all simply move beyond that at will, that they were able to simply choose to slough off the cumulative accrual of centuries of systematic anti-black negativity. But, that is not a power people possess.

Carson in his prelude to answering Kelly's question had already suggested that people are simply not like pieces divided up in a game of chess, the whites and the blacks. And his implicit criticism of Kelly applies equally to that of Blow. There is an obvious contradiction. There is no actual identification of individuals by skin color, but nonetheless so-called blacks are thought to be distinct from so-called whites.

> The framing of the state of race relations as a 'divide' to my mind creates a false impression, an equivalency. It suggests a lateral-ness. But this discussion is about hierarchy.

Millions and millions of people in the US and around the world are sickened by what they literally see as a never-ending rampage of racist beatings and killings by police forces across the nation, urban and rural. And as an immediate response people are taking organized actions of one sort or another to try to deal with it. As such, there is an equivalency of human beings within those millions and millions, and *not a racial divide.* Both Whites are there and Blacks.

The issue at hand, as Carson ambiguously says, is "hierarchy." To be more specific, the US throughout its history has been a racist State, both domestically and globally. The freeing of those enslaved was accomplished by many, many citizens and otherwise, independent of skin color. People struggled and still struggle mightily against the social hierarchy of the US. Blacks and Whites in a chess game is not a correct metaphor.

In the US in particular, the issue of *racists* and *racism* is such that self-identity is confused by the fact that powerful external forces distinguish individuals based on skin tone. These are not only racists; it includes those who believe only in racism as well.

A key source of Blow's confusion I believe is a lack of distinguishing r*acism* from *racists.* As I understand it, the latter are those who believe both in: 1) existence of distinct races, i.e., racism; and 2) there is a superior race and inferior ones. In the United States, especially the issue of *racists* and *racism* is such that self-identity is confused by the fact that powerful external forces distinguish individuals based on skin tone. These are not only racists. They include many who are not racist but nonetheless believe in racism.

Charles Blow certainly does not believe in superiority/inferiority relationships of races. I imagine he would have a hard time saying what another's character is like, who they are, what they think, do they like you or not, not on the basis of skin tone. At the same time, however, he does believe in racism, albeit social and not biological, and in that sense whether he appreciates this or not, he is at one with racists.

What is Carson's critique of the social construct of race that Charles Blow tightly holds on to? An internal contradiction of *identity politics* emerges. Other than the racist's mistaken belief that there is a superior race, there is in fact no Black social construct in the first place. Blow fails to see the significance of the fact that skin-tone does not have a link to a subject.

This is exemplified for instance by the Black Power movement of the late 1960's through the 1970's and which still is a major influence in dealing with racists, individual and institutional. It is at complete odds with Martin Luther King in this respect and several others.

The movement proved prisoner of socially-constructed African-Americans that simply do not exist (except for a replacement of the word Negro). Their attempt was to leave the US and settle in their supposedly real homeland, various African countries. Those who were Americans on the one hand, and those in the African countries receiving them, on the other, proved the fallacy of racism. Just because they each had dark skin, culturally the two groups proved to be strangers.

The result has been while racists run wild politically *racism* is championed by almost all. Identity politics serves to keep people apart through little more than such a silly thing as skin-tone. And yet, Blow ends the column with an assertion that one would hope he regrets having written, but for our purposes demonstrates how poisoning identity politics can be.

> All lives matter maybe one's personal position, but until this country values all lives equally, it is both reasonable and indeed necessary to specify the lives it seems to value less.

Addendum

The above should not be taken to mean I supported in any way shape or form Carson's brief run for the presidency. To the contrary!

The Story of Rachel Dolezal

Rachel Dolezal—a volunteer president of an NAACP chapter in Spokane, Washington—caused quite a stir when it came into the open that she had been thought Black, but was really White. Among many others this hit a nerve of Charles Blow, as reflected by a column he wrote in the *NY Times* (June 17, 2015), entitled Delusions of Rachel Dolezal.

From his first words Blow reveals himself to believe in racism, as defined here. He immediately makes a biological distinction between Blacks and Whites based on heritages.

> Rachel Dolezal, a woman with no known *black heritage*, has apparently, through an elaborate scheme of deception and denial, claimed for years to be a *product of black heritage*.

But in an exchange with Ben Carson a few months later, Blow, himself wrote of "The absurdity of race as a biological construct."

It is clear from the many interviews of Dolezal, TMZ, that she fantasized as early as five-years old being a person treated badly by the social order on the basis of dark skin. In her early teens she took on the mothering of two very young dark-skinned siblings, who were adopted by her parents. She is the guardian now of one of these in his early twenties. In that sense, as she tries to explain in many of her interviews, she has lived as dark-skinned with a body that is not without cosmetics.

Typical sections of interview reports:

On what she means when she says she is black:

> I have really gone there with the experience in terms of being a mother of two black sons and really owning what it means to experience and live blackness. And that's one aspect.
>
> Another aspect would be that I from a very young age felt spiritual, visceral, this feeling of central connection with black is beautiful, you know, just the black experience and wanting to celebrate that. And I didn't know how to articulate that as a young child, at the age of kindergarten or whatever, like you don't have words for what's going on. But certainly, that was soaked in. I was totally conditioned to not own that and to be limited to whatever biological identity was thrust upon me and married to me and so I kind of felt pretty awkward a lot of the time with that.

On the struggles with her identity and how they have affected her own parenting of her two adopted sons, who are black:

> "I felt very isolated with my identity most of my entire life that nobody really got it and that I didn't really have the personal agency to express it," she said. "And certainly, I kind of imagined that maybe at some point, especially, you know, for after, because I was graduated from high

> school and in an adult stride that maybe I'd be able to really process that, own it publicly and discuss the kind of complexity."

In the end, to suit her self-identity, much as is the case of changing gender by changing the body, Rachel adjusted her skin-tone color to suit who she was inside. Trans-gender is applauded by Blow, why not Rachel Dolezal, as rare as her case might be?

Blow's answer to this is rather confused at best. He understands accepting a movement of Black to White, because it is a source of added value socially, but not White to Black. The latter is not a source of social value, and therefore Blow criticizes it as an infiltration and corruption of the Black race:

> The whole notion of transracial as it has been applied to Dolezal is flawed in part because it isn't equally available to all. Racial passing has been a societal feature probably for as long as race has been a societal construct. But it was more often practiced by a person who was not purely white by heritage passing herself off or himself off as such. In some ways, this may have been understandable, even if distasteful, as these people identified as white in a society that privileged whiteness and devalued, diminished or attempted to destroy — both spiritually and physically—others.
>
> Whiteness in this country has historically been incredibly narrowly drawn to protect its purity, and this was not simply enforced by social mores, but also by law. Conversely, blackness was broadly drawn, serving as something of a collecting pool for anyone with even the minutest detectable and provable Negro ancestry. If you weren't 100 percent white, you were black. This meant that society became accustomed to blackness presenting visually in an infinite spectrum of possibilities, from pass-for-white lightness to obsidian darkness lacking all ambiguity.

Absent a biological underpinning, race, as Blow sees it, one is led into the absurdity of racism with or without being a racist. How can we know who really has black skin, who is a *real* member of the Black race, if someone like Rachel corrupts the biological race. And so, Blow's racism means separation of Rachel Dolezal from a community she most feels comfortable to be in, and who was serving voluntarily the NAACP, simply because her heritage does not include any relatives with naturally dark skin.

Langston Hughes:

Rachel had a baby, born February 16, 2016, and had broadly announced her baby's name plan before in December. She had the "brilliant audacity," it was reported, to name her baby boy Langston Atticus Dolezal (Atticus, the hero of *To Kill a Mockingbird.*).

> I'm naming him Langston because of Langston Hughes poem, 'Mother to son'. Life hasn't been easy for me at all, but I keep going. I'm still climbing, so don't you sit down and stop. You keep going, and I want that to be a lesson for all my sons (TMZ).

And indeed a representative of the Hughes clan, Arnold Rampersad executor of the Hughes' estate, wrote to her when he'd heard of the prospective name:

> The choice is more perfect than you'd think. The Harlem Renaissance poet frequently wrote about sexual relations between different races, and understood the pains of what used to be called a voluntary Negro, a term for a white person who chooses to fight for black rights. In that sense, it's perfect. This blackened name, either way, helps the self-identified trans-racial 38-year-old further succeed in her lifelong treachery.

Thou Shalt Not Kill

Benjamin, from the piece Critique of Violence (1921):

> The question 'May I kill' meets its irreducible answer: 'Thou shalt not kill.' This commandment precedes the deed. But just as it may not be fear of punishment that enforces obedience, the injunction becomes inapplicable, incommensurate once the deed is accomplished. It exists not as a criterion of judgment, but as a guideline for the actions of persons or communities. (p. 298)

The Law here is entwined with the shape of time. In open time to kill is a social taboo. The nature of a particular killing that has occurred is incommensurate with it. It exists in closed time, the deed done. In open time, of course, reaction to a killing is to be expected, because it is a social taboo. But that is not, per se, related to the command. It does not inform a particular judgment in closed time, nor is the judgement commanded by it.

In passing I must mention that Benjamin *rejects* the notion that the commandment implies sanctity of life as such.

> *The doctrine of sanctity professes that higher even than the happiness and justice of existence stands existence itself.* As certainly as this last proposition is false, indeed ignoble, it shows the necessity of seeking the reason for the commandment no longer in what the deed does to the victim, but in what it does to God and the doer. (p. 298)

The late-Leonard Cohen's final album was finished days before he died. The first two stanzas of the song Treaty:

I seen you change the water into wine
I seen you change it back to water too
I sit at your table every night
I try but I just don't get high with you

I wish there was a treaty we could sign
I do not care who takes the bloody hill
I'm angry and I'm tired all the time
I wish there was a treaty
Between your love and mine.

Returning to the main road, Benjamin's key insight bears upon the incommensurate relation, *don't do that* and *I did that.* On the one hand in open time there is gross US mistreatment of Blacks as Blacks, to the point of mass enslavement, torture and killing, ever since the US has existed. On the other hand, in closed time there are separate judgements of individuals.

Several family members of the churchgoers killed in Charleston in 2015 spoke in court. In the spirit of Martin Luther King each face to face said in different ways to the young man who had done such a horrible irrational act "You took something very precious from me, but I forgive you."

Forgiveness does not mean injustice. It does not require repentance even, nor does it need to discourage others to do such heinous acts. Rather, it moves thought away from punishment, taking revenge on a pathetic boy trapped in a wild *racist* social construct, including fixation with guns. Instead, it might move us all to come to terms with how destructive the racist-State of the US has been, from the very first, and still is.

Identity politics, however, creates obsession with answerability (guilt), by way of judgment of the individuals in closed time. Instead, following the movement headed by MLK in open time attack pacifically, but directly at racist institutions, calling upon the ridding of all in the leadership and on down that have engaged in racist practices. Police departments and prisons are clearly upfront in the line.

The Clintons' Fusion of Parties

The Bill Clinton presidency firmly established a *fusion* of the two dominant parties, Democratic and Republican. Since then the State has become more than just an instrument of corporate oligopolies. It has been integrated into the government, the latter, then, serving as their protective shield.

Identity politics serves to cast a shadow dimming the fusion from the public eye, while sewing the private military and banking oligopolies more and more into the cloth of the government; doing their most significant work directly in the employ of the State, through the government directly or contracting out, plus bribing in the form of government lobbying, financing only those in political office that serve them and so on.

From a practical standpoint, to the extent that there is a largely unspoken consensus of the two parties, then identity politics naturally fills much of the void. It still is not seen by many that, what were crucial splits of the two parties as late as the 1970's, by the end of 1990's they'd been well-patched; and to a great extent by the Clintons.

Gone was the financial system centered by the Glass-Steagall Act of the 1930's. Gone also has been the neo-Keynesian policies—complementary fiscal and monetary—used by Kennedy, Johnson, Nixon and Ford to soften both inflationary expansions and under-employment recessions. Policies that in many ways proved successful during the golden age of post-WWII capitalism, from the mid-fifties through the seventies.

It is not sufficiently appreciated that under the auspices of Bill Clinton the existing financial system was replaced. Under Ronald Reagan and George H. Bush there had been calls for such a de-regulation. But it was Clinton that achieved the fusion of the Democratic party and the existing Republican push of doing away with the reformation of the 1930s in the of the with two parties by that it was done without much of a protest, given its importance to US politics.

While it was happening, a notable silence, at best, emanated from within the orthodox wing that dominates the economics discipline. To the contrary, leading orthodox economists, e.g., Lawrence Summers, made their careers providing rare expertise in justifying the unhinging of the corporate banking oligopoly from its moorings. Like magicians, the economists served the Clintons' objective of transforming the government from a well-thought out regulator and guarantor of a banking system served the public, to being the bank oligopoly's protector, ultimately its financial guarantor.

In the process neo-Keynesian economic policies, aimed at short and shallow recessions—positive growth coupled with low percentages of unemployment—were put aside by the Clintons. Only after the 2007–2008 crisis, some twenty years later, have Keynesian policies been put forward again. The latter has included a minority of orthodox economists—e.g. Paul Krugman and George Stieglitz—but primarily it is coming from virtually all the populaces of the western industrial nations, rebelling against what has come to be called *neo-liberalism*.

However, Keynesian employment policy through fiscal demand is still being rejected by almost all those in power. Instead, other than the military-industrial complex and large corporations, national-economy policy has been, since the Clintons, reducing as much as politically possible government subsidization and direct financing of basic needs: education, housing, health-care, safety, producing and maintaining infra-structure and so on.

On the other side of the coin, there has been a never-ending funneling of investment money away from truly non-profit institutions, as well as even *product capital* industries in their own rights. Instead investments are sucked and into complex markets of debt ownership, the latter ultimately becoming concentrated in extremely small numbers of individuals.

Clinton, aided by investment banker Robert Rubin, ushered in the all-purpose bank and the freeing up of speculation in virtually every market of every kind, including *derivatives* and *swaps*. In 1999, Clinton proudly signed the bill ending altogether what by then was little left of the Glass-Steagall Act, the last remnant of the economic golden-age.

The Clintons were masterful in the fusions with George H. Bush on the one end of Bill's presidency and George W. on the other end (Obama, coming into his first term proved shockingly adept, himself, at retaining the fusion passed on by George W.). In the broadest and deepest issues of the time, as is still the case, the two parties have been fused together due to the Clintons. Hence, in the midst of identity politics, the lack of conflict between the parties has led to it being more or less unknown, let alone questioned in political discourse.

Bill Clinton raised up the *neo-cons* who across the parties served the military, and by creating a dangerous monster out of Saddam Hussein. The effect was to cut off the Peace organizations on the left wing of the Democratic Party, making them outcasts. These had bloomed in the late-fifties through the sixties and then again at the end of the catastrophic Vietnam War.

The Clintons took advantage of the first Iraq war, triggered by his Republican predecessor, Gorge H. Bush, so as to finally establish the military's grand circuit: never-ending demands for weapons around the globe, creating never-ending war.

Hilary Clinton as New York senator voted for the tragic invasion of the second Iraq in 2002. She did not disown it until in the face of her second run for the presidency. She felt politically left with no choice. In her word for it, she made a mistake.

Whatever the mistake was she didn't learn much from it. As Secretary of State she was consistently one of the leading *hawks* within the upper-echelons of the White House, hand in hand with the military. She was gung-ho in stretching out the war in Afghanistan, she was central to the decision to bomb Libya and then Syria, latter of which was stopped by negotiations with Russia apparently against her will.

Altogether, as Secretary of State, Hillary Clinton conducted no significant diplomacy employing genuine dialogue leading to as satisfactory agreement on both parts. Hilary Clinton and those around her settle problems, instead of through economic blackmail, not selling weapons or selling to others, and direct or military threats. It is telling perhaps that her successor, John Kerry, was able to make an agreement with Iran in a relatively short span, including the US lifting the sanctions that have punished the Iranian people for many years, and, yes, sanctions ardently supported by Secretary-of-State Clinton.

Both for-profit prisons, and for-profit teams of mercenaries—contracted out to the US armed forces flourished during the Clintons' administration and has more or less ever since. He fused the Democratic Party's position in this regard, the Republicans' going back to the Reagan administration. Throughout the Reagan/Bush 1980's and the Bush/Clinton 1990's the positions were identical. The number of private prisons and use of mercenaries increased exponentially over the two decades, Republican and Democrat hand in hand.

The Clintons also fused the Democratic Party to the Republican in the longstanding Republican attack on the welfare entitlements of the poor and needy, mostly put into place in the Sixties; passing legislation that eliminated some of the major federal entitlement programs. Entitlement in this context is elasticity according to need. That is, all those who qualify for a certain entitlement receive it, adding to the overall funding. Instead, the Clintons enacted in law provision of a fixed block grant funding allocated to the fifty states. In effect the State, as the unitary social entity no longer meets the social principle of guaranteeing each individual basic life-needs no matter how poor.

It should be remembered that the Clinton administration was the first to follow the end of the Cold War in 1989. Clinton also was the first Democrat in the presidency after twelve years. The Iraq war waged by George H. Bush had reached an uneasy stasis when Bill Clinton took office. It was the Clintons then who fused the Parties by not only rejecting Keynesian economic policies but also fusing the Democratic Party to the military-industrial complex along with the Republicans.

The Clintons throughout their administration imposed even more severe sanctions on Iraq than did Bush. They continued no-fly zones over Iraq, policed by the US, and allowing it to bomb Iraq at will. It is the Clintons' constant demonization of Hussein and Iraq in general over almost a decade that prepared the way for the invasion to come.

In 1998 Clinton announced another bombing of 'military and secure targets in Iraq.' Reading the transcript of it some fifteen years later one cannot miss Clinton's fusion with George W.:

> Earlier today, I ordered America's armed forces to strike military and security targets in Iraq. They are joined by British forces. Their mission is to attack Iraq's nuclear, chemical and biological weapons programs and its military capacity to threaten its neighbors.
>
> Their purpose is to protect the national interest of the United States, and indeed the interests of people throughout the Middle East and around the world.
>
> Saddam Hussein must not be allowed to threaten his neighbors or the world with nuclear arms, poison gas or biological weapons.
>
> I want to explain why I have decided, with the unanimous recommendation of my national security team, to use force in Iraq; why we have acted now; and what we aim to accomplish.
>
> First, we must be prepared to use force again if Saddam takes threatening actions, such as trying to reconstitute his weapons of mass destruction or their delivery systems, threatening his neighbors, challenging allied aircraft over Iraq or moving against his own Kurdish citizens.
>
> The credible threat is to use force, and when necessary, the actual use of force is the surest way to contain Saddam's weapons of mass destruction program, curtail his aggression and prevent another Gulf War.

In a primary debate (November 14), an exchange between the two major Democratic candidates picked up the ears of social media and such. The *NY Times* wrote an editorial the next day, entitled *Mrs. Clinton's Wall Street Blunder*. It took the position that it was a mistake for her to try and parry a Sander's attack (The *Times*' use of words) with a non-sequitur.

> SANDERS: Here's the story. I mean, you know, let's not be naive about it. Why over her political career has Wall Street been the major campaign contributor to Hillary Clinton? You know, maybe they're dumb and they don't know what they're going to get, but I don't think so.

> I have never heard a candidate, never, who has received huge amounts of money from oil, from coal, from Wall Street, from the military industrial complex, not one candidate doesn't say, 'oh, these campaign contributions will not influence me. I'm going to be independent'. Well, why do they make millions of dollars of campaign contributions? They expect to get something. Everybody knows that.
>
> CLINTON: Oh, wait a minute, senator. You know, not only do I have hundreds of thousands of donors, most of them small. I'm very proud that for the first time a majority of my donors are women, 60 percent.
>
> (APPLAUSE).
>
> So, I represented New York, and I represented New York on 9/11 when we were attacked. Where were we attacked? We were attacked in downtown Manhattan where Wall Street is. I did spend a whole lot of time and effort helping them rebuild. That was good for New York. It was good for the economy and it was a way to rebuke the terrorists who had attacked our country.
>
> So, you know, I looked very carefully at your [Sanders'] proposal. Reinstating Glass—Steagall is a part of what very well could help, but it is nowhere near enough. My proposal is tougher, more effective, and more comprehensive because I go after all of Wall Street not just the big banks.

The glaring non-sequitur was remarked upon in a NY *Times* editorial which reported:

> Predictably, Twitter exploded with demands to know what campaign donations from big banks had to do with New York's recovery from 9/11. Answer: little to nothing.

The editorial ends with a rather vague and contradictory, w*hat is to be done?*

> She should make a fast, thorough effort to explain herself by providing a detailed plan for how she would promote measures protecting middle-class Americans from another financial crisis.

But the dialogue surely goes much deeper than that. The editorial is just unwilling to dig for what they might dig up? Is it denial on the part of the *paper of record*? In words that conjure up sports coaches passing-off their star athlete's error: the editorial writers shrug their shoulders and sighs: "[It's] what happens when Hillary Clinton the candidate gets complacent."

Going deeper then, as Sanders says *everybody knows*, but it is almost never spoken of in public by those in the congressional/presidential circles, nor by their courtiers in the mainstream US press. He does it in an elegantly blunt: "Well, why does [Wall Street] make millions of dollars of campaign contributions [to Hilary Clinton]? Answer: they expect to get something."

The editorial, to its credit, leaves no doubt that Sanders is accurate. Hilary Clinton—she who is running for president for the second time—has for the last fifteen years been openly and at a grand scale financed by the banking oligopoly and its ancillaries, the same oligopoly that was de-regulated by Bill Clinton in the 1990's.

In the exchange during the debate, and the reason for Hillary Clinton's trouble parrying Sander's thrust, is that Bernie at that moment was shining a white light on the major fusion of the two Parties before a large interested audience. Lo and behold it became obvious, if briefly, to the true being of the Democratic Party.

Interestingly, The *Times* editorial makes no reference to another parry of Hillary's in the same dialogue, which also is a non-sequitur. "I'm very proud that for the first time a majority of my donors are women, 60 percent."

This one gives some insight into how automatic and successful Hilary Clinton has become in distracting her audience from things like the huge obvious payments to her by Wall Street interests, by referring to her identity as a woman. And yes, at least in the moment Hillary *was successful.* That statement was the only one in the entire dialogue exchange quoted above for which there was any applause to speak of at all, for either Bernie or Hillary. Moreover, it was not just polite applause either, it seemed to come from a real passion that no matter what she is being paid, by whom and what she does for it, Hillary Clinton, by God, is nonetheless a Woman and Bernie is not.

Self-identification Against Democratic Socialism

An unexpected turn of time occurred in the Democratic Party during the primary campaign for the 2016 presidency; a bright fire flickering in the darkness to which it soon returned. The context in which it happened goes back to the heretofore hidden fusion of the two dominant US parties spear-headed by the Clintons in the 1990's, and which has led in the US to a thoroughly corrupt and severely malfunctioning government at all levels.

A sign of the turn was the major dilemma suddenly faced by Hillary Clinton and her supporters, notably the corporate media. Virtually for the first time they were confronted with the exponential flow of money, in the millions, over some twenty-five years, that has gone into the Clintons' coffers, both personal and institutional.

Her patrons are the major oligopolies, notably, the private banking industry and the military industrial complex. Now, the question was being raised implicitly, *aren't you corrupt?* And openly, a question posed at each debate with Bernie Sanders was—in the generally understood language of capital—*Mustn't there have been a return?*

So thorough has been the corruption of US governance that for the most part it is taken for granted by the populace, although perhaps less by them than the politicians who are involved in it. Enmeshed, as so many of them are, in the culture of liquidation. The politicians correctly view their obsessive begging for money as investment in human-capital, while closing their eyes in one way or another to the fact that as an identity each is *debt-owned.*

What might be thought of as a simple flick of the switch, bringing to light such undemocratic behavior has proved to be not so easy. From the 1980's on a less and less effective public financing of campaigns accelerated reaching the Citizen-United judgment of the court, not that money is speech, but that it should be listened to, is obviously undemocratic.

Serious candidates for the presidency, whichever of the two parties, have been seriously at the mercy of debt-owners for over thirty years. But corruption for all those years has not been a presidential election issue. It is not difficult to explain this. Each candidate in every election has lived in their own glass house, knowing better than to throw rocks at others in theirs.

This time, however, there was Senator Bernie Sanders, independent democratic socialist, a figure that reminds one of Henry Wallace, possibly William Jennings Brian, although that may have been something of an illusion. Since he was not financed at all by the corporate oligopolies, nor himself a debt-owner of others, rocks for the first time could be and were hurled at the Clintons' glass mansion.

I don't wish to go deeply into Sander's history here. But, it is of note that his notion of democratic socialism comes from a post-war heritage with an American origin, one that naturally was at basic odds with the Democratic Party, particularly since the Clintons' presidency.

Sanders seems to have been influenced by Michael Harrington, known as the author of the extremely influential book of the Sixties, *The Other America*, that had a great effect on both Lyndon Johnson and Martin Luther King. Harrington along and Tom Hayden were major founders of US democratic socialism, notably Students for a Democratic Society (SDS). SDS had no ties at all to communism or to the communist States, and, indeed openly disassociated itself from the Soviet Union.

Harrington, looking back at his early days is quoted as saying of the social democrats of that time: "They were determined but unhysterical anticommunists engaged in seemingly Talmudic exegeses of the holy writ according to Karl Marx."

Hayden, leader of SDS, was identified with what was known as the New Left, which rejected completely Marxism, theoretically, let alone communism, and was neither pro nor con with it in practice, adopting a political stance in this regard not much different than left-wing US liberals of the time.

Being a practical person, then, Sanders' politics have no roots in communism whatsoever. As Sanders said during the campaign, the political economy that he identifies himself with is akin to that of the Scandinavian social democracies, and beyond that, in certain basic respects most Western European nations as well as Japan and South Korea to one degree or another.

My purpose of mentioning the above is to remark upon an echo triggered by the voice of Sanders, the democratic socialist. Not, I think, intentionally, but nonetheless he reprised in the 2016 campaign, an historic clash going back to some fifty years ago, in the days of the US entrance into the Vietnam War; a clash within the civil rights movement that occurred from around 1966 to King's death in April of 1968. It pitted King against the identity politics of the major civil rights organizations.

At the beginning of his famous 1967 speech, King articulated what he had to do, what his future path was to be, in the face of the Vietnam-War, and with it the seeming end to the US government commitment to ending poverty in the US and ultimately in the World at large.

> A few years ago [1960–1964] there was a shining moment in [our] struggle. It seemed as if there was a real promise of hope for the poor, both black and white, through the poverty program. There were experiments, hopes, new beginnings. Then came the buildup in Vietnam, and I watched this program broken and eviscerated as if it were some idle political plaything of a society gone mad on war. And I knew that America would never invest the necessary funds or energies in rehabilitation of its poor so long as adventures like Vietnam continued to draw men and skills and money like some demonic, destructive suction tube. So I was increasingly compelled to see the war as an enemy of the poor and to attack it as such.

> Perhaps a more tragic recognition of reality took place when it became clear to me that the war was doing far more than devastating the hopes of the poor at home. It was sending their sons and their brothers and their husbands to fight and to die in extraordinarily high proportions relative to the rest of the population. We were taking the black young men who had been crippled by our society and sending them eight thousand miles away to guarantee liberties in Southeast Asia which they had not found in southwest Georgia and East Harlem. So we have been repeatedly faced with the cruel irony of watching Negro and White boys on TV screens as they kill and die together for a nation that has been unable to seat them together in the same schools. So we watch them in brutal solidarity burning the huts of a poor village, but we realize that they would hardly live on the same block in Chicago. I could not be silent in the face of such cruel manipulation of the poor.

The stance adopted at that time both by Roy Wilkins, head of the NAACP, and Whitney Young, head of the Urban League, was a blunt rejection of King's identification with the poor as such; those that for MLK carried much of the burdens and tragedies of the War, independent of race. Instead—then and since—these major organizations have followed a mandate that political and economic objective of the organizations are to be limited to those within the color-bound sphere of race, although more recently of certain gender identities as well.

John Lewis is a giant of the civil rights movement prior to the US entrance into Vietnam. As a college student, he headed the Student Non-violent Coordinating Committee (SNCC)—formed in 1960—beginning in 1963. Once the 1965 voting-act, the crown of the civil rights movement, was finally passed, Lewis remained with King.

By the end of 1965, as foreseen by MLK, Lewis among others—e.g., James Farmer and Julian Bond—were being challenged by followers of the teachings and leadership of Malcolm X. In May of 1966, Stokley Carmichael became the head of SNCC. *Black Power* became Carmichael's calling. It overtly rejected King's principles of action: non-violence and integration.

On the other hand, SNCC and others like the Black Panthers aided the growing force against the War. In the interval from April, 1967 to April 1968, King's last year, Lewis was said to support him in his decision to work with them with respect to Vietnam, while the major civil rights organizations were at best silent and at worst some openly supported the War until sometime well into Nixon's first term.

After King's death, Lewis more or less left the public scene. Fifteen years or so later, though, he was elected to the House of Representatives from Atlanta, and has served there ever since.

As a congressman, Lewis realized that identity politics could easily blend with the Clintons' fusion of the two Parties in the 1990's, and which continued on in the George W. Bush administration and that of Barak Obama as well.

Lewis has been in the position over the years to guard as best he could the extremely important voting-rights Act that he had been so instrumental in bringing into being, along with various other achievements of the Sixties. Nonetheless, the same court which decided that money can be freely used by corporations to influence politicians also stripped the voting act of 1965 of its bite.

Lewis became an important figure not only in the governmental Congressional Black Caucus, but also a separate entity, the private Congressional Black Caucus PACS. In the presidential primaries of 2008, he was faced with a serious conundrum within the identity politics of race, adding a pinch of gender too. Lewis based on his long and close relationship with—and to some extent one can surmise his debts, to the Clintons over the years—found himself not endorsing Hillary for president.

Rather, identity politics dictated that Lewis endorse a one-term Senator who he barely knew by comparison to the Clintons. It was a pure case, however, albeit an unusual one to say the least. Obama's dark-skin, in the context of his possibly becoming the first person with that to be elected US president was overriding for a major figure of the fight against institutional racists.

In the days of the Democratic primaries of 2016, there was right away a two-headed and very effective, even if not warranted critique of Sanders in terms of identity politics. Leading up to the very early New Hampshire primary the well-known feminist of the 1970's, Gloria Steinem, along with ex-Secretary of State, Madeleine Albright, half-jokingly but half not were seen urging younger women to understand female obligations: Hillary Clinton would be the first woman to be elected US President.

As it happened, enough young women—and no doubt some men and some women who were not young, at all—responded by stripping away the cloak covering gender identity. Simply put, individual identity is not a function of gender. Steinem and Albright were compelled to say they'd misspoke, and after that the criticism of Sanders as not being a woman did not rise up much in Hillary's rallies, debates and so on.

But a second critique of Sanders was voiced by John Lewis in the days leading up to the next primary, South Carolina, considered a bell weather of southern Democratic votes. At a press conference announcing the endorsement of Secretary Clinton by the Congressional Black Caucus PACS, Lewis charged Sanders with grossly exaggerating a trivial association with the civil rights movement.

Something like merely attending the Washington march of 1963 for instance he suggested. And he said that he never encountered Sanders in his years as head of SNCC. But he did know Hillary Clinton. Lewis later admitted that his first encounter with her was actually a decade after his years in SNCC.

This became an event of sorts. The press had no problem finding out that Sanders was in fact a local student-activist in SNCC while at the University of Chicago. Bernie was, one might say, a proto baby-boomer. Born in the last years of WW II, he was one of a host of college-age students born around 1941 to 1946, who joined the civil rights movement beginning in the late fifties.

Most of them remained anonymous, outside personal connections. Like the emergence of the Beatniks, these young people were strong roots of the developing of the *Sixties*. Lewis's statement quickly went through the various social media, flowing no doubt from aging baby-boomers, proto and otherwise. They made the obvious point that droves of students were not familiar to John Lewis, an iconic figure.

Lewis quickly clarified this statement of his:

> "The fact that I did not meet him in the movement does not mean I doubted that Senator Sanders participated in the civil rights movement, neither was I attempting to disparage his activism. Thousands sacrificed in the 1960's whose names we will never know, and I have always given honor to their contribution."

The public dialogue ended there, it being agreed that John Lewis's *faux pas* was due to a lack of awareness that Sanders had actually played a real, if small part of the famed civil-rights movement led by Martin Luther King. Like the latter, Sanders and those who were coming to view him as the leader of a movement, effectively rejected *race* as an objective entity.

Both *racist* institutions, which are socially destructive, and *racism*, which is composed of a toxic belief in more than one human race, constitute serious political issues and policies. In truth identity is not a function of skin-color any more than it is of gender. It follows that without race, identity politics give way to a politics of social life.

Lewis's careless remarks about Sanders' past would seem to have been an instinctive attempt to cover up the fusion of the two parties, by confronting Sanders in the milieu of identity politics.

It does not seem a stretch to see why this tactic in 2016, for the first time, was different. One of the candidates was not financing his campaign by debts owned by corporations. In the years beginning around the 1990's and since, the corruption of one candidate cancelled out that of the other. This time, Sanders was a free agent.

Going further on this path, one can surmise that Lewis was attempting to discredit Sanders through the politics of identity so as to cancel out Sander's attack on the major role played by the Clintons within the culture of liquidation. Sanders would be painted as one who not only told a childish lie to everyone about his role in the civil rights movement, but also who in the process confirmed his stark lack of contact with issues of racism.

Interestingly, in Lewis's attempt at dis-crediting Sanders he opened himself up to criticism of his own indebtedness. The organization he represented that was endorsing Hillary Clinton—*The Congressional Black Caucus PACs*—itself has on its Twenty member board eleven corporate lobbyists, in addition to seven officials elected by the *Congressional Black Caucus* itself, within the government, and thirdly two officials employed by the PAC.

The lobbyists that had a say in endorsing Clinton came from such industries as pharmaceutical, private prison, tobacco, Walmart (the largest gun distributor in the US and on whose Board sits Hillary Clinton), and so on. In addition, the PAC received a flow of money from the large private banks used to finance her campaign. Lewis's status, however, has been respected by Sanders so that—along with the help of the establishment who did not want to make a fuss over it either—Lewis has been rescued from Sanders' critique of Clinton, at least for the most part.

And this, then, is when the turn in time happened, the flicker in the dark. In the politics of democratic socialism, the light suddenly shined upon the Clintons, corrupting and corrupted on a vast scale. In that flicker Bernie Sanders went from an icon's accusation of being a liar about his past, to a socially-concerned local leader at an early age fighting segregation at the University of Chicago.

In a flicker of light one sees MLK fifty years ago calling out for a politics that transcended the colors of human skin identifying others and indeed one self. And a baby boomer might hear the faint echoing of Sixties greetings, hearing at departures again from the current generations. The v-shaped fingers of one hand held up, and the words *Peace/Love* from each to the other.

MLK and the Clintons

Martin Luther King believed that those in the civil rights movement whom he'd led against the forces of racism had a mission to go much further than even that. They would lift themselves and others out of impoverishment and mistreatment.

> I choose to identify with the poor. If it means dying for them, I'm going that way, because I heard a voice saying, 'Do something for others.' (August 1966)
>
> We must see now that the evils of racism, economic exploitation and militarism are all tied together you can't really get rid of one without getting rid of the others the whole structure of American life must be changed. America is a hypocritical nation and we must put our house in order. (May 1967)

King chooses to identify with the poor, and not be a member of a faux race. That is, he rejects not only racists but also racism itself; indeed that there is no actual social construct of a Black any more than there is one of a White.

The re-emergence in the post-WW II period of identity came about in the years surrounding the death of King. It was connected initially to the black-power movement, whose very name is an identification of people by skin-tone. The post-sixties then saw the rise of the feminist movement and a bit later the gay/ lesbian/ /trans-gender movement(s).

For their part, leading civil rights organizations—notably the NAACP and the Urban League—refused in 1967/68, to join King's self-identification with the poor. Subsequently they have openly taken the stance that the capitalist system in its own right was not to be questioned, only how the system is currently functioning. In other words, it presumes that the struggles of those attacked by racists can succeed within and through existing political and legal forces, forces that sustain racism.

A difficulty of the stance taken by these organizations, as well as movements based on a self-identified race altogether, is that skin-tone is not a language. It cannot communicate *who* an individual subject is. "You are"—or within the subject "I am"—can only be communicated in experiences in open time. False identification based on biological characteristics prevents communication of experiences of the subject. This contributes to the hatred that racists have for the Other. The subjects are not communicated, but are solely in the imagination.

The surprisingly quiet ending of the economic golden-age, and the complete replacement of its core by the end of the 1990's, is marked by three intertwined developments that transcend the issues of identity politics, but are obscured by them.

1. Privatization occurring on a grand scale of previously nationalized industries as well as non-profits and heavily regulated industries; e.g., an on-going process of privatizing prisons, hospitals, mental

health-care and child-care provisions, local transportation and sanitation, mail delivery, and early education. What were formerly responsibilities of the public through the employment of the State are continually shifted to that of debt-owners maximizing their return on these institutions.

2. Dominance of speculative capital over product capital, the accumulation and increasingly concentrated money through debt ownership. A minute percentage of the population sits on enormous credit in their names, while there is expanding impoverishment and mounting debt of families and communities in the US and throughout the world. The various cultures in which subjects live are being destroyed by this.
3. Near-perennial warfare engaged by the US, with all its horrors, driven by an industrialized military established for the first time in the Cold War years after WW II. In the 1980's and 90's it went further, to the extent that the armed-forces themselves became to a great extent contracted out, the military privatized too. Hence expansion and constant technological advances by the US weapon industry means sucking in money so long as there are ongoing wars, and further threat of them.

At the same time the government, as noted, has an exception to neo-liberalism when it comes to financing the military-industrial complex. It is financed by the State, to such a degree that no one knows the money going into the military from the government. There has not been conducted a whole audit of the defense budget for many years.

Lest one thinks so, the integration of the State into private capitalist industries as just described is not what is generally meant by fascism. The latter is usually thought to be a system in which the private sector has been ingested into the State. Here it seems to be the reverse. The State, as such, has been being hollowed out to the point that it itself only exists inside a privatized system of which it is one specific component among others.

In particular, the State serves as a thick shell, shielding unlimited debt ownership and increasingly accumulating and concentrating money and power to accumulate more. This means the global munition industries, along with the major corporate oligopolies—among others, oil, pharmaceutical, agricultural, communications—and of course, the enormous banking system on which debt ownership is based. Of course, simultaneously the State shields the system from affording people as much as possible the pursuit of happiness.

Identity politics has been cutting deeply into the US political discourse since the Nixon administration's Southern Strategy. It took off further in the years of Reagan through the Clintons and then again with the election of President Obama. Cumulatively it has drawn clear divisions between the Democratic and Republican parties along identity lines.

But in doing so it has bypassed deeper and broader perspectives on the social Totality. It creates a passive silence concerning a discourse, as King understood it that encompasses race, gender and sexuality by identifying with poor people and people of all kinds with the rights of living a decent life are being robbed from them.

During the 1980's and 90's, the integration of the State into the culture of liquidation occurred, in tangent with corporate suppliers of war and their finest weapons around the world. The previous restrictions on the banking oligopoly—set by the Glass Stegall law in the 1930's, and which remained robust up to the mid-1970s—was no more. And yet, this historically momentous alteration, or at least its consequences were barely known until it was long-completed.

The central role of Bill and Hillary Clinton in the use of identity politics has been largely overlooked. Looking back, the Clintons were leaders of the Democratic Leadership Council (DLC), established within the Democratic Party in 1985 (They controlled it for virtually its entire existence; and when it ceased to function in 2011, all its records and various paraphernalia were left to the Clinton foundation).

Supporters of the DLC were known as New Democrats, but they were not so new. After Nixon's landslide victory over McGovern in 1972, the Coalition for a Democratic Majority (CDM), led by Henry (Scoop) Jackson, was similarly formed within the Democratic Party. Both the CDM and DLC fought for a radical departure from such Democratic Party economics staples as Keynesian economics in favor of a neo-liberal notion of balancing budgets, restrictive monetary policies, radical reductions of government control over the financial system, especially the Glass-Steagall restrictions on the banking oligopolies handling of government-guaranteed bank deposits.

In addition, both CDM and DLC supported wider military interventions globally. CDM helped spawn the Committee on the Present Danger. The latter, in the post-Vietnam Jimmy Carter years (1976–80) fought to sustain, at least, the existing scale of the military despite it being a rare peace-time. The committee was comprised of the soon-to-be-called neo-cons. In short, the new democrats signaled the dystopia that Martin Luther King visualized but could do nothing about: The evils of economic exploitation and militarism tied together.

Anthem

The birds they sang at the break of day
Start again I hear them say
Don't dwell,
on what has passed away
Or what is yet to be

Ah the wars they will be fought again
The holy dove she will be caught again
Bought and sold,
and bought again
The dove is never free

Ring the bells that still can ring
Forget your perfect offering
There is a crack,
a crack in everything
That's how the light gets in

We asked for signs the signs were sent:
The birth betrayed the marriage spent
Yeah the widowhood,
of every government
Signs for all to see

I can't run no more with that lawless crowd
While killers in high places say their prayers out loud
But they've summoned,
They've summoned a thunder cloud
They're going to hear from me

You can add up the parts you won't have the sum

You can strike up the march there is no drum
Every heart,
Every heart to love will come
But like a refugee

Ring the bells that still can ring
Forget your perfect offering
There is a crack,
a crack in everything
That's how the light gets in

Yes, that's how the light gets in
Words & Music: Leonard Cohen
CD *Leonard Cohen I'm your Man* sung by Perla Batalla and Julie Christensen

References

Agamben, Giorgio. *State of Exception*, Chicago: University of Chicago Press, 2005

Anders, Gunther. *Franz Kafka*, London: Bowes & Bowes, 1960

Babbage, Charles. *On the Economy of Machinery and Manufactures*, JCGtesting; circa 1832

Bakhtin, Mikhail. Author and Hero in Aesthetic Activity, *Art and Answerability: Early Philosophic Essays*, Texas: University of Texas Press, 1990; original 1919

Bakhtin, Mikhail. *Toward a Philosophy of the Act*, Austin: University of Texas Press 1993; original circa 1922–1924

Beasley-Murray, Tim. *Mikhail Bakhtin and Walter Benjamin: Experience and Form*, New York: Palgrave McMillan, 2007

Benjamin, Walter. Trauerspiel and Tragedy, *Early Writings 1910–1917*, Cambridge: Harvard University Press, 2011a; original 1916

Benjamin, Walter. The Role of Language in Trauerspiel and Tragedy, *Early Writings 1910–1917*, Cambridge: Harvard University Press; 2011b, original 1916

Benjamin, Walter. Fate and Character. *Reflections: Essays, Aphorisms, Autobiographical Writings*, New York: Schocken Books, 1978; original 1919

Benjamin, Walter. On Language as Such and on the Language of Man. *Reflections: Essays, Aphorisms, Autobiographical Writings*, New York: Schocken Books, 1978; original 1916

Benjamin, Walter. Critique of Violence, *Reflections: Essays, Aphorisms, Autobiographical Writings*, New York: Schocken Books, 1978; original 1921

Benjamin, Walter. Theological-political Fragment. *Reflections: Essays, Aphorisms, Autobiographical Writings*, New York: Schocken Books, 1978; original 1920–1921

Benjamin, Walter. Theses on the Philosophy of History, *Illusions: Essays and Reflections*, New York: Schocken Books, 1968; original 1940

Benjamin, Walter. Two Poems by Friedrich Holderlin, *Selected Writings* Vol. 1, Cambridge: University Press, 1972; original 1914–1915

Benjamin, Walter. To the Planetarium, Section of: One-Way Street, *Selected Writings* Vol. 1, Cambridge: Harvard University Press, 1996; original 1928

Benjamin, Walter. Myslovice—Braunschweig—Marseilles, *On Hashish*, Cambridge: Harvard University Press, 2006; original 1928

Benjamin, Walter. *On Hashish*, Cambridge, Mass: Belknap Press of Harvard University Press, 2006, original 1930

Benjamin, Walter. *One-way Street and Other Writings*, London: Penguin, 2009, original 1923–26

Berle & Means, Adolph. *Modern Corporation and Private Property*, New Jersey: Transaction Publisher, 1991; original 1932

Blinder, Alan. What's the Matter with Economics, The *New York Review of Books*, December, 2014

Blow, Charles. 'Black Lives Matter' and the G.O.P., *New York Times*, August 9, 2015

Blow, Charles. Delusions of Rachel Dolezal, *New York Times*, June 17, 2015

Braverman, Harry. *Labor and Monopoly Capital*, New York: Monthly Review Press, 1998; original 1974

Buckland, W.W. and A.D. McNair, *Roman Law and Common Law*, Cambridge: Cambridge University Press, 2nd edition, Cornell Library Digital Collections Reprint 2008; original 1936.

Carson, Rachel. *Silent Spring*, New York: Milestone Editions, 1960

Clark, Edwin Charles, *Early Roman Law: The Regal Period*, Cornell University Library: Digitalized by Microsoft; original 1872

Cohen, Leonard. Anthem, *I'm Your Man*, Verve Forecast, CD, 2006

Cohen, Leonard. Chelsea Hotel, *I'm Your Man*, Verve Forecast, CD, 2006

Cohen, Leonard. Treaty, *You Want It Darker*, Columbia Records, 2016

Coleman, David. Unemployment Rates by President: 1948–2016, historyinpieces.com, 2016

Deleuze, Gilles and Guattari, *Kafka Toward a Minor Literature*, Minneapolis: University of Minnesota Press, 1986; original 1975

Douglas, CH. *The Douglas Theory: A Reply to Mr. JA Hobson*, London: BIBLIOLIFE 2009; original 1922

Douglas, CH. *These Present Discontents*, London: Forgotten Books, 2012; original 1922

Douglas, CH. *The Labor Party and Social Credit*, London: Forgotten Books, 2012; original 1922

Douglas, CH. *The Control and Distribution of Production*, Miami: Hardpress Publishing (Print); original 1922

Douglas, Mary. *Primitive Rationing: A Study in Controlled Exchange, Themes in Economic Anthropology*, London: Tavistock Publication, 1967

Dover, Connie. Summer Before The War, *The Wishing Well.* by Hue Williams, Kansas City, Mo: Taylor Park Music, 1994

Dowden, Stephan. *Kafka's Castle and the Critical Imagination*, Columbia, SC: Camden House, 1995

Editorial Board. Mrs. Clinton's Wall Street Blunder, *New York Times*, November 16, 2015

Eisner, Robert. *The Great Deficit Scares: The Federal Budget, Trade, and Social Security*, New York: Twentieth Century Fund, 1997

Eisner, Robert. *The Great Deficit Scares: The Federal Budget, Trade, and Social Security.* New York: Twentieth Century Fund, 1997

Eisner, Robert. *Social Security: More not Less*, New York: Century Foundation Press, 1998

Emerson, Ralph. *Gifts, in A Series of Essays*, Middletown, DE: Bravo Ebooks, 2016; original 1844

Fenves, Peter. *The Messianic Reduction: Walter Benjamin and the Shape of Time*, Stanford: Stanford University Press, 2010

Firth, Raymond. *Themes in Economic Anthropology*, London: Tavistock Publications, 1967

Danielle Fox, "Welcome Back: Professionals Speculate on the Progress of Pitt's Chancellor Search," *Pitt News*, Jan. 9, 2014

Foucault, Michel. *The Order of Things*, New York: Vintage Books 1994; original 1966

Freud, Sigmund. *Civilization and its Discontents*, New York: WW Norton Books, 1962; original 1930

Galan, EW. : *Historic Structures: The Prague School Project 1928–1946*, Austen: University of Texas, 1984

Meyer, Marvin W. & Bloom, Harold. *Gospel of Thomas, The Hidden Sayings of Jesus*, San Francisco: HarperSanFrancisco, 1992

Guattari, Felix. *The Three Ecologies*, London: Athlone Press, 2000; original 1989.

Gospel Q, Lost *The Original Sayings of Jesus*, Berkeley Cal.: Ulysses Press, 1996

Harrington, Michael. *The Other America: Poverty in the United States*, Penguin Books, 1963

Hesse, Hermann. *The Glass Bead Game: (Magister Ludi)*. New York: Picador USA, 2002; original 1943

Hesse, Hermann. *The Journey to the East*, London: Owen, 1956

Hesse, Herman. *Siddhartha*. New York: New Directions, 1951; original 1922

Hesse, Hermann. *Demian: The Story of Emil Sinclair's Youth*, Cutchogue: Buccaneer Books, 1976a; original 1919

Hesse, Hermann. *Steppenwolf*, Cutchogue: Buccaneer Books, 1976b; original 1927

Hilferding, Rudolf. *Finance Capital* 1910

Hillis Miller, J. The Sense of an Un-ending: The Resistance to Narrative Closure in Kafka's Das Schloss, *Franz Kafka: Narration, Rhetoric, & Reading*, Columbus: Ohio State University Press, 2011

Ho, Karen. *Liquidated, An Ethnography of Wall Street*, Durham: Duke University Press, 2009

Hobson, J. A. *The Science of Wealth*, London: Williams and Northgate, 1911

Homer, *The Odyssey*, New York: Penguin Books, translator Fagles, 1996

Huxley, Aldous. *Brave New World: A Novel*, London: Chatto & Windus, 1932

Kafka, Franz. *The Man Who Disappeared (aka: Amerika), translator Hofmann, 1996*; New York: New Directions Book; original circa 1912 (pub. 1927).

Kafka, Franz. *The Trial, translator by Mitchell*, New York: Schocken Books, 1998; original circa 1914 (original publication, 1925).

Kafka, Franz. *The Castle, translator by Harman*, New York: Schocken Books, 1998; original circa 1922 (original publication, 1926).

Kantor, Jodi. A Historic Day for Gay Rights, but a Twinge of Loss for Gay Culture, *New York Times*, June 27, 2015

Karcevskij, Sergej. The Asymmetric Dualism of the Linguistic Sign, *Prague School: Selected Writings 1929–1946*, Austin: University of Texas, 1982; original 1929

Kelton, Stephanie. *Eisner's Radical Approach to Social Security—Tell the Truth," Keynes and Macroeconomics after 70 Years: Critical Assessments of The General Theory*, Northampton Mass: Edward Elgar Publishing, 2008

Kelton, Stephanie. Eisner's Radical Approach to Social Security - Tell the Truth!, *Keynes and Macroeconomics After 70 Years: Critical Assessments of The General Theory*, ed. L. Randall Wray & Mathew Forstarter, Northampton: Edward Elgar Publishing, 2009

Keynes, John Maynard. A Treatise on Money, London: Macmillan, 1930

Keynes, John Maynard. *The General Theory of Employment Interest and Money*, London: Macmillan, 1936

King, Martin Luther. *Beyond Vietnam*, Palo Alto, California: Altoan Press, 1967

King, Martin Luther. *The Other America*, San Francisco, CA: KQED-TV, 1967.

Kristof, Nicolas. Professors, We Need You!, *New York Times*, February 15, 2014

Lapavitsas, Costa. *Profiting Without Producing: How Finance Exploits Us All*, London: Verso, 2013

Lazzarato, Maurizio. The Making of the Indebted Man: An Essay on the Neoliberal Condition, Los Angeles, CA: Semiotext(e), 2012

Levine, David. *Economic Studies: Contributions to the Critique of Economic Theory*, London: Routledge and Kegan Paul, 1977

Levine, David P. Economic Theory Vol. 1: The Elementary Relations of Economic Life, London: Routledge and Kegan Paul, 1978

Lowrey, Annie. Warren Mosler, a Deficit Lover With a Following, *New York Times*, July 4th, 2013

Lyotard, Jean-Francois. *God and the Puppet, The Inhuman: Reflections on Time*, Stanford: Stanford University Press, 1991; original 1988

Maynard Keynes, John. *Treatise on Monday: The Pure Theory of Money, Volume V*, London: Royal Economic Society, 1971; original 1930

Maynard Keynes, John. *General Theory of Employment, Interest and Money*; original 1936

Malinowski, Bronislaw. *Argonauts of the Western Pacific*, London: George Routledge & Sons, 1932; original 1922

Mandeville, Bernard. *The Fable of the Bees*. original 1714

Mann, Thomas. introduction to *Demian*, by Hermann Hesse, 1947

Martin, John. "Ballet: Bolshoi Troupe's 'Giselle' Bows; Old Work Given New Texture at 'Met' Zhdanov and Raissa Struchkova in Leads" New York Times, April 29th, 1959

Marx, Karl. *Das Capital volume 1: A Critical Analysis of Capitalist Production*; New York: International Publishers, 1967a; original 1867

Marx, Karl. *Das Capital volume 2: The Process of Circulation of Capital*, New York: International Publishers, 1967b; original 1893

Marx, Karl. *Das Capital volume 3: The Process of Capitalist Production as a Whole*: New York: International Publishers, 1967c; original 1894

Mauss, Marcel. *The Gift: The Form and Reason for Exchange in Archaic Societies*, New York: ww Norton, 1990; original 1950

McMurtry, John. *The Cancer Stage of Capitalism: From Crisis to Cure*, New York: Pluto Press, 2013 [second edition]

Menger, Carl. *Principle of Economics*, New York: New York University Press, 1981: original 1871

Menger, Carl. On the Origin of Money, *Economic Journal*, 1892

Miller, Arthur. *Death of a Salesman*, Play Service, 1949

Mommsen, Theodor. *History of Rome Vol. 1*. Cornell University Library: Digitalized by Microsoft, 2008; original 1886

Nordhaus, William D. The Pope & the Market, *The New York Review of Books*, New York: October 2015

Orwell, George. *Nineteen Eighty-Four*, New York: Everyman's Library, 1987; original 1949

Polanyi, Karl. *Great Transformation*, Boston: *Beacon Press*, 2001; original 1944

Pope Francis, *Laudat Si, Encyclical*, June 2015

Raymond, Firth, *Primitive Polynesian Economy*. New York: Norton Books, 1975; original 1936.

Randall Wray, L.: *Modern Money Theory*, Palgrave Macmillan, 2012

Robert, Marthe. *The Old and the New: From Don Quixote to Kafka*, Berkeley: University of California Press, 1977

Ricardo, David. *Oh Principles of Political and Taxation*; original [3rd edition] 1821

Sahlins, Marshall. *Social Stratification in Polynesia*, Seattle: University of Washington, 1958

Samuelson, Paul Anthony. Economics: An Introduction Analysis, New York: McGraw-Hill Book Comp, 1948

Securities and Exchange Commission. *SEC Approves Registration Rules for Municipal Advisors*, Washington D.C., September 18, 2013

Smith, Adam. *The Wealth of Nations*; original 1776

Solzhenitsyn, Alexander. *One Day in the Life of Ivan Denisovich*, New York: Introduction by Marvin Kalb. EP Dutton & Co. 1963

Steinberger, Peter J. to the Editor, *New York Times*, February 16, 2014

Stigler, George. *Essays in the History of Economics*, Chicago: University of Chicago Press, 1965

Taylor, Frederick. *The Principles of Scientific Management*, Norton Books, 1967; original 1911

Twilight Zone, Rod Sterling, Metro-Goldwyn-Mayer Studios, 1959–64

Uno, Kozo. *Principles of Political Economy: Theory of a Purely Capitalist Society*, Brighton: Harvester Press, 1977; original 1964

Wray, L.R. *Monetary and Fiscal Policy for Sovereign Currencies: What Should Government Do?*, London: Macmillan, 2012

Wray, L. Randall. *Modern Money Theory: A Primer on Macroeconomics for Sovereign Monetary Systems*, Basingstoke: Palgrave Macmillan, 2012

Vardoulakis, Dimitris. *The Doppelganger: Literature's Philosophy*, New York: Fordham University Press, 2010

Index

www.ingramcontent.com/pod-product-compliance
Lightning Source LLC
Chambersburg PA
CBHW070925030426
42336CB00014BA/2535
9781608461028